D1299992

PRINTING PLACES

PRINTING PLACES

LOCATIONS OF BOOK
PRODUCTION & DISTRIBUTION
SINCE 1500

Edited by
John Hinks
and Catherine Armstrong

OAK KNOLL PRESS
&
THE BRITISH LIBRARY
2005

© 2005 The Contributors

First published in 2005 by
Oak Knoll Press
310 Delaware Street
New Castle
DE 19720
and
The British Library
96 Euston Road
London NW1 2DB

Cataloguing in Publication Data
A CIP Record for this book is available
from both the British Library and
the Library of Congress

ISBN (Oak Knoll) 1-58456-165-3
ISBN (BL) 0-7123-4906-5

Typeset by Ella Whitehead
Jacket design by Geoffrey Matheson
Printed in England by St Edmundsbury Press, Bury St Edmunds

Contents

Introduction

THE ANNUAL *Print Networks* conferences have a tradition of hosting a wide variety of papers within the fairly broad parameters of the history of the British book trade and its links with the former colonies and dominions. The desirability of choosing a theme for each conference has been considered and rejected, for the present at least, the organizing committee preferring to continue a broader, more inclusive approach. While this makes for diverse and interesting conferences it does not help with the choice of a title for each annual volume. However, it sometimes happens, quite fortuitously, that some common ground – rather than a 'theme' as such – emerges from a particular set of papers, suggesting a relevant title. This was notably the case with the earlier volume in the series, *The Human Face of the Book Trade*, which reflected a developing interest in the people who were involved in the trade, not just as book-sellers, printers and suchlike but also as individual men and women who were part of various communities: social, cultural, economic, religious, political, civic, and so on. Many of the essays which comprise the present volume, while meeting this now generally agreed need to put flesh on the bones of book-trade history, have a particular focus on the importance of location. The town in which a book was produced, or where a business was situated, is an important and sometimes neglected factor – and it usually was a town, for the making and distribution of books are primarily *urban* activities.[1]

In offering this volume of papers with the title of *Printing Places* the editors are deliberately emphasizing this theme of location which they found emerging from the papers presented at the conference held at the University of Exeter. This was in July 2002, when regular delegates were saddened by the recent sudden death of Professor Peter Isaac, founder of the series of conferences and of the British Book Trade Index, the History of the Book Trade in the North and many other valuable contributions to book trade history. Nevertheless, the mood of the conference was upbeat and there was a positive emphasis on taking forward Peter Isaac's hard work and enthusiasms.[2] He would have enjoyed the variety of papers presented at Exeter and had been looking forward to presenting his own paper, reporting on his further research on the Murray archive. Those who knew

Peter Isaac will not be in the least surprised that his paper was so meticulously prepared that it was virtually ready for publication without further editing. Iain Beavan has kindly added a brief postscript to acquaint readers with some additional contextual findings of recent research.

In addition to their broad scope the *Print Networks* conferences and series of books also benefit from a wide date-range of contributions. Typically, the medieval trade in manuscripts and early printed books is touched upon and there are often papers on aspects of the late nineteenth- or early twentieth-century book trade, with many papers focusing on the centuries in between. The present volume is no exception, its medieval interest being ably supplied by Lucy Lewis, who examines the edition of Boethius's *Consolation of Philosophy* printed at Tavistock Abbey shortly before the Reformation. Catherine Armstrong's chapter discusses the production and distribution of literature designed to enlighten readers in early modern England with knowledge of the 'New World'. As research reveals time and again, the book trade has played a leading role in the spread of new ideas; ideas about America were no exception. David Stoker has studied the book trade of Norfolk for many years and has contributed a number of essays to this series; he focuses here on books 'published' in Norwich in the seventeenth century, a period of particular interest in book trade history, not least because of the rapid and often turbulent spread of new religious and political thought. The Scottish book trade has been well represented in this series, and rightly so for Edinburgh in particular was an exceptionally important location for book production and distribution: Peter Isaac's paper discusses Oliver & Boyd as agents for John Murray II, while the late eighteenth-century periodical press of Edinburgh, and the activities of James Tytler in particular, are surveyed in an entertaining paper by Stephen Brown.

Peter Borsay's concept of the 'English Urban Renaissance' forms a thought-provoking framework for many studies of book trade history.[3] Ian Jackson prefaces his essay on eighteenth-century newspaper advertising with Borsay's remarks on the newspaper as both cause and effect of urban cultural change, before taking what we might see as a 'geographical turn' in his very informative study of the extensive advertising carried by the *Northampton Mercury* and the *Reading Mercury*. Most provincial news-papers depended upon advertising for their financial viability and Lisa Peters offers a fascinating essay on medical advertising, with its often exaggerated claims, in the Wrexham press from 1855 to 1906.

The 'English Urban Renaissance' benefited mainly the established gentry and the rising 'middling sort'; one needed a degree of surplus wealth to take part in the new cultural developments. Avoiding the historiographical quicksands of a polarization between 'high' and 'low' culture, it might reasonably be observed that so-called popular culture is also an essential focus for the history of the book, and of the book trade. This is ably demonstrated by Alice Ford-Smith's perceptive study of execution broadsides from the Midlands – a very popular and quite localized form of 'street literature'.

Locality – in particular the idea of the 'imagined' community – is an important feature of Graham Law's paper on three Victorian newspaper novelists. Starting from the ideas of Benedict Anderson, Law demonstrates that the 'imagined community' is a useful construct at local as well as national level and is a particularly fruitful approach to book history.[4] The possibility of moving, relatively easily and cheaply, between locations – if only for a holiday or weekend trip – was one of the new-found delights of the nineteenth century. The rapid spread of the railways had a huge impact not only on the landscape but also on many aspects of life and culture. Stephen Colclough's research into the impact of railways on the book trade is wide-ranging; the focus of his essay is the development between 1840 and 1875 of the railway bookstall, a highly innovative location of book-trade activity.

Many essays in this series remind us that it would be unwise to make too many assumptions about the provincial book trade. The exact nature of the trade and its practitioners in different places could vary considerably and sweeping generalizations are usually misleading. David Hounslow demonstrates the individual character of several book-trade people in York and Gainsborough in his paper, also reminding us that the evidence of imprints needs to be used with great care.

These conferences, held in various parts of the United Kingdom, often benefit from a paper or two on the local region. The Exeter conference was no exception, with two papers focusing on the West Country. The fortunes of subscription and circulating libraries, a number of them in seaside resorts, are discussed by Keith Manley, while Ian Maxted's essay on the production and distribution of topographical prints of Devon exemplifies the delicate balance between London and the provinces which was a key feature of much of the history of the book trade.

The editors hope that this volume of papers presented at Exeter in 2002 demonstrates that the study of the history of the book trade, so ably inspired by the energy and enthusiasm of the late Professor Peter Isaac, is thriving.

John Hinks

Acknowledgements

The editors wish to record their good wishes to Barry McKay upon his relinquishing of editorial involvement with this series and their thanks to Ian Maxted for his assistance with proof-reading.

Notes

1. This observation is well demonstrated by a recent collection of essays: *Printed Matters: Printing, Publishing and Urban Culture in Europe in the Modern Period* edited by Malcolm Gee and Tim Kirk (Historical Urban Studies Series), (Aldershot, 2002).
2. Barry McKay's appreciation of Peter Isaac is included in the previous volume in this series, *Light on the Book Trade: Essays in Honour of Peter Isaac* (2004), pp. ix-x, together with a list of his publications, pp. 213-16.
3. Peter Borsay, 'The English Urban Renaissance: the development of provincial urban culture, c1680-c1760', *Social History*, vol. 2 (1977), reprinted in *The Eighteenth Century Town: a reader in English urban history*, edited by P. Borsay, 1990, and P. Borsay, *The English Urban Renaissance: culture and society in the provincial town, 1660-1770* (Oxford, 1989).
4. Benedict Anderson, *Imagined Communities: reflections on the origin and spread of nationalism* (London, 1983, revised edition, 1991).

Contributors

Catherine Armstrong was one of two British Book Trade Conference Fellows for 2002 and has recently been awarded her PhD from the University of Warwick on the topic of Representations of 'Place' and 'Potential' in North American Travel Literature 1607-1660. She is currently working as a seminar tutor at the University of Warwick.

Iain Beavan is Senior Curator (Projects) in Historic Collections, University of Aberdeen. He has written widely on the Scottish book trade, especially in the nineteenth century. His recent research has centred on the Edinburgh firm of Oliver & Boyd, publishers and booksellers.

Stephen Brown is the Master of Champlain College at Trent University in Ontario Canada and the 3M Fellow in the Department of English. The author of over fifty articles and book chapters and editor of the manuscripts of the Scottish eighteenth-century printer, William Smellie, he is currently engaged as co-editor of volume two of the Edinburgh History of the Book in Scotland.

Stephen Colclough is a research fellow at the Centre for Writing, Publishing and Printing History in the Department of English, University of Reading. He has published on the history of reading in the long eighteenth century and the poetry of John Clare and is currently working on a history the distribution and retailing of texts in nineteenth-century Britain.

Alice Ford-Smith is the Assistant Librarian at the Wellcome Library for the History and Understanding of Medicine, London.

David Hounslow is a former children's bookseller.

John Hinks was Research Fellow on the 'British Book Trade Index on the Web' project (see www.bbti.bham.ac.uk) at the University of Birmingham (2002-2005) and is now an Honorary Visiting Fellow at the Centre for Urban History, University of Leicester, where he is pursuing his research interests in the history of the book trade and print culture.

Peter C. G. Isaac (1921-2002) was Professor Emeritus of Civil and Public Health Engineering at the University of Newcastle upon Tyne and a keen bibliophile. He served as President of the Bibliographical Society and founded both the British Book Trade Index and the annual seminars on the history of the British book trade which continue as the 'Print Networks' conferences.

Ian Jackson was one of two British Book Trade Conference Fellows for 2002. He completed his doctoral thesis in History, entitled 'Print in Provincial England: Reading and Northampton, c.1720-1800' at the University of Oxford in January 2003, and he currently works for the Australian War Memorial in Canberra, Australia. His research interests include eighteenth-century provincial newspapers, and how the book trade influenced the evolving relationship between metropolitan and provincial cultures in the long eighteenth century.

Graham Law has been teaching in Japan since 1981 and is now Professor in the School of International Studies, Waseda University, Tokyo. He is co-editor of the Wilkie Collins Society Journal and his main interests are in periodicals and serialization in the Victorian period.

Lucy Lewis completed her doctoral thesis in 2000 at London University on 'British Boethianism 1380-1486'. She is now based at Cambridge University Library.

K. A. Manley is a Bibliographical Services Librarian, Institute of Historical Research (part of the University of London Library Services) and was editor of *Library History* from 1988-2004.

Ian Maxted has been County Local Studies Librarian for Devon since 1977. Since the 1970s he has compiled the Exeter Working Papers in British Book Trade History, a series which is at present available on the internet at www.devon.gov.uk/library/locstudy/bookhist/ He is currently working on illustrated topographical works and the printmakers associated with them in the period 1750-1875.

Lisa Peters is a librarian at University College Chester working in the field of online learning. Her main research interest is North Wales newspaper history.

David Stoker is a senior lecturer in the Department of Information and Library Studies of the University of Wales, Aberystwyth. He has been interested in the early Norwich book trade since 1970.

The Tavistock Boethius:
One of the Earliest Examples of Provincial Printing

LUCY LEWIS

PRINTED ON THE EVE of the Reformation, the Tavistock Boethius reflects the independence and prosperity of the Abbey in which it was produced. It is a volume at once traditional and forward-looking: traditional in its contents – a translation into English of Boethius's *Consolation of Philosophy* made by John Walton in 1410 – and forward-looking in its techniques and methods of presentation. The printer Thomas Richard undertook to present Walton's translation with an accompanying (anonymous) commentary which appears in a smaller type-face interspersed intermittently through the main text. Although textual arrangements of this kind were relatively common in medieval manuscripts, they presented certain technical challenges to the inexperienced printer, and these challenges are met on the whole successfully by Richard. Whether Richard had had any previous experience in printing is not clear, but it seems unlikely, and the 1525 edition of Boethius is certainly the first production of the press established at Tavistock. Indeed, it was one of the earliest productions of a provincial press anywhere in England.[1] It is the ambition and confidence of the undertaking, combined with Richard's editorial practice in preparing the text and its intriguing commentary for sixteenth-century readers, which constitute the chief interest of this edition and which will form the subject of this paper.

The book, number 3200 in the *Short Title Catalogue* of Pollard and Redgrave, is in quarto format, quired in eights.[2] Sheets are signed on the first four leaves of each quire beginning with A and ending with R. A black letter type is used which may originally have been designed for Latin (or possibly French) texts, as 'w' is usually replicated by printing two 'v's together, as if the 'w' character were in short supply. Woodcut initials are used fairly frequently throughout and there are two woodcut images, one at the beginning and one at the end of the edition. The title page shows an image of Christ in judgement surrounded by the four evangelists, Matthew, Mark, Luke and John. This image is itself surrounded by elaborate

1

woodcut borders. On the final page of the edition appears the coat of arms of Robert Langdon, whose role as patron of the enterprise is acknowledged in the colophon:

Enprynted in the exempt monastery of Tauestok in Denshyre By me Dan Thomas Rychard monke of the sayd Monastery To the instant desyre of the right worshipful esquyer Mayster Robert Langdon. Anno d. M D xxv. Deo Gracias.

The involvement of Langdon, a member of the Cornish gentry, suggests that the Abbey maintained strong and fruitful links with the secular world outside its walls. Indeed, the second (and last) production of the Abbey's press was a decidedly secular publication, the *Statutes of the Stannery*, containing the regulations of the Devonshire tin-mining industry.[3] A single copy of this survives in the library of Exeter College, Oxford, which also holds the only perfect copy of the Tavistock Boethius. The fact that Exeter College was founded by a Bishop of Exeter, William Stapeldon, for the education of scholars from the West Country, goes some way to explaining the presence of these two rare volumes in this location, but more will be said about provenance below.[4]

The fostering of connections with secular society by the Abbey may be seen as consistent with its attempt to establish an autonomous identity independent (or at least relatively so) from ecclesiastical authority. The word 'exempt' in the colophon refers to the 1519 ruling in favour of the Abbot of Tavistock, who resisted the claim of the Bishop of the diocese to visit his Abbey.[5] The Abbot at that time was Richard Banham and the Bishop was Hugh Oldham. The high status of the Abbot of Tavistock at the end of the Middle Ages was reflected by his wearing of a mitre and by his enjoyment of many of the privileges of a bishop. He also enjoyed a seat in the House of Lords, a privilege granted only to twenty-nine abbots. The Abbey can therefore be seen as a powerful, not to say worldly, institution which was highly conscious, and indeed jealous, of its place in society.[6] The choice of Boethius's *Consolation of Philosophy* as a text to inaugurate the Abbey's press is therefore an interesting and appropriate one. Boethius was a Roman senator steeped in the traditions of classical philosophy but also conversant with the doctrines of the Christian church, which he may or may not have adopted. The *Consolation* seems poised on the borderline between two worlds. Christianity is nowhere explicitly affirmed in the text and yet nowhere is it flatly contradicted (although there are one or two points which are not consistent with orthodox Christianity). In spite of the doctrinal ambiguity of the text, there can be no doubt that it upholds traditional morality and values, recommending a contempt for worldly pleasures and an acceptance of the providential scheme. Framed as a dialogue between the prisoner Boethius and the allegorical figure of Lady Philosophy, the work incorporates sections of lyrical poetry and mythological narrative which enhance its appeal. The work's popularity among medieval readers may partly be explained by its ability to echo and confirm traditional morality while at the same time offering an escape, or at least an imaginative release, from the familiar world of medieval religious didacticism.

The *Consolation of Philosophy* was certainly just as popular amongst the laity as amongst the religious. John Walton's 1410 translation of the work into English – the one printed at Tavistock – was commissioned by a wealthy secular patron, Elizabeth Berkeley, daughter of Thomas the Magnificent.[7] The existence of a patron is first hinted at in the 'Prefatio Translatoris', although the person is not named. In this translator's preface, Walton disclaims responsibility for having conceived the project, emphasizing that he undertook the task at the request of an honoured superior. The name of the patron and the translator form an acrostic which is spelled out over four stanzas appended to the work in the text printed by Thomas Richard.[8] Until recently, it was thought that only the printed edition preserved this version of the text, with the extra stanzas. Although nineteen extant manuscripts were recorded by Mark Science, the work's modern editor, none of these (according to Science) contained the acrostic stanzas.[9] In fact, one manuscript (which Science had presumably not examined although he had recorded it) does contain the acrostic; moreover, this manuscript – MS. Thott. Royal Library, Copenhagen – also contains the commentary text reproduced in the 1525 edition, and was apparently used as printer's copy by the Tavistock printer, Thomas Richard.[10] This manuscript, dated to the early fifteenth century, was owned by the Cornish antiquary William Borlase, who inscribes his signature along with the date, 1737. The fact that a West Country provenance can be traced far back confirms other physical evidence (such as marks in the text) linking it with Richard's 1525 edition.

The commentary present in the Copenhagen manuscript and the 1525 edition is of particular interest because it seems to be one of the first commentaries on the *Consolation* written in English. Of course it was preceded by a long and rich tradition of Latin commentaries, out of which it grew, but nevertheless this represents a new and exciting phase in the history of Boethianism.[11] The author of the commentary is not known, although it seems likely that Walton himself composed it in conjunction with his verse translation of Boethius's Latin text. In order to compose his translation, Walton would have consulted various sources, and evidence for this survives in the lexis of the work.[12] Meditating on this material, he may have decided that he wished to present to his readers some of this additional information and explication without over-burdening the translation proper. The strict separation between explanatory material and direct translation was not always observed by medieval translators and so Walton's practice (if Walton can be taken as the commentary's author) would have been somewhat novel, even forward-looking. Chaucer, who had translated the *Consolation* into English prose in the preceding century, was more traditional in that he incorporated explanatory material (mainly paraphrases from Nicholas Trevet's Latin commentary) into the body of the translation itself. The textual connections between Chaucer's translation, the *Boece*, and Walton's will be explored further below in a discussion about Thomas Richard's role as inheritor of the English tradition of Boethianism. Richard was himself credited with authorship of the commentary in the Tavistock print, but the recent 'discovery' of the same text in the Copenhagen manuscript has definitively laid that theory to rest. Richard's decision to print commentary and text together, though largely determined by the copy he had to hand, may have been influenced by continental editions which gave the *Consolation* with commentary text. One example (though others could be cited) is the 1476 edition printed in Nuremberg by Anton Koberger. This presents Boethius' Latin text in a central text-box, surrounded by the Latin commentary of Thomas Aquinas in smaller type on all four sides, a tidier arrangement than that found in the Richard edition, which simply inserts chunks of commentary text at the appropriate place. The Nuremberg edition is a small format volume of similar dimensions to Richard's Boethius. Another edition, printed in 1477 by Colard Mansion in Bruges, gives a French translation of the *Consolation* together with a commentary by Regnier de S. Trudon. Colard Mansion's association with Caxton means that his work may have been more familiar to Englishmen like Richard than that of other continental printers. However, there are few similarities with Richard's edition, for Mansion's *Consolation* is a large format volume with lavish illustrations added by an illuminator and coloured paraph marks and was clearly a de luxe book. A single type size is used for both text and commentary, and the commentary is continuous with the text rather than separated from it: the word 'Glose' indicates a piece of exposition.[13] Some early English editions (though not Caxton's *Boece*) presented original source texts with commentary texts, and Richard may well have seen books like Richard Pynson's print of the pseudo-Bonaventuran *Imitation of the Blessed Life of Christ*, translated into English by Nicholas Love and accompanied in the printed edition by marginal glosses.[14]

The commentary in the Tavistock print shares certain similarities with a work called *The Boke of Coumfort of Bois*, surviving in one manuscript, MS Bodleian Auct.F.3.5.[15] This fifteenth-century text paraphrases and expands on the first book only of Boethius's *Consolation*. Free translation and commentary are melded into one continuous discourse, in a fashion typical of medieval scholarship. Although the similarities between this and the Tavistock text are close enough to suggest possible influence, it appears that they are more probably due to a common source: Nicholas Trevet's Latin commentary. The debt to Trevet needs to be fully acknowledged before speculations about the motives of the English commentators can be made. N. H. Kaylor Jr, in his article on *The Boke of Coumfort*, is rather too quick to assume that the Christianizing tendencies in that text are original and new. The examples that Kaylor cites actually turn out to be traceable to the Trevet commentary. For example, the discussion of exile and the city of reason in Book I prose 5 of the *Consolation* is used by the author of *The Boke of Coumfort*, and by the commentator in the Tavistock edition, to introduce the idea of the kingdom of heaven. The equation of the kingdom of heaven with reason is present in Trevet's commentary and it seems that the two English commentaries draw on that. Trevet's Latin reads:

Sed non sic de patria Boecii, per quam mansionem infra terminos racionis intelligimus. In hac enim est tantum unus princeps, scilicet Deus, qui est principium et regula recte racionis, unde et unusquisque in terra uiuit secundum rectam racionem in quantum quis uiuit secundum rectam racionem in tantum manet in patria et ciuitate propria cuius Deus est princeps, patet quod in tantum quis manet in patria in quantum subicitur Deo.[16]

This is echoed very closely in the two English texts. The commentary in the Tavistock edition reads:

But in thys realme of resonablete that specially be longeth to the court of heuen / ther ys but one lorde and souereyn, the vyche is God / principle and ruler of reson /

vherfore in so mouche as any man leneth after reson / in hove moche he is subgett to the rule of goddess lavve. And in hove moche he leneth after reson / and so moche he abydeth in hys contre and in hys proper cyte. In vvyche god alone ys prince and gouernour.

The text in *The Boke of Coumfort* reads:

For if thou remember of what cuntre thou were borne? That is heuene hit is not gouernede be emperoures ne be gouernayle of multitude as were the cuntrees of Athene but oon lorde oon kynge that is god he is lorde of thy cuntree The weche lorde reioysed him and is gladde of the duellynge of cytezenes, that menes in his cytee of reson. And he ordeynes nought to be put ought in to exile of the weche lorde it is a souereyne fredom for to be gouernede be the brydel of him and to obeye to his ryghtwisnes.

The Boke of Coumfort is closer to a translation of Boethius, but nonetheless reflects the emphases in Trevet's commentary clearly. Many other examples could be given to demonstrate the dependence of the English commentators on Trevet.

Science prints most of the commentary present in the Tavistock edition in an appendix, but unhelpfully omits some shorter pieces of commentary text without acknowledging that he has done so. The omissions (which are probably oversights) seem rather arbitrary, as some shorter pieces of commentary are included, but on what basis (if any) the selection has been made is not explained. One fairly substantial paragraph that Science omits (or overlooks) occurs on A3^a of the Tavistock edition, between stanzas 8 and 9 of the 'Prefatio Translatoris'. The paragraph is a mythographical gloss and reads as follows:

Caliope as poetes fayneth ys one of the sonnes doughteres & ys one & chef of the ix muses & they cal her goddas of eloquence. She hath iii welles Gramatica Dialetica & Retorica of whom ys driued [*sic*] al craft of eloqu[e]nce Also they feyneth to be in hel iii susters called furyas or vengeresses that punishe men for ther mesdedes the one ys called Alecco a nother Megner & the iii Tessiphone. These also be called muses of morning that tecyth & enformeth men to make sorouful complayntes

Another piece of commentary text omitted by Science from his appendix occurs on D4^a of the Tavistock edition. A brief definition of tragedy is inserted between stanzas 182 and 183, which is Fortune's speech in her own defence, Book II prosa 2. The definition reads as follows: 'Tragedyes ben dytes made of made of certen persons vyche begynnethe in welthe and prosperyte and endeth in myscheffe & aduersyte'. This echoes Chaucer's

Boece, which our commentator probably had in mind at this point. Chaucer's gloss reads: 'Tragedye is to seyn a dite of a prosperite for a tyme, that endeth in wrecchidnesse'. This definition differs in a small but significant way from Trevet's commentary at this point. Trevet passes moral judgement on the victims of tragedy whom he portrays as wicked, whereas Chaucer simply states that they are unfortunate.[17] Trevet's gloss reads: 'tragedia est carmen de magnis iniquitatibus a prosperitate incipiens et in aduersitate terminans'. The crucial words here, of course, are 'magnis iniquitatibus'. The decision by the anonymous commentator to follow Chaucer rather than Trevet here can be seen as a conscious decision, since there is evidence that he clearly had access to the Trevet commentary as well as to the *Boece* and would have been in a position to choose.

There is some evidence that the printer Thomas Richard altered Walton's text in places where he thought Chaucer's translation more appropriate or effective. For example, the word 'songes' in Book I, stanza 32 of Walton's translation has been changed in the printed text to 'dytes', echoing Chaucer's 'delitable ditees'. Similarly, 'trewth' in Book I stanza 94 has been changed to 'soth', again echoing Chaucer; 'minde' in Book V stanza 12 has been changed to 'soule' echoing Chaucer's phrase 'enprented into sowles'. Other examples are given by Science in his introduction.[18] Other changes, not attributable to the influence of Chaucer, are made. Richard seems to have attempted to update the language of Walton's translation, a text composed some hundred years before the printed edition was made. For example, the word 'cleped', which had apparently become archaic by 1525, was substituted, often by the word 'called'. Certain other changes are less easy to explain and seem to reflect editorial whim more than anything else. For example, the word 'wilful' and its cognates like 'wilfulnesse' seem to have been replaced whenever they occur in Walton's translation. The last stanza of Book I metrum 7 provides an example of this (although it occurs many times). The two versions of this stanza are given in full below because there are other subtle differences worthy of comment. First, Walton's translation in the manuscript tradition:

> Ne ioye þou noght of worldly wilfulnesse,
> Ne drede þe noþing of þis worldly dynne,
> Ne hope þou noght þat transetorie es,
> Ne sorwe þou noght but only for þi synne,
> For euery þoght þat þis regneþ ynne
> Ful trouble and derk it is and may noght see

> He is so wrast away he may not wynne
> And brideled sore what þat euer he be.

In the edition printed by Richard the text reads:

> Ne Joy thou nought of worldly welthynes
> Ne dred ye nothynge of thys worldly dyne
> Ne hope thou not that transeytory ys
> Ne sorow thou nought but yf yt be for synne
> For euery thofte that thes regneth in
> Troble & derke yt ys & may not se
> He ys so wrast a way he may nofte wynne
> And brideled so that he may not be fre

The version printed by Richard seems to retain the deference that we would expect from a presentation-copy version of the text, and the Copenhagen manuscript (used as printer's copy by Richard) probably was such a text. The deference is present in the modification of 'þi synne' to simply an impersonal and generalized 'synne'. Deference is also detectable in the suppression of the idea that worldly status and power is not equivalent to freedom: the phrase 'what þat euer he be' is replaced by the more neutral 'so that he may not be fre'.

Richard's interventions as editor and his active engagement with the text reflect the relevance and perennial fascination of the *Consolation* for late-medieval readers: it was a text to be reassessed, made new and brought up to date, not a fossilized relic. Although Walton's language may have seemed a little dated by the early sixteenth century (dated enough at least to require occasional modernization), it is clear that the themes and subject matter of Walton's Boethius were still deemed relevant. Philosophical and ethical works like the *Consolation of Philosophy* (a category distinct from purely religious works) had, after all, been a mainstay of the early printers at the close of the fifteenth century, and Richard's choice of this text to inaugurate his printing career reflects an awareness of recent successes by Caxton and other printers, successes which he no doubt hoped to emulate. Caxton's edition of Chaucer's *Boece* would have been perhaps the most obvious model for Richard's experiment. The Caxton *Boece* would not, however, have been perceived as exceptional or experimental by early readers of printed books, simply for the reason that it was often bound with other, related texts, and I have discussed the phenomenon of sammelbande in an earlier paper.[19] These combinations, whether the result of conscious, analytical classification or driven by more pragmatic considerations (such as the economic advantage of binding several texts of the same dimensions within one cover, however random the selection) would have shaped readers' understanding of such material. Whether by accident or design, the *Consolation of Philosophy* was made available to early print readers as part of a body of material, part of a complex of knowledge. The relative responsibility of readers, printers and booksellers for sammelband combinations is a question which I addressed in my earlier paper, and which Alexandra Gillespie also discussed in a recent useful article.[20] It is not always easy to determine at what stage the decision to combine texts was made, but a mutual collaboration between these three groups (readers, printers and booksellers) seems to have been likely.

A brief discussion of a sammelband volume viewed recently in the library of Exeter College, Oxford, will help to give a sense of the literary context out of which Richard's edition emerged. The volume contains four early editions bound within an early binding. The titles, in order of their appearance in the volume, are: the *Orcharde of Syon*, printed by Wynkyn de Worde in 1519, then Caxton's 1484 edition of Cato's *Distichs*, called *Caton*, followed by Caxton's 1478 edition of the *Boece*, and finally Lydgate's *Book of Our Lady* printed, again by Caxton, in 1484.[21] The ownership signature 'Lodovicus Joh[a]nnes' appears on the first leaf of the *Orcharde of Syon*, a name intriguingly similar to one inscribed in the Richard edition also in Exeter College Library where the signature reads 'William Lodovici'. Perhaps 'Lodovici' is a genitive, meaning 'of Lodovicus'? Could Johannes be the father and William the son? It certainly seems likely that the Richard edition and the sammelband shared an early provenance. The collocation of the *Distichs* of Cato with the *Boece* is interesting, though perhaps not surprising. Both texts can be described as ethical, though not austerely scholastic: they would have appealed to the serious-minded though not necessarily academic reader. Interestingly, the same combination occurs in a volume in the Bodleian Library, Oxford, shelfmark Arch.G.d.13. In that volume the *Caton* and the *Boece* are bound with the 1484 edition of *The Knight of the Tower* and the 1484 edition of Aesop's *Fables*.[22] The fact that three of these editions in the Bodleian volume share a publication date is surely no mere coincidence and hints at early marketing strategies on the part of printers and booksellers.

The Exeter College sammelband is a good example of the kind of volume that Richard and his contemporaries would have used – the kind of volume, indeed, in which they may first, or most readily, have encountered Boethian material. The combination of texts contained in the sammelband reflects the complementarity of philosophical and more orthodoxly religious material, and such a combination would have been appealing to the more sophisticated clergy – men like the printer Thomas Richard. Although not included in that particular volume, Walton's translation of Boethius's *Consolation* occupies a key position within this ethical tradition, as is demonstrated by its inclusion with the *Dicta Philosophorum*, translated by Earl Rivers in the Newberry manuscript copied in 1480.[23] The Exeter College sammelband contains, alongside the printed texts, a macaronic, Latin/English lyric copied in an early sixteenth-century hand, and apparently unrecorded until now.[24] The lyric appears on the reverse of the last page of the *Caton*, facing the first page of the *Boece*, appearing to link them. The lyric's fusion of Latin and English echoes the polyglot nature of the *Boece*, a text which, although written all in English, introduced several new words into the language, mostly philosophical terms.[25] The heterogeneity or mixed nature of the macaronic lyric also seems to reflect in miniature the mixed form of the *Consolation of Philosophy*, a prosimetrum written in alternating verse and prose sections, although Chaucer's translation is all in prose. Perhaps the author or copyist of the lyric intended to supply a perceived deficiency in Chaucer's all-prose *Boece* by offering this verse companion. The juxtaposition of appropriate verse material with the *Boece*, perhaps for similar reasons, occurs in an important manuscript now in Cambridge University Library, MS Ii.3.21. The verse matter in this case, however, was of less obscure origin, being the work of Chaucer himself: his short, Boethian lyrics *Fortune* and *The Former Age* are copied along with the translation. The lyric in the Exeter sammelband recommends self-knowledge as the basis for virtue and is composed in an aphoristic style reminiscent of the *Caton*. The importance of not abandoning self-knowledge is central to the teachings of Philosophia in the *Consolation of Philosophy*, and in this respect the lyric echoes the thematic as well as the linguistic nature of the text it accompanies. A full transcription of the lyric is not necessary here but I intend to publish it in a separate journal article in due course.

Manuscript annotations in copies of the Richard edition are more functional, less inspired. They do, nonetheless, provide useful insights into how early readers used and construed the text. Most annotation in the Exeter College copy is in Latin, suggesting a fairly learned reader, perhaps the William Lodovici whose ownership signature is inscribed along with the date 1550. According to the library's catalogue, Lodovici died in 1583. Underlining of key words by the annotator is fairly frequent, and especially dense in Book III prose 3, the philosophical heart of the work, which describes the nature of sovereign good, Boethius's 'summum bonum'. Two copies of the edition in the Bodleian Library provide further examples of early reader-annotation. One, still preserved in its original binding, contains the ownership signature of Humfrey Wanley, whose interest in the text seems to have been largely philological judging by the kind of annotations he makes. For example, he notes that 'reden' is an infinitive and that the word 'correcteth' has an Anglo-Saxon termination. After Wanley, who lived in the seventeenth century, the book passed into the ownership of the Earl of Oxford and then to Thomas Hearne. Hearne was responsible for supplying the missing last page of text, with the coat of arms woodcut, in manuscript. The other copy of the Richard edition in the Bodleian contains annotation of a rather more random nature. These jottings seem to bear little relation to the text. Hastily-scribbled sums and pen trials are frequent, but what appears to be a rather more considered statement in a sixteenth-century hand occurs on D5ᵃ. This is the beginnings of a formal, almost legalistic, declaration which may have been the practice draft of some fuller document. Written twice, one line below the other, are the words: 'Be it knowne vnto all men by these p[re]sente that I Timothee Caxtos (?)'. The conjectured surname 'Caxtos' is not at all clear. This is the most formal of the various jottings in the volume.

The casualness, almost irreverence, of the annotations in the last-mentioned copy raises the question of aesthetics. Was Richard's edition regarded by its early readers as a piece of fine printing, an aesthetic object, and had Richard intended it to be viewed as such? Or was it viewed as a merely utilitarian volume to be treated with no special care? The use of woodcut initials throughout the volume reveals an endeavour to give variety and graphic interest to the page. The introduction of speech headings not present in Walton's text ('Philosophia loquitur', 'Boetius loquitur', or simply 'Boecius' and 'Phia') serves more to clarify content than enhance appearance, but is done discreetly and does not overcrowd the page. Some blank half-pages indicate that there was difficulty estimating space to accommodate the prose commentary. However, in at least one place, a page lay-out which seems initially odd turns out to be judicious and considered, revealing that Richard thought carefully about the relation of text to commentary. At the foot of $Q8^a$, the first line of stanza 957 appears alone, separated from the rest of the stanza by a large chunk of prose commentary which takes up the whole of $Q8^b$ and two thirds of the next page, $R1^a$. Although this separation seems awkward at first, there is a kind of aptness to the hiatus, as the topic being discussed at this point is time and eternity. The disruption of the stanza's finite form, as printed in Richard's edition, seems to illustrate the very concept that Philosophia is expounding to Boethius: that the world is perpetual, without end. The stanza begins: 'Loo Plato sayth thys worlde hath euer ybe' and continues, after the hiatus: 'And to an ende hyt shal neuer be brought | They say ther fore hyt hath eternyte'. Whether or not this marriage of form and content was intended by Richard is debatable but his edition is certainly an intelligent one, particularly in its fusion of traditional material with new trends, and perhaps he should therefore be given the benefit of the doubt.

Richard's edition makes bold and ambitious use of available materials and disposable resources to carry the tradition of British Boethianism through into the age of print. Richard shows discretion in his sparing modifications to Walton's text, and manages the difficult task of balancing text and commentary on the page with comparative (though not total) success. The commentary he preserves for us is of especial interest in being perhaps the earliest English commentary on Boethius's text and this enhances the literary significance of the edition. Above all, however, it is the ambition of the project for a newly-established provincial press that is impressive. It reflects the confidence of a community grounded in the traditions of the past and in the Christian faith but yet outward-looking. In a time of such rapid change as the Reformation, perhaps a text like the *Consolation of Philosophy*, with its emphasis on stoical forbearance and its lack of religious zealotry, was especially valuable.

Notes

1. On the earliest printers in the British Isles, see W. K. Sessions, *A Printer's Dozen: The First British Printing Centres to 1557 after Westminster and London* (York, 1983).

2. *Short Title Catalogue of Books Printed in England, Scotland and Ireland, and of English Books Printed Abroad, 1475-1640*, ed. by Alfred G. Pollard and G. W. Redgrave, rev. by W. A. Jackson, F. S. Ferguson and Katharine F. Pantzer, 2nd ed., 3 vols (Oxford, 1976-1991), hereafter referred to as *STC*.

3. *STC* no. 6795.6.

4. On the history of the college, see *The Victoria History of the Counties of England: Oxfordshire*, vol. III (London, 1970).

5. See G. H. Radford, 'Early Printing in Devon', *Transactions of the Devonshire Association*, 60 (1928), 51-74 (p. 62).

6. For a detailed account of the Abbey's role, see H. P. R. Finberg, *Tavistock Abbey: A Study in the Social and Economic History of Devon* (Newton Abbot, 1969).

7. On the Berkeley family and their patronage, see Ralph Hanna, III, 'Sir Thomas Berkeley and His Patronage', *Speculum*, 64 (1989), 878-916.

8. On the use of acrostics in the work, see I. R. Johnson, 'New Evidence for the Authorship of Walton's Boethius', *Notes and Queries*, 43 (1996), 19-21.

9. *Boethius: De Consolatione Philosophiae Translated by John Walton Canon of Oseney*, ed. by Mark Science, Early English Text Society, original series, 170 (London, 1927).

10. A detailed description of the Copenhagen manuscript, of Richard's edition, and of the connections between the two, is given by Brian Donaghey, Irma Taavitsainen and Erik Miller in 'Walton's Boethius: From Manuscript to Print', in *English Studies*, 80 (1999), 398-407.

11. On the tradition of British Boethianism, see my unpublished doctoral dissertation, *British Boethianism, 1380-1436* (Queen Mary and Westfield College, University of London, 2000). Chapter six is a discussion of Walton's translation.

12. See M. V. Aldridge, 'An Annotated Glossary, with Introduction, to John Walton's Translation of Boethius, De Consolatione Philosophiae (1410)' (unpublished doctoral thesis, University of Oxford, 1967).

13. A copy of each of the continental editions is held at the Cambridge University Library. The former is shelf-mark Inc.5.A.7.2[898], the latter is Inc.1.F.3.1. For a useful survey of different commentary/text layouts in early printed books, see Gerhardt Powitz, 'Text und Kommentar im Buch des 15. Jahrhunderts', in *Book and Text in the Fifteenth Century*, ed. by Lotte Hellinga and Helmar Hartel (Hamburg: Hauswedell, 1981), pp. 35-45. See also M. McFadden Smith, 'Form and Its Relationship to Content in the Design of Incunables' (Cambridge PhD Thesis, 1983).

14. *STC* no. 3623.

15. See N. H. Kaylor, Jr, 'Interpolations in *The Boke of Coumfort of Bois*: A Late-Medieval Translation of Boethius's *De Consolatione Philosophiae*', *Fifteenth-Century Studies*, 23 (1997), 74-80. A projected edition of *The Boke of Coumfort* by Brian S. Donaghey has yet to appear.

16. Trevet's Latin commentary is available in an unpublished microfilm edition made by E. T. Silk, which is the one quoted here: 'Nicholas Trevet on Boethius. Exposicio Fratris Nicolae Trevethii Anglici Ordinis Predicatorum Super Boecio De Consolacione'.

17. On Chaucer's definition of tragedy, see Henry Ansgar Kelly, *Chaucerian Tragedy* (Cambridge, 1997).

18. See *Boethius: De Consolatione Philosophiae*, ed. by M. Science, p. xxviii.

19. See 'For No Text Is An Island, Divided from the Main: Incunable Sammelbande', in *Light on the Book Trade: Essays in Honour of Peter Isaac*, ed. by Barry McKay, John Hinks and Maureen Bell (New Castle & London, 2002), pp. 13-26.

20. Alexandra Gillespie, 'Caxton's Chaucer and Lydgate Quartos: Miscellanies from Manuscript to Print', *Transactions of the Cambridge Bibliographical Society*, 12:1 (2000), 1-25.

21. The *STC* numbers of these four, in order, are: 4815, 4853, 3199 and 17023/4. However, *STC* omits to mention the Exeter College copies of all these editions, a surprising oversight.

22. *STC* numbers for *The Knight of the Tower* and Aesop's *Fables* are: 15296 and 175.

23. See R. A. Dwyer, 'The Newberry's Unknown Revision of Walton's Boethius', *Manuscripta* (17) 1973, 27-30. The text of the *Dicta Philosophorum* contained in this manuscript was, according to Curt Bühler, copied from Caxton's edition. See Bühler's article in *Anglia* (74) 1956, 281-91. A rich and fruitful interchange between manuscript and print culture was characteristic of the close of the fifteenth century, and Bühler's example is only one among many.

24. Reference sources checked and found not to mention it are: William A. Ringler, Jr, *Bibliography and Index of English Verse in Manuscript 1501-1558*, prepared and completed by Michael Rudick and Susan J. Ringler (London, 1992); Carleton Brown and Rossell Hope Robbins, *The Index of Middle English Verse* (New York, 1943); Rossell Hope Robbins and John L. Cutler, *Supplement to the Index of Middle English Verse* (Lexington, KT., 1965).

25. See Morton Donner, 'Derived Words in Chaucer's *Boece*: The Translator as Wordsmith', *Chaucer Review*, 18 (1984), 187-203.

The Bookseller and the Pedlar: the Spread of Knowledge of the New World in Early Modern England, 1580-1640 [1]

CATHERINE ARMSTRONG

I am an adventurer, if not to Virginia, yet for Virginia, for every man that prints, adventures.

John Donne: *Sermon before the Virginia Company*, 1622.[2]

Thine, bound in what I may...

William Wood:
Epistle Dedicatory 'To the Reader' of *New Englands Prospect* (London, 1635).[3]

Thou mayest in two or three hours travaile over a few leaves, see and know that which cost him that writ it yeares and travaile over land and sea.

William Wood: as above.[4]

THESE THREE QUOTATIONS epitomize the mind-set of those engaged in spreading knowledge about America. The first is taken from John Donne's 1622 sermon to the Virginia Company in London, given to reassure and inspire members as news reached England of the massacre of over three hundred of the colony's settlers. Donne, the Dean of St Paul's Cathedral, never went to America but was a passionate supporter of the Company whom they hired to preach on important occasions, and who aspired to be its secretary. As Donne's rhetoric here shows, he felt that the job of recruiting new supporters was as important as that of maintaining the colony itself. It is a coincidence of history that European contact with America occurred when the products of print culture were becoming more accessible in many ranks of English society. This paper examines how the writing of authors such as Donne was distributed throughout London and the provinces to eager consumers of information about the new world.

The second author quoted here is William Wood who did make the journey across the Atlantic, spending some time in the Massachusetts Bay colony before returning to England to write the promotional tract *New*

15

Englands Prospect, published in 1635. In his epistle dedicatory Wood signs off with this remark, which indicates that he thought the success of his book was inextricably linked to the success of the colony about which he was writing. The author and the message are one and the same, with the same destiny, the same 'prospect'. The author and the reader are also bound together: the author 'travailling' across the world, the reader through the book. Wood's remarks show an awareness of his place in the early modern networks of communication of which the book trade is one significant aspect.[5]

During the 1580s, exploration of America by Englishmen was begun in earnest and the first attempt was made to establish a permanent settlement at Roanoke in present day North Carolina. This ended ignominiously with the probable murder of all surviving colonists during the escalation of the war with Spain when no ships could be sent out from England to relieve them. Some members of the English elite had already developed an interest in geography and America in particular as shown by the popularity of translated works such as Richard Eden's version of Monardes's *Ioyfull Newes out of a Newe Found World*.[6] Occasionally enthusiastic amateurs translated these books but mostly the work was commissioned by a publisher; Richard Eden was an influential member of Phillip Sidney's circle at court and he had edited and translated many continental texts about North and South America.[7] Eden seems to have had no ulterior motive, unlike Richard Hakluyt the younger who, working from the 1580s onwards, also collected and edited texts with the intention of encouraging English colonization of America for the greater good of the commonwealth.[8] But the role of individual authors, and how their texts impacted on the history of English settlement is outside the scope of this essay, which instead follows the distribution of printed knowledge about the New World from the pens of settlers, visitors or commentators to the shores of Southern England or the streets of London and then outwards to the rest of the country.

Printed knowledge came in many forms, with different literary genres being employed for various effects including travel journals, letters, promotional tracts, sermons, exploration narratives. There were two distinct ways in which a text about America achieved publication during the late sixteenth and early seventeenth century. The first is what I have called the 'deliberate' acquisition of information, usually undertaken by what we would call the 'publisher', who could be an interested patron, a colonial company or a successful printer. These books were written with the intention of being printed, widely distributed and then read by a cross-section of society. Included in this category are sermons, promotional material published by the Virginia Company, and texts sent from New England to be published in London.[9] The Massachusetts colony established its own printing press in 1638 but nothing printed there during the early years was sent to England for distribution.[10] All texts that travelled east across the Atlantic were in manuscript form and published in London or Oxford.

The second category of texts is the 'commandeered' works. These include letters, diaries and tracts intended for a very small readership, a friend or group of friends of the author, and intended to remain in manuscript form.[11] Many of these works found their way into the hands of someone who believed that they should be published for the benefit of further colonization. An example is a letter from the explorer Sir Humphrey Gilbert written to his brother that was somehow seen by George Gascoigne who promptly sent it for publication.[12] Books or pamphlets were sometimes printed entirely without the author's knowledge. *A True Relation of such occurrences as hath happened in Virginia* was published in 1608 without acknowledgement of its true author, Captain John Smith. A certain I.H. declared in his preface to the text that this oversight was unintentional and he acknowledged Smith in print.[13] The role of collectors and editors such as Hakluyt and his successor Samuel Purchas must be acknowledged here.[14] They accepted information about America from letters, journals, family papers and other private literature, and edited and printed them, publicizing them for contemporary readers and preserving them for historians. It is important to acknowledge that authors intending their work to be seen by small private audiences still worked within conventions of a constructed readership that may seem impersonal today. Hence the content of the two types of literature may not radically differ because an awareness of some sort of readership, and a reluctance to reveal oneself as author, can be seen in both sorts of text.

Before travelling into the provinces, it is important to take a look at the London trade for a moment. During the early modern period the book trade remained centred on London. The printing trade was monopolized by the Stationers' Company, which received its charter from Queen Mary in 1557; Elizabeth on her accession confirmed its incorporation, and the Company purchased premises, appointed offices and hired servants. A register was established to record regulations, the binding of apprentices and granting of printing licences. Consequently, the printing industry was under the supervision of both the monarch and the Company itself.[15] Many printers during the early modern period were treading a fine line between legal and illicit activities, though the majority of those who were punished had produced a book licensed to someone else, rather than a totally proscribed one.[16] All the members of the Company operated in London so the distribution of books and the knowledge contained within them depended on trade networks with the capital. By 1577 there were 175 printers operating in London plus an unknown number of apprentices. The Stationers' Company register is a great resource for historians studying early modern printing in London, giving an account of every book licensed for publication as well as who presented it and printed it. The only printers allowed to operate outside the Company's remit were the university presses at Oxford and Cambridge, and only one book on America was printed outside London before 1640: John Smith's *A History of Virginia* printed in Oxford in 1612. William Simonds, a Doctor of Divinity at Magdalen College, provided additional commentary material for Smith's work, which may explain this anomaly.[17]

The London printing and bookselling trades are the only parts of the early modern distribution network that have been thoroughly examined by historians. It would be a mistake to think of practitioners of this trade as merely printers or booksellers. They took an active role in collecting and distributing knowledge and an active interest in overseas travel, indeed the title of 'publisher' might more accurately describe the role of these men. Publishers in the modern sense, taking responsibility for financing and distributing a text, did not exist independently of booksellers during this period. Instead members of the Stationers' Company would print books having been commissioned to do so by a bookseller who would then sell them in their shops. So, four people would be involved at the initial stage of creating a book: the author, the patron, the printer and the bookseller. But writers did occasionally try to acquire publication for their own manuscript with the help of a patron. William Strachey's *Historie of Virginia Britannia* is an example of this – he never got the manuscript published during his lifetime and was shunned by three patrons including Francis Bacon.[18] Printers were a powerful third party in this business arrangement, and became important figures in the literary world; occasionally they would even perform the tasks of cutting and piecing together of texts themselves. The three publishers of the largest number of travel and geographical texts during Elizabeth's reign also happened to be among the wealthiest printers in London.[19] However, even this status did not prevent them from an occasional brush with the law. Richard Jugge was one of the earliest to recognize the value of books on navigation, printing English versions of the work of Peter Martyr and Martin Cortes. Henry Bynneman was both a printer and bookseller who owned two shops in London from 1566 to 1583. He printed numerous travel narratives during this period and was also the holder of several monopolies. Though he was prosecuted in 1580 for printing a libellous letter, he remained a printer of scholarly material, with a special interest in the new sciences including geography. Bynneman acquired accounts of Frobisher's 1578 journey from a source close to one of his captains at a southern port town on their arrival back in England.[20] The scale of Bynneman's success is revealed by the inventory of his property at his death in 1583. He owned many books on the New World: forty-five copies of *The conqueste of the Weste Indians* valued at 30s, 350 copies of *Portes creekes havens of the W. Indyas* (printed in 1578, this was the earliest information on navigating the New World) valued at 12s 6d, and finally 150 books of *Survey of the worlde* valued at nine shillings.[21] After Bynneman's death in 1583, Edward Allde took over his mantle as one of the most prolific printers, putting his name to many of the later narratives. He operated between 1584 and 1624 from the 'Gilded Cup' in Cripplegate. His work brought him to the attention of the authorities twice: once for printing a Catholic confession, and later for printing some heretical texts that were seized and burnt.[22] There is no evidence that any of the texts printed in Elizabeth's reign relating to geography and travel were the subject of any investigation.

London printers and booksellers, as well as being promoters, were active in the commandeering of manuscripts to be turned into books and they also commissioned works once it became clear that there was a market for information about the exploits of Englishmen in the New World. *The Relation of Maryland,* a tract encouraging gentlemen adventurers to invest money and servants in Lord Baltimore's new colony, written in 1635, was financed and distributed in London by 'Master William Peasley at his house on the backside of Drury Lane near the Cock Pit theatre' who also was the agent who would take money for the passage of a man and his servants, and provide information on the provisions needed to be a successful settler.[23] Printed advertising was beginning to appear in books during the early modern period. Pages would be added or comments inserted in introductions recommending reading material by the same author or on the same topic. For example, on the title page of *The Arte of Navigation*, by Martin Cortes, translated by Richard Eden, appeared the following note:

Whereunto may be added at the wyl of the byer another fruitefull and necessary booke of navigation translated out of Latine by the sayde Eden.[24]

Not only publishers and booksellers but also the London clergy were helping to promote the sale of books on exploration during this period. The Bishop of London personally instructed all preachers in his diocese to promote and advertise the sale of the 1622 tract *Discourse on the Discoverie of the New Found Land* by Richard Whitbourne.[25] The reasons why some clergy went to America, while others promoted settlement there and even encouraged the marketing of books about America from their pulpits are complex. The interest of the clergy during late Elizabethan and early Stuart England in the social problems of the country has been well documented.[26] Ever since Richard Hakluyt wrote his pioneering work *Discourse on Western Planting* in 1584, America had been seen as a receptacle for England's surplus population for the good of the rest of the nation and for the benefit of the poor themselves, as in America they might be able to find spiritual fulfilment through work as well as material comfort. The clergy were also enthused about the possibility of a large new congregation to minister to – the native Americans – seeing it as the Englishman's duty to civilize and educate the Indians, as well as a convenient way to rival the proselytizing Spanish and French.[27]

So there is evidence not only of practitioners in the book trade but also ministers of the church encouraging the sale of books about America. How does the historian go about tracking the distribution of knowledge during the early modern period? This is more easily said than done! It is very difficult to compile statistics on the readership of any book in the sixteenth century. This period witnessed the development of what Louis B. Wright called 'a middle-class culture' in England involving not only an increase in literacy but also a development in the taste for the printed word; an interest in print culture was emerging for the first time outside the universities.[28] The main point of my argument here though is that travel narratives were accessible both to the educated reader and the lower status listener.[29] Firstly this paper will examine how books may have reached the reader traditionally recognized by the historian, and then look at how information on America also found its way via the book trade to the lower sort of person, not often considered a consumer of the written word.

Identifying the owners of a particular surviving text can be fruitful, but is misleading in this case. Those copies of a book preserved for the modern eye are often those left in the hands of antiquarian collectors who chose to keep and bequeath the book. This surely alters the way a historian must examine surviving copies; he or she must acknowledge others who did not choose to preserve a book, who may not have treated it with so much care. Inventories are a useful place to start, both of an individual's property and also of booksellers' stock.[30] However, a problem encountered when studying inventories is that small books were not valued as artefacts in themselves and were not usually categorized individually. This is extremely frustrating for the historian who comes tantalizingly close to seeing concrete evidence of an interest in books on America only to be foiled at the last. For example, the minister William Crashaw donated his library to the church at the end of his life but none of his books was individually identified, only the monetary value was calculated. Crashaw preached to the Virginia Company and even invested £240 of his own money in the colony so it is almost certain that he would have owned books and pamphlets on the subject, but we have no proof.[31]

During this period, provincial bookshops rarely had catalogues, so it is hard to track the availability of particular texts across the country. General stationers throughout the country also sold books but these too leave us no record of their business. Occasionally an inventory on the death of a provincial bookseller will reveal individual book titles. For example, when John Denys of Cambridge died in 1578, his shop contained four accounts of Martin Frobisher's voyages, valued at 1d each.[32] Roger Ward's shop in Shrewsbury was inventoried at his death in 1585, and he owned 'one book on the West Indias' and 'one booke in praise of Furbisher' among others.[33] However, it would be easy to exaggerate the spread of books to provincial bookshops. Other evidence reveals bookshops whose owners had no interest in the sale of books concerning America. The inventory taken in 1644 of John Audley's shop in Hull revealed that he owned no texts on America or geography at all, though a few small books did remain uncategorized at the end of the inventory; this is surprising because of Audley's location in a port town (though Hull's location on the north-east coast means that no ships would have docked there on their way to or from the New World) and also the prevalence of American literature during the 1640s when the inventory was taken. We can only speculate as to why this is the case. Audley may have owned books on America but already sold them all, or he may have had no interest in travel or the colonies at all. Perhaps none of the customers of Hull had ever expressed an interest in the New World so Audley had not sought out any books on that topic.[34] Bennett in his seminal work *English Books and their Readers* argues that in the London bookshops, especially in St Paul's Churchyard, a huge variety of books were sold, but that this was not true of the provincial bookshops. He thought that mostly religious and classical texts found their way there but very few contemporary works or plays. This was in spite of the fact that he estimated ten per cent of all works published during this period concerned history, geography or travel.[35]

Provincial book fairs were also an important part of the trade. They were held at Oxford, Bristol, Salisbury, Nottingham, Ely, Coventry and Stourbridge near Cambridge during this period, and probably other venues. As well as local fairs, the wealthy book dealer and buyer had the opportunity to go (or send an agent) to the bi-annual Frankfurt book fair.[36] Gentlemen in the English countryside also had the opportunity of having books delivered to their doorstep for them, brought by a friend or relation from London, or sent by a local carrier. In probably the first recorded example of a promotional book tour, John Smith travelled the country in 1624 to advertise his new work *A Generall History*, by handing out books and maps to the local gentry.[37] As well as promoting the sale of his own work, Smith obviously wanted to publicize the colonies of New England and Virginia (though by this time Smith was a little cynical about the virtues of Virginia, having been badly treated by the authorities there). The conjunction of the fortunes of colony and author so appreciated by Wood in 1634 was obviously on John Smith's mind during the mid-1620s as well![38]

It is worth taking a moment to examine the size of these works about America. Smith's *Generall History*, a weighty tome, was exceeded in size by such multi-volume collections as Hakluyt's and Purchas's travel narratives, and Theodore de Bry's thirty volumes on America, published in four languages between 1590 and 1634. These could all stand alongside Raleigh's best selling *History of the World* in granting kudos to the owner, displayed for visitors to admire in his library. The price of books during this period remained fairly constant, though illustrated works could be very expensive. The price of a book depended on the printing format (folio, quarto or octavo) and whether the work was bound or unbound. A large work such as Hakluyt's *Divers Voyages* cost nine shillings unbound, putting it far out of the price range of all but the wealthier sort of people.[39] Henry Percy, the Earl of Northumberland (nicknamed the Wizard Earl because of his interest in alchemy) was one of these people. He was a friend of Raleigh and owned several travel narratives, including an annotated copy of Hakluyt's *Principall Navigations*, another huge text that would have been unaffordable to the majority of readers.[40] Slightly cheaper were Monardes's *Ioyfull Newes*, and Raleigh's *Discovery of Guiana*, which cost one shilling each unbound.[41] However another group of works remain largely hidden from view, unrecorded in bookshop and library inventories. These are the small pamphlets, broadsides, individual laudatory poems that were often too paltry to be bothered with by large collectors or bookshop owners, or are described in documents under a blanket heading of 'small books'. Occasionally ballads appear concerning migration to America, especially during the 1630s when the much-maligned Puritans were leaving for New England, but the survival of these ballads is very rare.[42]

Smaller books and pamphlets were carried from London to the provincial markets and fairs by itinerant pedlars, and in many cases the same pedlars carried news from the provinces to be distributed at Paul's Walk.[43] These pedlars were often on the margins of society, prosecuted for vagrancy and suffering extreme financial hardship.[44] They mostly travelled between market towns but occasionally strayed off the main routes and visited smaller villages where a few people might buy their books and read them to the rest of the community. The pedlars would buy books in London or from packhorse carriers on the road, and would bring news of overseas travel to the lower status people who would have neither the money nor the inclination to buy larger volumes, in fact, pedlars were actually forbidden from selling larger volumes.[45] The level of mobility in early modern England was surprisingly high and this facilitated the spread of news and ideas.[46] Inns were a very important site in the spread of ideas and the informal sale of small books, as were fairs and markets of all sorts, especially on the country's communication arteries, the roads and rivers. The Home Counties acted as funnels for the traffic in and out of London and there the spread of news and written pamphlet literature was especially prevalent. As one might imagine, the further from London, the slower and more patchy the information received; packhorses only travelled about twelve miles a day.[47] It is not yet possible to paint a picture of systematic distribution of small books and pamphlets, but only to suggest a framework within which historians can search for concrete evidence.[48] It is misleading to imagine that information about the New World provided anything more than an interesting morsel in the staple diet of almanacs, ballads, religious commentaries and, from the 1640s, political news sheets and papers that made up the majority of the pedlar's wares. However, sensational news such as the massacre in 1622 of 300 settlers in Virginia by neighbouring native Americans did become the topic of discussion in many early news sheets, no doubt titillating some of its readers in a similar way to the more usual stories of executions, floods and monstrous births.[49] Broadsides were also a means of carrying printed information to the provinces, again often arriving in the pedlar's pack, or occasionally brought by a sailor or failed colonist, or an interested member of the local elite. Broadsides seem to be the forerunner of poster advertising, and were nailed to church doors, street corners, trees on commons and other public places and obviously encouraged public reading rather than private ownership of the printed word.[50] It is important to acknowledge the merging of the literate and oral traditions in early modern England, with the literate and semi-literate members of society reading aloud, or memorizing and repeating later the contents of a broadside for the benefit of non-literate members of their household and wider community. Sites used within a community to transfer this information were often public spaces such as the street, the alehouse or the church, though the tone of exchanges in these spaces would have been very different!

To sum up, I have identified two streams of printed knowledge about America that entered the supply chain from the pen of the author: the deliberate and the commandeered literature. These both then fed through the book trade in London, and were influenced by promoters, editors and printer-publishers and emerged as two streams of knowledge distribution. The larger works such as Hakluyt and Purchas were sold and disseminated through established London and provincial booksellers. These had more in common with other large books, such as works of classical literature and history that were bound and kept as artefacts by their owners. The smaller books were sometimes sold by bookshops and 'Paul's walkers' in London but were also carried to the provinces by chapmen and pedlars, reaching a far more diverse and sometimes only semi-literate audience. These works were often not preserved after reading and were akin to the hastily printed and cheaply distributed ballads, almanacs and chapbooks that circulated in the mid-seventeenth century.[51]

Turning back to London for a moment, the relationship between these two sorts of news distribution is symbolically represented at St Paul's Churchyard where booksellers congregated throughout this period.[52] The larger, more reputable booksellers had permanent shops, identified by a sign, with quite considerable buying power and direct connections to a printer-publisher. Alongside these shops, smaller texts were sold by stall-holders and wandering salesmen whose mobile nature meant they had a lesser reputation but an ability to turn a quick penny should the occasion arise. The pedlars provided a useful service. Throughout the seventeenth century one of their most popular wares was the cheap almanac, which provided information on fairs, highways, farming, posts and the calendar for a few pennies to those who might not normally have become readers. It is possible the pedlars provided a similar service to those of a lower status who were interested in the New World, not only providing the literature itself, but also throwing in a few tall tales of their own. The co-existence of these two forms of distribution side by side in St Paul's Churchyard symbolizes for me their coexistence in the cultural world of the early modern period.

In conclusion, then, this paper is asking for a reassessment of the much-contested distinction between high and low culture in early modern England.[53] In this case, it seems, the distinction is a valid one. Different sorts of printed literature disseminated information about America to different sorts of people. That is not to suggest a sharp polarity with a distinction between elite and popular literature, rather a continuous spectrum that also included a particular type of literature aimed at the middling sort of reader as the century progressed. However, it is a reality that very few could afford the large tomes collected by scholars such as the works of Hakluyt and Purchas. Enthusiastic gentry and aristocrats and interested parties pursuing learning in geography and navigation must surely have been the main consumers of these books. The few public libraries during this period also tended to be able to buy the larger works. Norwich library, founded in 1608, owned full sets of Hakluyt's and Purchas's travel narratives.[54] In Dorchester, a town that became famous in 1630 for organizing a migration to Massachusetts under the guidance of its Puritan preacher John White, the town library owned a copy of Purchas and one of its leading citizens, diarist William Whiteway, owned Purchas, John

Smith's work on Virginia, other geographical works and even some globes.[55] Even the wealthier literate few would not have considered such an outlay unless they had a special interest, either as patrons or as potential investors in the colonial enterprise. These texts certainly were not universally popular; the Devereux library of the third Earl of Essex surveyed in the mid-seventeenth century contained no works at all concerning the New World, apart from a theological pamphlet discussing the Antinomian crisis.[56]

Simultaneously, those of a lower status may have gained information about America by sharing a book, reading a public broadside or being read to by a sibling, colleague or friend within the community. Of course it was also possible for those of higher status to consume the cheaper literature as well. A few decades later Pepys was an avid collector of ballad literature. It is clear that the distinction between the literate and the illiterate has been drawn too sharply by historians; many people must have had basic reading skills, while needing help with complex or unusual texts.[57] The accessibility of the smaller works referred to is undeniable; many of these smaller books contain no Latin or Greek quotations or references for which a classical education would be required, but instead biblical references and basic, if rather wordy, common sense.

If space permitted, the spread of news by word of mouth would also need to be addressed, a means of communication that affected all ranks of society. It was especially important in the port towns of the South and West. Returning sailors and discontented settlers would have had their hour of fame, especially if they could embellish their experiences with a few tales of Spanish pirates, frightful natives and savage beasts.[58] But by concentrating on the book trade of late Tudor and early Stuart England we can identify a crucial development: the planting of the seeds of interest in America in the minds of the English. The period also saw a huge increase in the number of people with access to print, even if they were not wealthy enough to buy large works, or could not read every word of a book. The itinerant pedlars, finding an audience more receptive to the printed word, did a roaring trade too.

Notes

1. I would like to thank Bernard Capp, Maureen Bell and Ian Maxted for their helpful advice and encouragement during the preparation of this paper.
2. J. Donne, *Sermon given before the Virginia Company* (London, 1622), quoted in A. Fitzmaurice, 'The Rhetoric of the Virginia Company Sermons' in F. McCullough, *The English Sermon Revised* (Manchester, 2000), p. 37.
3. W. Wood, *New Englands Prospect* (London, 1635), sig. A3.
4. Wood, *New Englands Prospect*, sig. A3.
5. Wood not only saw his role as educational. He also hoped to dismiss 'many scandalous and false reports ... from the sulphurous breath of every base ballad monger'.
6. N. Monardes, *Ioyfull Newes out of a Newe Found Worlde, Englished by John Frampton* (London, 1577). Monardes' work was groundbreaking as it represented America as a botanical treasure trove having the potential to cure all the world's ills.
7. See A. L. Rowse, *The Elizabethans and America* (London, 1959) for a discussion of the role of the Phillip Sidney circle.
8. Richard Hakluyt's 'Discourse of Western Planting' (1584) distributed in manuscript form at the court of Elizabeth I set out his ideas for empire building and the benefits that overseas colonies would bring to the mother country. Though he was the first Englishman to do this, his thinking was strongly influenced by John Dee who had written of Britain's 'thalassokratia' (sea empire) in the 1570s.
9. For example: W. Crashaw, *A Sermon Preached in London before the Right Honorable the Lord Lawarre ... Feb 21 1609* (London, 1610); The Virginia Company, *Inconveniences which have transported themselves from England to Virginia* (London, 1622); W. Morrell, *New England, or a Briefe Narration of the Ayre, Earth, Water, Fish and Fowles of that Country ... in Latine and English verse* (London, 1625). Morrell claimed that he was persuaded by friends to write a tract for publishing but this seems to be a rhetorical device to prove authorial modesty.
10. The first texts to be published by the American press were a book of Psalms (commonly known as 'The Bay Psalms'), W. Pierce, *An Almanack for the Year of Our Lord 1639* (Boston, 1639), and *The Oath of a Freeman* (Boston, 1638). An introduction to the history of American printing is: T. Goddard Wright, *Literary Culture in Early New England* (New York, 1966).
11. For information on scribal publication in early modern England see H. Love, *Scribal Publication in Seventeenth Century England* (Oxford, 1993).
12. H. S. Bennett, *English Books and Readers 1558-1603* (Cambridge, 1965), p. 22.
13. M. Shaaber, *Some Forerunners of the Newspaper in England 1476-1622* (London, 1966), p. 268.
14. R. Hakluyt, *Principall Navigations* (2nd edition, London, 1599); S. Purchas, *Purchas, His Pilgrims* (Glasgow, 1957).
15. C. Blagden, *The Stationers' Company: A History, 1403-1959* (London, 1960) is the seminal work in this area. See also H. G. Aldis, *The Book Trade 1557-1625* (Cambridge, 1909).
16. E. Eisenstein, *The Printing Press as an Agent of Change* (Cambridge, 1979) p. 19.
17. *Printing and Publishing at Oxford 1478-1978: An Exhibition* (Oxford, 1978), p. 17.

18. W. Strachey, *Historie of Travell into Virginia Britannia*, ed. by L. B. Wright (London, 1951), p. xiii.

19. R. McKerrow, *A Dictionary of Printers and Booksellers in England, Scotland and Ireland 1557-1640* (London, 1910).

20. Bennett, *English Books and Readers*, p. 278.

21. M. Eccles, 'Bynneman's Books', *The Library*, XII (1957), 128.

22. McKerrow, *Dictionary of Printers and Booksellers*.

23. *A Relation of Maryland* (London, 1635), title page.

24. E. Bosanquet, 'English Seventeenth Century Almanacks', *The Library*, X (1929-30), 375.

25. L. B. Wright, *Religion and Empire: The Alliance between Piety and Commerce in English Expansion 1558-1625* (New York, 1943), p. 138.

26. A good survey text examining the social tensions in early modern England is J. Sharpe, *Early Modern England: A Social History 1550-1760* (London, 1984). Essays in *The English Sermon Revised* ed. by F. McCullough (Manchester, 2000) examine the role of the clergy as social commentators.

27. Current historical debates examine whether the intention to proselytize was merely a rhetorical device used by promoters to encourage settlement in America, or whether it reveals a genuine missionary zeal. I tend towards the latter argument, identifying the environmental conditions within America as a reason for failure to convert, and not lack of enthusiasm.

28. L. B. Wright, *Middle Class Culture in Elizabethan England* (Chapel Hill, NC., 1935). This is a controversial claim and it is perhaps a little ahistorical to use the term 'middle class'. However, I agree with his assessment of the changing nature of the reception of printed material.

29. It was also very likely that the 'better sort' of reader were also regular listeners, employing their staff and family members to read aloud. See K. Sharpe, *Reading Revolutions: The Politics of Reading in Early Modern England* (New Haven, CT., 2000) p. 271.

30. J. Barnard & M. Bell, *The Early Seventeenth Century Book Trade and John Foster's Inventory of 1616* (Leeds, 1994), p. 40. The authors identify thirteen existing early modern bookshop inventories, all of which will provide fruitful further study.

31. R. M. Fisher, 'William Crashaw's Library at Middle Temple', *The Library*, XXX (1975), 116.

32. T. Watt, 'Piety in the Pedlar's Pack', in *The World of Rural Dissenters*, ed. by M. Spufford (Cambridge, 1996), p. 258.

33. A. Rodger, 'Roger Ward's Shrewsbury Stock', *The Library*, XIII (1958), 251.

34. C. W. Chilton, 'A Provincial Bookseller's Stock', *The Library*, I, series VI (1979), p. 126. Ian Maxted has digitized the 1615 inventory of Exeter bookseller Michael Harte, and believes that customer demand may have played a part in his acquisition of texts.

35. Bennett, *English Books and Readers*, pp. 264-5.

36. Aldis, *The Book Trade*, pp. 403-8.

37. D. Cressy, *Coming Over* (Cambridge, 1987), p. 6.

38. John Smith was not only a well-known traveller throughout Europe, the Near East and the New World, but also one of the most widely read authors on America in the first

few decades of the seventeenth century. Copies of his book *A Map of Virginia* (Oxford, 1612), were sent back to the colony by the Virginia Company to help the settlers communicate with the natives: J. Axtell, *Natives and Newcomers* (Oxford, 2001), p. 317.

39. F. Johnson, 'Notes on English Retail Book Prices', *The Library*, V (1950-1), 92.

40. 'Library of the Wizard Earl', *The Library*, XV (1960), 257.

41. Johnson, 'English Book Retail Prices', 106-9.

42. A rare example is *A Proper Newe Ballet called the Summons to Newe England*. Bodleian Library, Tanner MS 306, ff. 286-7.

43. Shaaber, *Forerunners of the Newspaper*, p. 234.

44. For the role of pedlars and their wares, ministering to the 'unspectacular orthodoxy', see T. Watt, 'Piety in the Pedlar's Pack', pp. 235-70.

45. Bennett, *English Books and Readers*, p. 266.

46. M. Frearson, 'Communications and Continuity of Dissent in the Chiltern Hundreds', in Spufford, ed. *The World of Rural Dissenters*, pp. 274-7.

47. Ibid., p. 285.

48. Margaret Spufford has completed a survey of the distribution of pamphlet and chapbook literature for 1660 onwards in her work: *Small Books and Pleasant Histories* (Cambridge, 1985).

49. J. Frank, *The Beginnings of the English Newspaper 1620-60* (Cambridge, MA., 1961), p. 17.

50. An example of such a broadside is: *Proportion of Provisions Needfull for such as Intend to Plant Themselves in New England* (London, 1630).

51. For a history of early English newspapers see Frank, *The Beginnings of the English Newspaper*; for a comprehensive study of almanac production and distribution see B. Capp, *Astrology and The Popular Press* (London, 1979).

52. Aldis, *The Book Trade*, p. 398.

53. A recent book on the points of tension and contact between high and low culture is B. Reay, *Popular Cultures in England 1550-1750* (London, 1998).

54. C. Bridenbaugh, *Vexed and Troubled Englishmen 1590-1642* (Oxford, 1968), p. 346.

55. D. Underdown, *Fire From Heaven* (London, 1992), pp. 47, 55.

56. V. Snow, 'The Devereux Library', *The Library*, XXI (1966), 115.

57. For a recent assessment of this problem see A. Fox, *Oral and Literate Culture in England 1500-1700* (Oxford, 2000).

58. This was especially true during Elizabeth's reign when English sea dogs were undertaking the privateering war against the Spanish. For more information see K. Andrews, *Elizabethan Privateering 1585-1603* (Cambridge, 1964), p. 234.

Norwich 'Publishing' in the Seventeenth Century

DAVID STOKER

W HEN IN JANUARY 1731/2 three men were arrested in Norwich for 'publishing a seditious paper', those concerned had nothing to do with the production, finance, or sale of the item in question.[1] Their crime was either to circulate copies or possibly to read the contents aloud to an audience at a coffee house or similar public place. The meaning of 'publishing' was then related to the dissemination of information, not necessarily connected with printed matter, and bore little or no association with the financial responsibility for its production. The modern concept of a 'publisher' as one who undertakes and organizes the production and distribution of a printed work, acting as a middleman between the writer, producer, and retailer did not emerge until the late eighteenth century within large centres of book production such as London. The essential components of this role are that the publisher is investing in the publication directly, undertaking it on behalf of someone else for remuneration, and/or arranging for its distribution. By the middle of the seventeenth century, members of the London book trade were beginning to specialize into the different functions of printer, bookbinder, stationer, wholesale bookseller, retail bookseller, or even financier, which was a precursor to the emergence of a publishing trade. There was far less such specialization in the provinces. Most provincial towns had no printers, and their booksellers might be acting as stationers, bookbinders, newsagents, vendors of patent medicines and of other wares. Nevertheless, from the imperfect evidence of contemporary imprints it is clear that some of the financial and distributive functions associated with publishing, were being carried out by large numbers of provincial booksellers at this time, albeit intermittently, and as one sideline along with other more profitable trades.

This paper will seek to examine such publishing activity in Norwich during the seventeenth century and discuss those printed items which have a local bookseller named in their imprints, either in the capacity of undertaker (usually designated by the phrase 'printed for') or distributor

31

(designated by 'sold by'). The works would of necessity have been printed elsewhere as there was no press in Norwich between 1572 and 1701. For want of a more precise term, they will be described as 'Norwich publications'. Imprints are not always reliable, and were sometimes used to mask complex financial relationships or disguise the responsibility for controversial works. However, with respect to books sold in the provinces during the seventeenth century, they are usually straightforward and mean what they say. It is noteworthy that once printing returns to Norwich in 1701, when the bookseller and printer were able to negotiate more easily, and local printers became part-time booksellers, the variety and complexity of imprints grows noticeably.

One hundred and twenty-three Norwich publications dating from the seventeenth century have been identified out of a total of 701 known for England and Wales.[2] However, these numbers are inevitably approximate and it would be misleading to suggest that Norwich publications truly represent 17.5% of the total. The Norwich imprints have been collected over a thirty-year period using a range of library catalogues, and by examining items in local collections, whereas the remainder have been compiled only from online bibliographies and catalogues. An educated guess would be that Norwich represented between 12.5 and 15% of the overall total, and was easily the largest provincial centre for such publishing.[3]

An analysis of these 123 titles, shows that 72% were 'printed for' a Norwich bookseller, and 37% 'sold by' (9% have both forms). A number of the items are variant issues of London titles, published with different imprints, and several items exist in two 'Norwich' states each one with the name of a different local bookseller. One hundred and twelve titles (91%) were printed in London, five in Cambridge, and one each in Oxford, Edinburgh and Rotterdam! Two-thirds (68%) were quarto, 28% octavo, and 4% duodecimo (no larger or smaller formats are included). The average number of printed sheets used in these publications was 11.3 (ranging between one sheet only for *The History of the Protestant Reformation*, and 116 sheets (928 quarto pages) for John Collinges's *The intercourses of divine love*, of 1683).[4] Nearly ninety percent of the publications were on religious subjects, with 57 (46%) sermons or collections of sermons, 36 (29%) works of religious discourse, 17 (14%) works of religious controversy, and one catechism. The remainder included three works of history, three on medicine, three auction catalogues, one masque, one narrative poem, one Latin textbook and a treatise on witchcraft.

All of the publications appeared between 1615 and 1700, with three discernible periods of activity. Only eleven titles were published in the quarter century before 1640. The following three decades saw a growth to 17 publications for 1641-1650, and 18 for 1651-1660, and then a sharp decline to eleven titles between 1661 and 1670. Thereafter there is a steady increase with twenty or more items published in each of the last three decades. These statistics do not however explain why particular titles are linked with Norwich booksellers, whereas other works – frequently by the same authors – are not. The following account of several titles and those who were responsible for their publication, will therefore seek to do so, examining each of these periods in turn.

Norwich Publishing before 1640
The bookseller Nicholas Colman is named on the imprint of two broadsheet ballads concerning a disastrous fire in Beccles, printed in 1586.[5] Yet this local publishing venture was exceptional and apparently not repeated in nearly thirty years. The first significant item naming a Norwich bookseller was an English translation of Alexander Neville's, *De furoribus Norfolciensium* entitled *Norfolkes furies*, printed for Edmund Casson at the sign of the Bible in 1615.[6] Casson became a freeman stationer of Norwich in 1613 having previously served an apprenticeship with William Firebrand, a London bookseller.[7] This book of 80 pages was aimed at a local market, and contained an account of the rebellion led by Robert Kett in 1549, which had taken control of the city. Spare pages were also filled with lists of mayors, sheriffs, and bishops, together with a brief account of notable happenings within the city. It was a wise choice, and in 1623 Casson undertook another edition.[8]

The next Norwich publication is puzzling since it was printed in Edinburgh for Christopher Ponder, at the Angel in Norwich, 1616. *The execution of Neschech* is a discourse on usury by James Spottiswood, a Scotsman, who was then rector of Wells in Norfolk.[9] The connection with the Edinburgh printer Andrew Hart occurred through the author who was then staying in that city and saw his book through the press.[10] The link with Ponder who apparently undertook the publication, is harder to establish.[11] Publications between 1617 and 1623 were all commemoration sermons by local clergymen. William Younger's *The nurses bosome* and *Judah's penance* were together printed for Edmund Casson, in 1617,[12] followed by the author's *The unrighteous judge*, for Henry Featherstone in

London but sold by Ponder (1621).[13] Two further sermons, both preached before the judges at the Norfolk assizes by Samuel Garey were *Jentaculum judicum* together with *A manuell for magistrates* printed for Matthew Law in London and sold in Norwich by Casson.[14] Nothing seems to have been published during the succeeding eight years until two further booksellers became involved as local distributors for works published in London. Thus, Thomas Carre's name appears on the imprint of a sermon by John Brinsley of Great Yarmouth, *The preachers charge and peoples duty*, in 1631,[15] and similarly Edward Martin on *Three sermons ... delivered upon severall occasions in Norwich*, by Thomas Reeve.[16]

Edmund Casson's last such venture was one of two issues of Ralph Knevet's *Rhodon and Iris*, a satirical play in verse performed at an annual pageant in praise of Spring, organized by the Society of Florists, in Norwich in May 1631. The growing puritan element of the city government disliked the Florists' Feasts, and the play mocked many leading figures in the magistracy, who took offence at the performance. However, it was popular amongst most of the spectators and Knevet claimed that he published the work to show the population just how innocuous it was. A more likely reason for publication was to cash in on a small-scale local controversy.[17]

The next two early works are also puzzling work as there is no obvious connection with Norwich by their authors. George Foxle's, *The groanes of the spirit*, printed at Oxford in 1639, exists in four states with title pages naming booksellers in Leicester, Bristol, and London as well as Abraham Atfend, another bookseller recently arrived in Norwich.[18] Atfend's second venture was *Christ's victorie and triumph* by the metaphysical poet Giles Fletcher, first published at Cambridge in 1610, and consisting of four narrative poems on Biblical themes. It was reprinted there in 1632, and again in 1640, with one issue of the later edition sold by Atfend.[19]

Thus, by 1640 five Norwich booksellers had become aware of the possibilities of under-taking small-scale publishing, and that the financial risks involved were not great. Both the range of subjects and types of book were surprisingly varied. Most, but by no means all, had some local connection that would commend them to readers in the city, and all of were literary works on a small scale. The precise reason why one particular title and not another had a Norwich imprint however is not always apparent and often must have been the result of entirely accidental factors.

The Civil War, Commonwealth and Restoration (1641-1670)
Norwich was not directly involved in any military action during the Civil
War, but the city suffered economic disruption and there appears to have
been no publishing activity from 1641 to 1646. The aftermath of the war
saw an increase in local publishing, initially with a rash of controversial
religious tracts, as the political and religious differences of the community
began to be reflected in the literature on sale, and the traditional controls
on the press broke down. Several of these tracts reflect the growing division
of the Puritan party into the Presbyterian and Independent factions. The
differences were brought to a head in August 1646 by the publication in
London of a vituperative pamphlet entitled *Vox populi, or the peoples cry
against the clergy*, denouncing Presbyterian designs for reforming religious
worship in Norwich, and blaming that party for creating the religious
division in the city and driving a wedge between the people and the
parliament.[20] The Norwich bookseller Edward Martin, sensing a major
controversy, published a Presbyterian reply entitled *An hue and cry after Vox
populi*,[21] but some copies survive with the imprint 'printed for William
Frankling' pasted over the original.[22] The controversy was still smouldering
in October when William Franklin, published a second rebuttal *Vox
Norwici, or the cry of Norwich*.[23] In 1650 an attempt was made to reconcile
the differences between the Independent and Presbyterian concepts of
religious reform with *A peace making jurie*.[24] Similar printed statements and
proposals by groups of clergy for religious reforms regularly feature such as
The attestation of the ministers of the county of Norfolk and Norwich, 1648.[25]

Published sermons likewise begin to reflect the tide of religious and
political events at this time. John Carter, Minister of St Peter Mancroft,
preached a series of influential and controversial sermons before the
municipal authorities in the 1640s. 'The nail hit on the head and driven
into the city and cathedral wall of Norwich' was the first Guild-Day
sermon to be preached in his church, following the desecration of the
cathedral a few weeks before.[26] Carter assured his listeners that to support
the Parliament was to oppose an evil Court circle but not the King. By
1647, he had become disappointed by the lack of religious reform, due to
the inertia of the Municipal Assembly. In a surprisingly frank Guild-Day
sermon 'The wheel turned by a voyce from the throne of glory', he turned
against the local magistracy. His two sermons gained such fame that they
were published jointly in London and Norwich in 1647.[27] In 1650 another
controversial Guild-day sermon by John Carter caused a sensation. In 'A

rare sight or, the lyon: sent from a farr country and presented to the city of Norwich', he accused the magistracy of hypocrisy and failure to maintain good order:

Who amongst you will strike down a disorderly alehouse, if the brewer that serves it be an alderman, a rich man, or a friend?[28]

Pressure from the authorities resulted in Carter's removal from St Peter's, and so when *A rare sight*, together with another of his sermons, was published by John Sprat, another Norwich bookseller, the author was described as 'minister of the Gospell and as yet sojourning in Norwich'.[29] Carter was however popular among the common people, and was soon elected by the parishioners of St Laurence church to be their rector, where he remained until his death in 1656. Carter's popularity is also reflected by the publication of his funeral sermon *Elisha's lamentation for Elijah*, preached by his disciple John Collinges and printed for William Franklin.[30] Collinges was to become a prolific and voluminous local author before his death in 1690, and was an important figure in reviving and re-organizing the Norwich City Library in the 1650s.[31]

The uncertainty of the times is also reflected in two sermons published by Franklin in 1650. On Christmas day 1646 and 4th January 1647, Thomas Rous preached sermons on the theme of Isaiah 9.6. At a time when the celebration of Christmas was discouraged, these innocuous sermons attracted criticism. Rous's enemies fomented and exaggerated the tale until it was widely believed that he had committed a serious heresy, and had his property sequestrated. His sermons were therefore printed for William Franklin, 'for the vindication of the author'.[32]

Religious controversy on a personal level also begins to appear particularly from the pens of the Presbyterian ministry. In 1652 Franklin published John Collinges' *Responsoria ad erratica pastoris* a voluminous reply to *The peoples privelidges* by William Sheppard published in London.[33] Collinges followed this in 1654 with *Provocator provocatus*, attacking a sermon by a Mr Boatman. This drew a reply from Theophilus Brabourne, another local minister, but which was published at his own expense.[34] Collinges' many further controversial works from this period were published by London booksellers perhaps indicating that the dispute had broadened. Brabourne engaged in further religious controversy with *An answer to Mr Cawdry's two books of the Sabbath*, printed for Franklin, in Norwich, in 1654.[35]

Other publications by Norwich booksellers during the 1640s included *A plaine and easie catechisme,*[36] John Robinson's *Miscellaneous propositions and quaeres,*[37] (one of three medical works) and a famous tract on witch hunting. During 1645 and 1646, Matthew Hopkins, the self-styled 'Witch-finder General', led a crusade throughout the eastern counties against hundreds of suspected witches. In fourteen months, he was responsible for 400 executions, but ultimately some enlightened members of society took issue with his methods of obtaining confessions. His enemies drew up a series of questions for consideration by the judges of the 1647 Norwich assizes, expressing reasoned doubts about 'this torturing witch-catcher'. Hopkins published the questions together with his answers in *The discovery of witches* hoping to justify himself.[38] One of the two issues of this pamphlet was sold by Edward Martin in Norwich. However, his attempted vindication was unconvincing and he retired to Manningtree and died soon afterwards.[39]

The Restoration of Charles II in 1660 was the signal for celebration and relief by all sections of society. During a brief honeymoon which followed, political, legal and religious problems and the bitterness created during the Civil War were shelved, and a rash of loyal sermons were preached in the churches up and down the country, including some by men who had previously censured the last Stuart administration. All of the small books published in Norwich during the early years of the Restoration reflect this combination of relief and loyalty felt by all sections of the community. Theophilus Brabourne wrote *A defence of the Kings authority* in 1660, printed for the author, but sold in Norwich by William Nowell, which was so popular that a second enlarged edition was published almost immediately.[40] He then wrote and published *God save the King and prosper him,* a 'justification... of the King's gracious proffer for liberty of conscience', also sold by Nowell.[41] William Franklin, whose name is found on several Presbyterian tracts, published James Warwell's *Votiva tabula; or a solemn thanks giving,* and Henry White's *A thank offering to the Lord for the happy recal of our dread sovereign, in 1660.*[42] The following year William Oliver, a young bookseller recently arrived from London, published two sermons by John Winter, celebrating King Charles' coronation and commemorating the anniversary of the execution of his father.[43]

The year 1662 marked both the beginnings of the persecution of non-conformists (which was to last, in various degrees of severity, until 1689), and also the re-introduction of strict controls over printing in the form of the 'licensing act'.[44] Much of the bitterness that had grown up amongst Royalist and Anglican sympathizers was poured on to the representatives of the non-conformist churches, who were initially denied opportunity to reply. This shift in attitudes is reflected in the tenor of local sermons. Thus John Winter's *Honest plain dealing*, published in Norwich by William Oliver in 1663, refers to the Presbyterians as:

the height of impudence, the depth of maliciousness, the length of wilfulness, and the breadth of licentiousness are the four dimensions of a fanatic body, which hath neither right side nor right end.[45]

Thus, after 1664 there seems to have been a lull in such publishing activity for eight years, due to the licensing regulations and the silencing of the non-conformists in the city.

Norwich Publishing 1671-1700

The decline in local publishing during the late 1660s was relatively short-lived and the last three decades of the century saw a considerable increase in both the size and the number of books published, due entirely to the work of three fairly prosperous bookselling businesses; those of the Oliver family, George Rose, and Edward Giles. Each of these men had a significant influence on the books published in the city.

William Oliver was an ardent Royalist and supporter of the Church of England, the son of a Somerset clergyman. Two of his three sons had distinguished careers in the post-Restoration church. He was also a friend of Sir Thomas Browne, author of *Religio Medici,* who bought books at his shop and used him as an agent for the supply of news.[46] He was a pious man, employed by the Corporation to provide hospitality on their behalf to those clergymen visiting Norwich to preach at the cathedral. This brought him into contact with many of the authors he published. Oliver's output of 22 titles before his death in 1689 were largely loyal sermons by local clergy, commemorating events of the Restoration or relating to the King or bishop of Norwich. Other works were of religious discourse such as two editions of Robert Conold's *Notion of schism stated* (1676-7) or a *Discourse on the repugnancy of sin.*[47]

After Oliver's death, his widow Elizabeth published two auction catalogues,[48] but once their third son, Samuel, was old enough to take over the business he followed the publishing tradition begun by his father. Samuel Oliver's name is found on the imprints of several local sermons, particularly those preached in Norwich cathedral, such as Erasmus Warren's *Divine rules*, or John Jeffery's *Duty and encouragement of religious artificers*.[49] He appears to have developed a working relationship with the Cambridge printer John Hayes, who produced five works for him. Samuel Oliver was also named as the distributor of a work in Latin printed in Rotterdam. This was *De naturali religione liber*, a substantial work by Pierre Chauvin the minister of the Walloon refugee church in Norwich.[50] This was one of the few local works advertised in the 'Term Catalogues' for Easter 1693,[51] provoking an anonymous reply in French published in Rotterdam in the same year.[52]

The bookseller George Rose was a far more worldly and less virtuous man than William Oliver, for example in 1695 he was convicted of fathering an illegitimate child, and then had to make a public apology for referring to the justices concerned as 'two fooles and an infidell'.[53] However earlier in his career he was more respectful and the main supplier of books and stationery to the Norwich Corporation. He was a supporter of the established church, but more for reasons of convenience than any positive attachment to its principles. Rose's output was smaller than that of William Oliver, but also consisted mainly of local sermons. His first enterprise resulted from his connection with the city authorities, who drew up an agreement that he should publish at his own expense a sermon preached before the Mayor and Aldermen by Robert Conold.[54] Conold's sermon sold well and encouraged him to finance another book by the same author, *The notion of schism stated*, which he did in partnership with William Oliver in 1676.[55] His name is also found on the imprint of a curious work by John Harris called *The divine physician*, which claimed to provide rules for the cure and prevention of most diseases by moral reform and strict adherence to the teachings of the Bible. This book exists in two states, one printed for Rose and another sold by him.[56] It could not have sold particularly well as in 1700 Rose published an auction catalogue which contained nine copies of this work.[57]

By 1677 Rose had come to a working agreement with the London bookseller Robert Clavell the publisher of the *Term Catalogues*, who appears to have been active in the development of links between the London and provincial trades.[58] Sir Thomas Browne refers to 'the new catalogue of bookes sett out by Clavell' in 1681.[59] He also took advantage of the arrangement with Rose when he wanted to transmit money to his son in London. Rose and Clavell also shared the costs involved in the publication of several items of Norfolk interest, including traditional commemoration sermons but also *A compleat treatise of preternatural tumours* by the Norwich surgeon John Browne.[60]

By far the most important figure in Norwich publishing during the seventeenth century was Edward Giles, a man whose name never figures in the Corporation records as having been employed by the city, nor was he patronized by the Cathedral clergy.[61] He was probably a Presbyterian but acted as the publisher for several dissident groups and their ministers. The tradition of non-conformity was so deeply ingrained in the population of Norwich that, despite official intolerance, the movement began to revive in the last quarter of the seventeenth century, and their bookseller began to prosper. Giles began his bookselling and publishing career in 1678 when the worst of the non-conformist persecution had abated, but the difficulties he encountered were nonetheless considerable. His output concerned mainly the works of Norfolk Presbyterians such as John Lougher, Francis English, or James Oldfield and he is said to have maintained a friendship with John Collinges, the most notable of them.

The difficulties experienced by the two main non-conformist groups after the Restoration brought them closer together, at least on an individual level. Thus, Giles' name is also found on the imprints of many works by Independent (Congregational) ministers such as Martin Finch, Thomas Allen, Timothy Armitage, and John Cromwell. These two religious groups constitute the major part of his output and consist mainly of sermons and bulky treatises on parts of the Bible, none of which were related to contemporary or local events. In 1686 Thomas Grantham, a famous Baptist preacher, came to live in Norwich and formed a church there and at Great Yarmouth. In 1691 he published in London, *A dialogue between a Baptist and a Presbyterian* attacking the Presbyterians in general and their minister John Collinges in particular, over their practice of infant baptism. Collinges died before the attack was published but Giles published *An answer to Mr Grantham's book* by Collinges's friend the Congregationalist Martin Finch.[62] The bookseller was interested in developing the controversy and so published Grantham's reply *A discovery-of audacious insolence,*[63] followed by Samuel Petto's *Infant baptism vindicated from the exceptions of Mr Grantham.* The controversy was only brought to an end by the death of Grantham in 1692.

One sect shared the contempt and intolerance of both the established church and the major non-conformist groups – the Quakers. The refusal of this group to compromise on any aspect of their conduct or belief served to incense their critics. Thus, Edward Giles published a virulent condemnation by Francis Bugg a former Quaker who had developed an obsessive hatred of the sect. *The Quakers-detected, their errours confuted, and their hypocrisie discovered* was published in 1686.[64] On a few occasions Giles published works by Church of England clergy, if they were of a conciliatory or friendly nature and tended to bridge the gap between the faiths. Examples of this type of work were Bishop Kidder's *Convivium caeleste* and Jonathan Clapham's exhortation to passive obedience in the sermon *Obedience to magistrates recommended*, reprinted for Giles within a year.[65]

Some of the most interesting titles produced by Giles have not survived and are known only because of entries in his catalogues, and so have not been considered in the analysis. Amongst these were three books for children, *Directions for learners to spell English right, The miracles of Christ*, and a catechism *The ordinary matter of prayer, drawn into questions and answers*.

During a thirty-three year career, ending in 1711, Giles published over fifty works, many of them of great volume, and nearly all by non-conformist authors. As such, he was probably the most prolific provincial publisher of his time. However compared with most London booksellers, his output was relatively small – Robert Clavell's name is found on nearly eight hundred imprints. John Dunton refers to Giles as an honest man, who 'has met with very good success in his way but the booksellers in the country cannot in a settled way, either ruin or enrich themselves so soon as those in London'.[66]

Therefore, a typical Norwich publication of the seventeenth century was a religious work such as a collection of sermons, written by a local clergyman, printed in London for a Norwich bookseller, in a quarto volume of about 90 pages. However there was a surprising range of other works published in the city. Many, but by no means all, of such publications would be of local interest, but well known local authors would not necessarily choose to have their works published locally. For example, Sir Thomas Browne knew and regularly used two of the principal booksellers of Norwich, but none of his works have their names on their imprint. The decision of a bookseller as to whether or not he should invest money in the publication of a book may have been influenced by a number of factors but was primarily an economic one. William Oliver may have published sermons by Anglican clergy who shared his views towards the church and the state, and Edward Giles published a large number of works by his friend John Collinges, but ultimately these works published only because the bookseller believed they would have a ready sale in the locality.

Notes

1. *Norwich Mercury*, 2 January 1731/2.

2. This figure does not include all provincial printing but only items where there is some publication statement in the imprint (thus 'Bristol: printed by William Bonny' would not be included, whereas 'Bristol: printed and sold by William Bonny' would). The 702 items identify 198 provincial booksellers working in 86 towns, mainly dating from 1630-1700.

3. The figures given do not include items printed in a provincial city, without any name of a local bookseller on the imprint, otherwise York and Newcastle would have been higher.

4. Based upon the two thirds of the books where detailed information was available about the pagination, compiled by dividing the number of leaves by the format.

5. Thomas Deloney, *A proper newe sonet declaring the lamentation of Beckles* (London: Robert Robinson for Nicholas Colman, Norwich, 1586) and D. Sterrie, *A briefe sonet declaring the lamentation of Beckles* (London: Robert Robinson for Nicholas Colman, Norwich, 1586).

6. Alexander Neville, *Norfolkes furies or a view of Ketts Campe, necessary for the malecontents of our time;* (London: printed for Edmund Casson, Norwich, 1615).

7. Casson was in business in Norwich 1613-1635, David Stoker, 'The Norwich book trades – a biographical directory', *Transactions of the Cambridge Bibliographical Society*, 8 (1981), 79-125, 89.

8. Alexander Neville, *Norfolke furies and their foyle, vnder Kett, their accursed Captaine. With a description of the famous citie of Norvvich* ([London] Printed for Edmund Casson, Norwich, 1623).

9. James Spottiswood, *The execution of Neschech and the confyning of his kinsman Tarbith. Or a short discourse, shewing the difference betwixt damned usurie, and that which is lawfull* (Edinburgh: printed by Andro Hart, for Christopher Pounder, Norwich, 1616).

10. *Dictionary of National Biography* article on James Spottiswood.

11. Ponder was in business 1615-1624, Stoker, 'The Norwich book trades', 115-16.

12. William Younger, *The nurses bosome. A sermon within the Greene-yard in Norwich on the Guild-day when their Maior takes his oath....* [and] *Iudahs penance, the sermon preached at Thetford before the judges* (London printed for Edmund Causon, 1617).

13. William Younger, *The unrighteous judge: or, Iudex Cretensis, the iudge of Crete: A sermon preached within the iurisdiction of the arch-deaconry of Norwich, at a generall court, in April last past, 16. 1621* (London: printed by G. Eld for Henry Fetherstone, ... solde by Christofer Puntar of Norwich, 1621).

14. Samuel Garey, *Ientaculum Iudicum: or, a breake-fast for the bench: prepared, presented, and preached in two sacred seruices, or sermons, ... before the two Assises at Thetford, at Norwich, 1619* (London: printed by B.A. for Matthew Law, and ... sold by Edmond Casson at Norwich, 1623).

15. John Brinsley, *The preachers charge. and peoples duty about preaching and hearing of the word: opened in a sermon* (London: printed for Robert Bird and are to be sold by Thomas Carre in Norwich, 1631). Carre was a bookseller in Norwich 1603-1645, see Stoker, 'The Norwich book trades', 88).

16. Thomas Reeve, *Three sermons ... delivered upon severall occasions in Norwich* (London: printed by A. Mathewes for J. Grismond, sold by E. Martin [Norwich], 1632). The sermons were also issued as *The churches hazard delivered in a sermon*, also with Martin as local distributor. Edward Martin was a bookseller at the Upper halfe-moone in Norwich 1627-1654, see Stoker, 'The Norwich book trades', 110.

17. Ralph Knevet, *Rhodon and Iris, A pastorall* (London: printed for M. Sparke ... sold by E. Causon, Norwich, 1631). See also, Amy Charles, *The Shorter Poems of Ralph Knevet* (Ohio, 1966), pp. 24-6, and R.W. Ketton-Cremer, 'The florists' feasts' *Forty Norfolk Essays* (Norwich, 1961), pp. 13-16.

18. George Foxle, *The groanes of the spirit, or the triall of the truth of prayer* (Oxford: L. Litchfield, sold by A. Atfend in Norwich, 1639). Atfend was in business in Norwich 1636-1653, see Stoker, 'The Norwich book trades', 81.

19. Giles Fletcher, *Christs victorie, and triumph in heaven, and earth, over, and after death* (Cambridge: printed by Roger Daniel for A. Atfend, Norwich, 1640).

20. The Norwich authorities were quick to react to 'Vox populi', on 2nd September the Assembly unanimously passed a resolution condemning the pamphlet and calling for the punishment of its authors. Norfolk Record Office Norwich Assembly Book 6 (1642-1668) f.45. See also J.T. Evans, *Seventeenth Century Norwich: Politics, Religion and Government 1620-1690* (Oxford, 1979), pp. 157-65.

21. *An hue-and cry after Vox Populi, or, an answer to Vox Diaboli, or a libellous pamphlet falsly styled Vox Populi; reviling the Magistracy and Ministry of Norwich* ([London] Printed by Ja. Cranford for Edward Martin, Bookseller in Norwich, 1646).

22. Franklin was a bookseller next to the George and at the upper halfe moone in Norwich 1645-1664, see Stoker, 'The Norwich book trades', 101.

23. *Vox Norwici: or, the cry of Norwich, vindicating their ministers ... from the foule and false aspersions and slanders, which arre unchristianly throwne upon them in a lying and scurrilous libell, lately come forth, intituled, Vox Populi* (London: printed for W. Franckling in Norwich and sold by Richard Tomlins, 1646).

24. *A peace making jurie, or twelve moderate propositions, tending to the reconciling of the present differences about church-combinations* ([London:] Printed by W.H. for Willliam Franklyng, Norwich, 1650).

25. *The attestation of the ministers of the county of Norfolk, and city of Norwich, in vindication of the ancient truths of Jesus Christ* (London: printed by R. Cotes, and sold by W. Franklyn, Norwich, 1648).

26. R.W. Ketton-Cremer, *Norfolk in the Civil War* (London, 1969), pp. 233-4 and p. 174.

27. John Carter, *The nail and the wheel. The nail fastyned by a hand from heaven. The wheel turned by a voyce from the throne of glory* ([London: Printed by J. Macock for M. Sparke, and sold by William Franklin in Norwich, 1647). See Evans, *Seventeenth Century Norwich*, pp. 165-9.

28. John Carter, *The tomb-stone and a rare sight* (London: printed by Tho: Rycroft for E. D. & N. E., and sold by John Sprat, Norwich, 1653). Sprat was a bookseller near the Norwich Guildhall 1653-1656, see Stoker, 'The Norwich book trades', 120.

29. Carter, *The tomb-stone and a rare sight* (London: printed by Tho: Rycroft for E. D. & N. E., and sold by John Sprat, Norwich, 1653).

30. John Collinges, *Elisha's lamentation for Elijah. Or, the just cause of a peoples mourning upon the losse of a faithful minister, ... Discoursed in a lecture sermon, ... upon occasion of the losse of ... John Carter* ([London:] printed by John Streater for W. Frankling in Norwich, 1657).

31. A. S. Hankinson 'Dr John Collinges of Norwich, 1623-1690', *Norfolk Archaeology, xlii* (1997), 511-19, for an account of his religious career and David Stoker, 'Doctor Collinges and the revival of the Norwich City Library 1657-1664', *Library History*, 5 (1980), 73-84, for his role as a librarian.

32. Thomas Rous, *Christ the saviour and governor of his church; or, two sermons on Isaiah 9. 6* (London: printed for W. Franklin, Bookseller in Norwich, 1650).

33. John Collinges, *Responsoria ad erratica Pastoris ... the Shepherd's wandrings discovered, in a revindication of the great ordinance of God* (London: printed for William Frankling, Norwich, 1652).

34. John Collinges, *Provocator provocatus. Or, An answer made to an open challenge made by one M. Boatman ... 13th of December, 1654. in a sermon* (London, Printed for William Francklyng, bookseller in Norwich., 1654).

35. Theophilus Brabourne, *An answer to Mr Cawdry's two books of the Sabbath* ([London: Printed for M.[i.e. W.] Franklin, in Norwich, 1654).

36. R.A. *A plaine and easie catechisme wherein the grounds and principles of Christian religion are briefly taught* (London, printed for William Franckling, Norwich 1649).

37. John Robinson, *Miscellaneous propositions and quaeres* (London: printed for R. Royston, and sold by Edward Martin, Norwich, 1649).

38. Matthew Hopkins, *The discovery of witches: in answer to severall queries, lately delivered to the Judges of Assize for the county of Norfolk* (London: printed for R. Royston and sold by Edward Martin in Norwich, 1647).

39. Ketton-Cremer, *Norfolk in the civil war*, p. 308.

40. Theophilus Brabourne, *A defence of the Kings authority and supremacy, in the church and church-discipline* (London: printed for the author, and are to be sold by William Nowell, in Norwich, 1660).

41. Theophilus Brabourne, *God save the King and prosper him; or, a justification of the word of God, of the Kings gracious proffer for liberty of conscience* (London: printed for the author, and are to be sold by booksellers in London, and by William Nowell, in Norwich, 1660).

42. James Warwell, *Votiva tabula; or a solemn thanks giving offered up to God the mighty protector of kings, for the wonderful protection and happy restauration of our gracious soveraign Charles the II.* ([London:] Printed for R. Royston ... sold by William Franckling, Norwich, 1660).

43. John Winter, *A sermon preached at East Dearham in Norf. May 29 1661 being the day of the coronation of our most gracious soveraign* (London: printed for William Oliver, Norwich, 1662).

44. *'An act for preventing the frequent abuses in printing'* 14.Car.II. c.33.

45. John Winter, [Greek title – *Aplos kai kaloz*] *honest plain dealing: or, meditations and advertisements offered to publick consideration* (London: printed by A. M. ... sold by William Oliver, Norwich, 1663).

46. Stoker, 'The Norwich book trades', 111-13.

47. Robert Conold, *The notion of schism stated according to the ancients, and considered with reference to the non-conformists* (London: printed by R.W. for William Oliver and George Rose booksellers in Norwich, ..., and Nath. Brooks ... in Cornhill, and R. Chiswell ... in St. Paul's Church-yard, 1676). The second edition, 1677, had only Oliver's name in Norwich. Also *A discourse upon the repugnancy of sin,* 2nd edition (London: sold by William Oliver, 1682).

48. *A catalogue of valuable books ... which will be sold by auction ... at Mrs Olivers house ... 16th December 1689 by Edward Millington bookseller* ([London: 1689]) and, *A catalogue of ancient and modern books ... which will be sold by Auction ..., at Mrs Olivers House, ... tenth of July 1693. by Edward Millington* ([London, 1693]).

49. Erasmus Warren, *Divine rules for Christian unity opened and urged. A sermon preach'd in the Cathedral Church of Norwich* (London: printed for Samuel Oliver bookseller in Norwich and sold by J. Robinson, 1692), and John Jeffery, *The duty and encouragement of religious artificers described in a sermon preached in the Cathedral Church of Norwich* (Cambridge: printed by John Hayes for Samuel Oliver, Norwich, 1693).

50. Pierre Chauvin, *De naturali religione liber* (Roterodami: Apud Petrum vander Slaart, sumptibus Samuelis Oliverii, Norvincensis, 1693).

51. *The Term Catalogues* II. 455.

52. *Eclaircissimens sur un liver de la religion naturelle, compose par Mr P. Chauvin* ([Rotterdam, 1693]). See also W. Moens, *The Wallons and their church at Norwich,* 2 vols (London, 1887), II. 236.

53. Stoker, 'The Norwich book trades', 117-18.

54. Norfolk Record Office, Norwich Mayor's Court Book 24 (1666-77) fol. 306, and Robert Conold, *A sermon preached before the Maior of the City of Norwich in the Cathedral-church ... January 31. 1674/5* (London: printed for George Rose in Norwich, ... and by Nath Brook, 1675).

55. See note 47 above.

56. John Harris, *The divine physician: prescribing rules for the prevention, and cure of most diseases, as well of the body, as the soul* ([London:] Printed for George Rose in Norwich, ... and by Nath Brook & Will Whitwood in London, 1676), and (London: printed by H. B. for Will Whitwood, and sold by George Rose, Norwich, 1676).

57. *A catalogue of ancient and modern books ... which will be sold by auction (or who bids most) ... at Mr G. Rose's house, on Monday, Decemb. 2d. 1700* ([London, 1700]).

58. B.L. Sloane Ms. 1847, and Sir Thomas Browne, *Works,* 4 vols (London, 1964), iv. p. 149.

59. Bodleian Library Ms. Rawl. D391 and Browne, *Works,* iv. p. 186.

60. John Browne, *A compleat treatise of preternatural tumours both general and particular* (London: printed by S. R. for R. Clavell, and sold by George Rose in Norwich, 1678).

61. Stoker, 'The Norwich book trades', 102-3.

62. Martin Finch, *An answer to Mr Thomas Grantham's book; called, a dialogue between a Baptist and a Presbyterian* (London: printed by T. S. for Edward Giles bookseller in Norwich, and Tho. Parkhurst in Cheapside, 1691).

63. Thomas Grantham, *A discovery of audacious insolence*, London: printed by Tho. Snowden for Edward Giles, Norwich, 1691, and Samuel Petto, *Infant baptism vindicated from the exceptions of Mr Thomas Grantham* (London: printed by Thos. Snowden for Edward Giles, Norwich, 1691).

64. Francis Bugg, *The Quakers detected, their errours confuted, and their hypocrisie discovered* (London: printed for the author ... sold by Edward Gyles, Norwich and Ralph Watson, St Edmunds-Bury, 1686).

65. Richard Kidder, *Convivum caeleste. 2nd edition with additions* (London: printed by John Richardson for Thomas Parkhurst and sold by Edward Giles in Norwich, 1684), and *Obedience to Magistrates recommended in a sermon preached upon Septemb. 9. 1683:* (London: printed by T. S. for Edward Giles, Norwich, 1683).

66. John Dunton, *The life and errors of John Dunton* (London, 1705), 316-17.

James Tytler's Misadventures in the Late Eighteenth-Century Edinburgh Book Trade

STEPHEN BROWN

O N WEDNESDAY MORNING, 11 January 1804, the body of a late-middle-aged man was found drowned in the wash on the north shore of the Neck Gate, not far from Salem, Massachusetts. The man turned out to be the editor of the local newspaper, *The Salem Register*, and had last been seen on Monday evening in a state of advanced drunkenness, crossing the spit from his home at Cat Cove on the Atlantic to a neighbour's house, where he had gone to borrow a candle. Apparently disoriented with drink, he had slipped from the spit into the tidal waters, drowned and was carried some distance along the shoreline. His funeral was well attended and several local dignitaries were among his pall bearers. A sum of $120 was raised for his widow and twin daughters.[1] The man was a Scot, James Tytler, an Edinburgh printer and journalist, and the story of how he came to die in America provides a narrative of the Edinburgh periodical press in the late-eighteenth century. Death by misadventure is somehow a fitting end for this man of extraordinary gifts and eccentric, even unbalanced sensibilities, whose life in the book trade was itself a series of compelling misadventures.

Before his flight as an outlaw to America by way of Ireland, James Tytler was involved with no fewer than eight weekly and monthly publications in Scotland between 1774 and 1792. He was editor and often the sole author for six of these periodicals and also contributed regularly to Edinburgh's three newspapers.[2] He built and operated his own printing press as well as working for three very successful printers, William Auld, Colin Macfarquhar, and John Mennons. He was employed at various times by William Creech, Charles Elliot, and Peter Hill, finishing his Edinburgh career in what should have been a lucrative association with the shady Cornelius Elliot but which instead resulted in prosecution for sedition. Tytler's most lasting work was done as editor, compiler, and chief writer for the second edition of the *Encyclopaedia Britannica* and as a major contributor to the third edition; his article on 'Electricity' would inspire a young Michael Faraday to give up book binding for science. Tytler had a peculiar talent for serializations in theology and history which he not only wrote but usually self-published, and as writer or editor he is credited with six works of geography and medicine, as well as numerous political pamphlets, broadsheets, poetry, and translations of classical texts.[3] He is the prototypical hack writer, and his life in the book trade provides a unique insight into the nature of popular publishing in late-enlightenment Edinburgh. Tytler's career as printer, journalist, and editor illustrates three defining aspects of the late eighteenth-century Scottish – and especially the Edinburgh – popular book trade: an emphasis on texts with scientific, medical and philosophical content; a tendency toward controversy and intellectual dissent; and a highly competitive sense of the marketplace that rewarded entrepreneurship, but only at considerable risk. The 1770s through the 1790s were the decades in which Edinburgh evolved its own distinctive periodical style, marked by an unstintingly democratic dissemination of knowledge, a craving for frank disputation, and a canny, exegetical attention to contentious language. That fondness for the con-tentious expression of opinion is particularly evident in Tytler's approach to magazine and review writing and is never more clearly stated than in his 1780 announcement 'To Our Correspondents' in the tenth number of his *Weekly Mirror* where he writes that while in most publications

the Editor of the Magazine himself for the most part keep[s] silence. With the *Mirror* the case is different. It is supposed to be done by a single person, or by a number of persons agreeing so much in their way of thinking that the Author's frequently spoke of in the singular number. Only one set of sentiments therefore can be admitted into it, and where letters are received differing very widely from those of the [Editor], he is obliged to make remarks upon them.[4]

While Tytler's editorial obligation 'to make remarks' often led him into criminal libel, it also made him popular with booksellers who wanted lively and controversial copy, not because they were pugnacious themselves but because verbal fisticuffs sold. And that very popularity would eventually lead to Tytler's literary demise in Scotland.

James Tytler was born on 17 December 1745 at Fearn in the county of Forfar in the northeast of Scotland, the third of four sons of the local min-ister, who taught his boys Latin and Greek before sending them to the local parish school. The father was a graduate of Marischal College and all three of Tytler's brothers studied at one or the other of Aberdeen's two colleges, the eldest, George, pursuing divinity before emigrating to America and the youngest, Henry, taking a medical degree. James attended classes only briefly, however, before becoming a surgeon's apprentice in Forfar at age sixteen. By the autumn of 1763, when he was eighteen, Tytler's name appears among those attending medical classes at the University of Edinburgh where he studied with Professors Cullen, Hope, and Monro, although Cullen's chemistry class would have the most lasting effect on Tytler's career. He left the University without a degree in 1765 when he signed on at Leith as ship's surgeon aboard the Greenland whaler *Royal Bounty* under William Ker. Shortly after his return to Edinburgh in September 1765, Tytler married Elizabeth Rattray, a solicitor's daughter, through whom he became involved with the small radical sect of seceders known as the Glasites, after their founder John Glas who had split from the Church of Scotland in 1726. Tytler next set up as a chemist in Leith, but business was poor and his finances deteriorated to the point that he fled Scotland sometime in 1767, eventually settling in Newcastle where he again attempted to practise as a chemist. By 1773, Tytler, now the father of five children, had returned to Scotland and established himself in Restalrig on the outskirts of Edinburgh, making his first attempt as an author while continuing to ply his trade as a preparer of medicines. Around this time, he became familiar with the printer William Auld, quite possibly through the Mary's Chapel Masonic Lodge, and was contracted by Auld to write, compile and edit the *Gentleman and Lady's Magazine*, which first appeared in late January 1774.

On his return to Edinburgh, Tytler achieved a certain notoriety within the book trade by setting up as a printer with neither qualifications nor premises. He somehow contrived to build his own press from scrap parts and began to print his own works, including *A Letter to John Barclay on the Doctrine of Assurance* – notable for its articulate insistence upon tolerance and its critique of dogmatism – and some competent translations of Virgil's *Eclogues*. As one might expect, Tytler's attempts at printing were inadequate even at their best, his type irregular and his inking uneven. Still, however bizarre it seemed to others, Tytler continued to issue his own various works from this homemade press for over a decade, training his eldest son George in the trade, whose imprint appears in 1782 on volume two of his father's *General History of All Nations, Ancient and Modern*, and steadily improving in his own efforts despite the primitive nature of his press. Tytler was certainly a decent writer, with a lively, identifiable voice and an extraordinary breadth of interests and learning. He was fluent in the classical languages and authors, knowledgeable in medical and natural science, intimately informed about the intricacies of Christian theology and insatiably curious. His intellect was of that promiscuous sort especially well suited to journalism and periodical writing, and these qualities would have been evident to William Auld, who enjoyed a long and successful career as a printer of almanacks, chapbook accounts of sensational trials, legal judgements, and Masonic texts, including the very popular and often reprinted *Freemason's Handbook*. Auld had been a printing partner in two fairly successful periodicals, the *Edinburgh Magazine*, a monthly which he published together with Walter Ruddiman from 1757 through 1762, and then the *Edinburgh Weekly Journal*, a newspaper issued first in partnership with Ruddiman from 1757 until 1765, and then with William Smellie and John Balfour.[5] The *Journal* ceased to publish some time after an acrimonious dispute between Smellie and Auld, in which Smellie attempted to assume control of the weekly, eventually leaving the partnership and convincing Balfour to withdraw his support for the publication.[6]

In 1773, Smellie had launched together with Gilbert Stuart, Charles Elliot, and John Murray, the initially very successful and widely promoted *Edinburgh Magazine and Review*, and Walter Ruddiman, three years after splitting with Auld, had begun in 1768 *The Weekly Magazine or Edinburgh Amusement*, which proved a great popular success and counted James Tytler along with the Scots vernacular poet Robert Fergusson among its many contributors. It ran until 1784, outliving its founder. It is not unlikely that Auld, witnessing the success of his two previous partners, was casting about for an author/editor when he met James Tytler. Auld, unlike Ruddiman and Smellie, never wrote, compiled or edited, remaining a silent printing partner in his periodical ventures; consequently, he would have been attracted to a literary talent such as Tytler's as a means of getting back into the periodical business. At any rate, Auld and Tytler formed a partnership to produce the *Gentleman and Lady's Magazine*, a weekly compiled and written entirely by Tytler.[7] And because Auld never demonstrated an interest in the content of the journalism he published, Tytler would have been allowed considerable freedom in putting together the *Gentleman and Lady's Magazine*. Certainly, over the twelve months of its run, Tytler's aggressive nature became increasingly apparent in his writing and editing decisions, eventually turning the publication into more of a review than a magazine. The periodical was 32 pages octavo, advertised itself as issued every Friday, and attempted – as its title indicates – to include matters of importance to women readers. Here Tytler's lifelong medical interests proved crucial, and he provided essays on childbed fever and recommendations for inoculations against the measles, alongside the more usual romantic tales and conduct lessons. A fair amount of the content was reprinted, although the original material is more substantial than was usual in a publication of this sort, and included numerous biographies, one of Tytler's favourite genres.[8] The magazine's premier number begins with a character of Samuel Johnson, whose tour of Scotland remained very much a topic of interest in Edinburgh. Drama proved a particular passion of Tytler's and he printed regular theatre reviews, despite what he identifies as 'a certain old Presbyterian prejudice in the minds of many readers against everything that savours of the stage'.[9] But Tytler's interests are most apparent in what he calls his 'literary reviews', four pages set aside in most numbers for extracts and discussions of titles currently for sale in the Edinburgh book shops. His choices made no concessions to his female readers and, predictably, reflected Tytler's own interests in medicine, natural history, politics, and theology. Selections range from demanding scientific titles such as John Pringle's *Discourse on the Different Kinds of Air* to a remarkable and lengthy review of Tytler's own serial publication, *Essays on the Most Important Articles of Natural and Revealed Religion*, a work which he intended should run to thirty numbers although only two were actually completed. This latter text was one which Tytler had printed on his homemade press, and in his 'Letter to the Editor' under the Literary Intelligence heading for 20 July 1774, Tytler describes his own achievements as

the most extraordinary Literary Phenomena that have appeared perhaps, since the invention of printing: you will be somewhat surprised, I suppose, to hear of a printing-house at Restalrig: – but you must be still more so, when I inform you, that the printer performs every part of his work himself: *Author, Printer, Compositor, Corrector, Pressman, Book-binder,* and *Book-seller* ... who not withstanding, never served an apprenticeship to any of these businesses ... but what would [your readers] say sir, to see an author, not writing, but actually printing a book from his *pericranium*, alone, without either scroll copy, heads, or previous M.S. of any kind.[10]

As much as it was common practice for booksellers to advertise and even puff their own titles in the newspapers and magazines in which they held financial interests, Tytler's rhetoric here is beyond the pale.

Tytler's democratic inclinations become increasingly apparent in the later stages of the run of the *Gentleman and Lady's Magazine*, when he begins to write long reviews that extend over more than one issue on political texts, exposing the abuses of the local government and the M.P., Sir Laurence Dundas. Here Tytler seems to be emulating the style employed by William Smellie and Gilbert Stuart in their *Edinburgh Magazine and Review*, a way of writing initiated in the first *Edinburgh Review* in 1755 and fully developed by Francis Jeffrey in the later *Edinburgh Review* of 1802. In Tytler's hands this approach to reviewing ranged from the brutal, mocking dismissal of books in a single line to detailed critical studies carried on over several numbers of the magazine. For example, the author of *Principles of Trade* is sent off as 'ignorant, affected and uncouth' while Allen's *The American Crisis* is put down as 'crude, silly [and] bombastic'. Tytler is fonder of Lord Kames, whose *Sketches of the History of Man* he describes as 'whimsical and speculative; but curious, historical, and entertaining'.[11] Tytler takes two numbers to review enthusiastically Gilbert Stuart's pamphlet exposing the gross financial mismanagement of Herriot's Hospital by the Town Council, applauding in particular Stuart's gift for libelling his opponents. Tytler next gives over three issues of the *Magazine* to review a lengthy satirical poem on the scandalous re-election of Sir Laurence Dundas as M.P. This Tytler supplements with a anonymous letter 'To the Printer' of his own composition in which he cleverly satirizes Dundas as a lottery cheat.[12] The final number of the *Gentleman and Lady's Magazine* is published on Wednesday 28 December 1774, the whole run having amounted to four volumes, twelve numbers to the volume. In a hastily inserted address 'To our Readers and Correspondents', Tytler complains about the usual financial challenges of the periodical marketplace, especially unpaid subscriptions, and to the question posed by one reader – 'Are all our Engravers dead?' – he replies that 'though the Engravers are still in life, yet Trade in general has been so dead, payments so dilatory, and their price so dear, that we found we could not do justice to ourselves and our readers both, had we continued to furnish the usual number of Plates.'[13] *The Gentleman and Lady's Magazine* is at times a strikingly distinctive effort which began its life emulating Ruddiman's *Weekly Magazine* before adopting the tone of Smellie's and Stuart's monthly *Magazine and Review*, whose style is more characteristic of the Tytler literary bent. But it finally succumbed to these two competitors in the tight Edinburgh market, having moved some distance in its political content from its original design as a *gentleman's* magazine that would also be fit reading for *the ladies*. In comparing the *Gentleman and Lady's Magazine* with the *Edinburgh Magazine and Review*, one finds that the two periodicals share a common style of reviewing, especially in Tytler's later numbers. Tytler seems to have been genuinely influenced by Gilbert Stuart's approach in particular and gradually adapted his own review writing to reflect a similarly aggressive stance. That confrontational posture probably cost the *Gentleman and Lady's Magazine* its readership or, at the very least, scared off the printer/publisher, William Auld. It would remain, however, James Tytler's hallmark as a journalist.

Suddenly lacking an income and having abandoned his chemist's business to become a literary man, Tytler was quickly overwhelmed with debt in early 1775. His wife left him at that point, abandoning their five children, and he sought refuge in the Sanctuary at Holyrood, where he remained until Colin Macfarquhar enlisted him in 1776 to compile, edit and write original articles for the second edition of the *Encyclopaedia Britannica*. Tytler then removed himself and his children to Duddingston, returning to Edinburgh only reluctantly during the nearly seven years he laboured over the *Encyclopaedia* (1777-83). His continuing problems with debt made him wary of settling within the town precincts, and when Tytler did finally come to Edinburgh, it was to take up occasional accommodations in Colin Macfarquhar's premises. MacFarquhar did this, not out of charity, but so that he could keep Tytler sober enough to stay on schedule with his compilation of the *Britannica* and to control his quixotic tendencies. Tytler received sixteen shillings a week for his efforts, which meant that despite the considerable demands placed upon his time by the *Britannica*, he still needed various hackwork and journalistic assignments to support his family. Tytler was clearly well known in Edinburgh and convivial – his moving obituary for Robert Fergusson in the *Gentleman and Lady's Magazine* testifies in its intimate knowledge of the poet to Tytler's sociability – and his lifelong friendship with Dr Robert Anderson,[14] who succeeded James Sibbald as editor of the *Edinburgh Magazine and Literary Miscellany* is a good indication of the intellectual respect shown Tytler by his journalistic colleagues. Anderson was a prime source of books and other research materials for Tytler throughout the *Britannica* years and was joined by the bookseller Charles Elliot and the printer/publisher John Mennons in offering Tytler work and support in his various undertakings.

It was no doubt friends of this sort who enabled Tytler to convince the Edinburgh Town Council to allow him the use of the new Registry Building to conduct his air balloon experiments in 1784 and who helped him through recurrent periods of insolvency.

The second edition of the *Britannica* is the best evidence of the scope of Tytler's intellectual interests: he wrote lengthy new articles on Edinburgh, Electricity, Fishery, Geography, and War, among many other subjects, as well as most of the biographies. His essays on whales and whaling draw on his own experiences and were carried over into later editions. Herman Melville used these extraordinary pieces extensively, and anyone who has read *Moby Dick*, has necessarily read some Tytler. When he wrote a lengthy addendum to his article on Air for the Appendix in volume ten of the second *Britannica*, Tytler included a substantial account of the science and history of balloon flights. Notwithstanding his demanding work on the *Encyclopaedia Britannica*, Tytler was also employed by Dr Andrew Duncan on the *Medical and Philosophical Commentaries*, prepared a general index for the *Scots Magazine*, wrote *A System of Geography*, a *History of Edinburgh*, and began his serialized *General History of All Nations*. Some of these works were printed by Tytler and his son on his homemade press, and others drew on material prepared for the *Britannica* – his duodecimo *History of Edinburgh* is one such example. He also briefly wrote and self-published a periodical, the *Weekly Review*, in 1779, in the manner of Defoe's *Review*, before writing, compiling, and editing a rather interesting magazine for John Mennons, called the *Weekly Mirror*, which made its first appearance on 22 September 1780. Each issue of the *Weekly Mirror* was sixteen pages octavo, and the magazine was designed to bring together the literary musings and essay style of Mackenzie's *Mirror* with a summary of recent political and public transactions. These 'Historical Memoirs' alternated with 'Literary Memoirs', which emulated the critical essays that Addison had originated with the *Spectator*. The proposal and subsequent newspaper advertisements for the *Weekly Mirror* described the new periodical as a 'collection of original essays on those subjects which are most generally canvassed in common conversation'.[15] The format afforded Tytler the opportunity to pass what the advertisement describes as 'remarks' upon the current state of affairs and, as was the case with the *Gentleman and Lady's Magazine*, Tytler was at his best when editorializing in the *Weekly Mirror*.

The first number includes an incisive retrospective critique of the government's failure in the American war, concluding that the current nature of party politics, electioneering, and increasing ministerial 'obsequiousness toward the Crown' does not bode well for the new parliament.[16] Throughout the duration of the *Weekly Mirror,* Tytler uses the example of what he calls the principled perseverance of the 'American Patriots' against the British government to illustrate by contrast the immodest divisiveness of Scottish politics. His political commentaries are often startlingly blunt and complemented by some darkly ironic essays. The colloquy 'On Smuggling' and 'A Modest Vindication of Smuggling' in the November numbers are particularly good examples of this, with their Swiftian criticism of government fiscal incompetence and a parliament that condones the robbery of the public purse. Tytler remarks in the persona of a smuggler:

Had Mr. Burke's oeconomy bills passed, there might have been some hopes of amendment, and perhaps I might have begun to entertain some scruples about smuggling myself – but when both these and the bill for taxing all places and pensions (voted in at the first motion by pensioners themselves) were at last thrown out by the Minister, I cannot entertain a doubt of its being my duty to keep as much of my money in my pocket as I possibly can.[17]

Everywhere in the *Weekly Mirror,* Tytler's anti-government sentiments are apparent. His is a particularly Scottish Whiggism whose suspicions are directed at the discrepancies 'between descriptions and realities', as they arise from the political language of dispatches and public oratory.

In the final number of the *Weekly Mirror* on Friday 9 March 1781, Tytler identifies the enemy of political liberty as what he calls 'the servile disposition of the vulgar'. Tytler begins by observing that

of late, I have found an opinion very strongly prevalent, that our political liberty consists only in *obedience* to the laws, without enquiring how these laws may be changed or perverted to bad purposes by the law-makers. It hath also been thought, and very much inculcated, that only a certain set of people have any right to *concern themselves* with *law-making,* and that in the exercise of this honourable profession, they are bound neither to consult the interests nor the desires of those who are to obey. If any of those whose province it is to *obey the laws* shall happen to be dissatisfied with this method of proceeding … they are considered as opposers of the *powers that be,* as rebels, turbulent, factious, and as coming within the *comprehending act,* or some of the almost obsolete arbitrary statutes of Charles II.

... Yet this it seems is *liberty* and the *most excellent constitution* that ever was invented by man!

Throughout this number of the magazine, Tytler emphasizes the responsibility of every man to exercise his right to self-determination, employing a Covenanter's perseverance in dissent and a seceder's zeal for independence in a Scottish re-invention of Wilkite language. Like many Scots of his political stripe – and this especially included rural Presbyterian ministers – Tytler took courage from the example of the American rebellion. He insists that 'no man has the right to oblige me to serve him unless I please' and that 'all human contracts are conditional, and the breaking of the condition on one part undoubtedly breaks it on the other also'. Therefore, Tytler concludes that 'in times of public calamity ... where the rights of the people are grossly invaded, the relation betwixt master and servant must cease'. Tytler stops short of inciting violence – his political journalism is always pacifist, employing the Glasite principle of passive resistance – but he strongly counsels self-respect and urges concerted negotiation to bring about reform: 'I do not recommend turbulence and confusion, but I recommend a determined resolution, and a proper value for ourselves.' But Tytler's sense of satire never deserts him, even in his most eloquently righteous moments. He concludes this paper by observing that some prime examples of the

servility of the vulgar are their extreme readiness to run out and look at the coaches of great men passing by [and] the putting into the news-papers that such a lord or duke or other dignified character, arrived at town on such a day. ... Thus the pride of the great is industriously fostered [and] they fancy themselves a kind of superior beings.[18]

How might the revolution begin in Edinburgh? Tytler suggests that a good first action would be for the vulgar simply to ignore the rich. It may be of interest to note here the cheap price of Tytler's magazine, which sold for one pence a number or a shilling one pence a quarter. Tytler and Mennons obviously hoped to reach readers among the lower trades and labourers.

With its final issue on Friday 9 March 1781, the *Weekly Mirror* managed numbers sufficient to just complete the proposed first volume. In a note to subscribers printed on the magazine's last page, Tytler apologizes for the 'irregularity of its publication these several weeks past' but insists that to have kept to schedule would have required him to have 'deviated from [his] first engagement of giving nothing but *originals*' in the magazine.

He pleads illness as a cause for the delay in composing his essays, and promises that number one of the second volume will appear on 'the 6th of next month', something which does not happen, and subscribers are subsequently notified that because of the continued 'indisposition of the author ... a final period has been put to [the magazine] on that account, and as they could not find another person capable of finishing it upon the same plan'.[19] Tytler's correspondence at this time with Dr Robert Anderson describes his efforts to recover his health from a collapse brought on by overwork,[20] and it is a shame that the demands of editing the *Britannica* prevented him from continuing what was an acutely perceptive political periodical. Nonetheless, Tytler did not forget his program for promoting liberal ideals at Edinburgh, and he would have another, even more radical, go at political commentary with the launch of his *Historical Register* more than a decade later in 1791. In the meantime, Tytler embarked on an adventure that would gain him an enduring if, ultimately, a somewhat humiliating place in the history of manned flight, as Scotland's first balloonist.

While he was completing the tenth volume of the second edition of the *Encyclopaedia Britannica*, Tytler found himself, however fleetingly, sufficiently well known and respected in Edinburgh to consider some new career directions. He returned to his early love of chemistry and began to experiment with various forms of magnesia and alternative compounds for bleaching. He also became fascinated with the accounts of balloon flights by the Montgolfiers in France. Contemporary sources suggest that Tytler raised some modest funds to pursue his interests in fire balloons by selling his formula for an improved bleaching process for cloth and by turning for patronage to some well-situated and recently acquired friends, notably the cabinetmaker and soon-to-be infamous housebreaker, Deacon William Brodie and Edinburgh's increasingly most innovative bookseller, Charles Elliot, who came to know Tytler well through their joint interest in the *Britannica*.[21] Tytler's extensive research on the mechanics and chemistry of balloon flight, as well as teaching him how to construct and fly a balloon, also furnished some of the last material published in the final volume of the second *Britannica*. Tytler sold subscriptions through Charles Elliot's bookshop in Parliament Square to underwrite the cost of building his balloon, with the promise that subscribers would enjoy a private viewing of the first ascent, along with a lecture on the scientific principles underlying manned flight. Although Tytler's efforts first to inflate and then float his balloon met with regular misfortune from bad weather to fire, his progress was carefully, if sceptically, chronicled by Edinburgh's three newspapers and, when Tytler did make a moderately successful flight on 28 August 1784, the papers were enthusiastic, despite his having ascended to only 350 feet and travelled less than half a mile. But as Tytler persevered in attempting to improve the performance of his balloon over the next two months, he lost public favour and the *Edinburgh Evening Courant* eventually called upon the Sheriff to put an end to Tytler's distracting activities.[22] Tytler's investors all fell away and he found himself once again insolvent and seeking sanctuary at Holyrood late in 1784, where he remained until John Mennons invited him to Glasgow to write and edit yet another new magazine, the *Observer*, in 1785.

Mennons had left Edinburgh for Glasgow sometime in 1782 and he began publishing the *Glasgow Advertiser* – forerunner of the *Herald* – on 27 January 1783. The *Advertiser* was a success from the outset and provided the foundation for Mennons' many publishing triumphs, including his adaptation of the Edinburgh *Town and Country Almanack* for west coast customers. Mennons was keen to provide Glasgow with news and political commentary equal to that in Edinburgh, and even London, and he hoped that his new periodical, the *Observer*, would achieve this under Tytler's editorship. Mennons trusted that the two of them might build upon the format developed in the Historical and Literary Memoir sections of the *Weekly Mirror*. The *Observer*, however, failed after just twenty-six weekly numbers, and Tytler returned to Edinburgh in January 1786, where Charles Elliot employed him to write for the third edition of the *Encyclopaedia Britannica*, just then getting underway.

Tytler's last and most distinguished periodical work would be the *Historical Register, or Edinburgh Monthly Intelligencer*, which first appeared 13 July 1791. Tytler's return to journalism followed his work on the somewhat controversial *Edinburgh Geographical, Commercial, and Historic Grammar*, and came at a time when the fear of insurrection and especially the spreading discontent associated with such reform groups as The Friends of the People were driving the government to suppress every manner of dissent. So fraught a political moment provided an ideal opportunity for Tytler to resurrect the intelligent critical commentary that characterized his *Weekly Mirror*. Furthermore, Tytler found a publisher for his new venture – Charles Elliot's nephew, Cornelius – who took pains to widely promote the periodical through newspaper advertisements and booksellers in

Edinburgh, Glasgow, Dublin, and London. No other magazine with which Tytler had been associated was so extensively distributed or met with such popular demand; William Auld had placed no advertisements whatsoever for the *Gentleman and Lady's Magazine*. Early numbers of the *Historical Register* quickly sold out, and notices were placed in all the Edinburgh newspapers throughout the winter months of 1791-92, promising fresh runs of the first six issues. Complete sets were advertised all through 1792, regularly selling out and requiring reissue. The magazine was printed on fine paper, with each number containing 48 pages octavo, stitched in blue covers and sold at six pence a copy. It appeared initially on the 13th of each month, although Tytler soon reverted to his past worst practice of delivering his text a week or more behind schedule. The content was entirely political: half the space was dedicated to national and international commentary, half to a miscellaneous chronicle of national and local events during the previous month. All the copy was original and written by Tytler who promoted a reform agenda from the outset. Predictably, he opposed Edmund Burke and championed Thomas Paine, though not uncritically. Tytler engaged his opponents by closely examining their rhetoric, and the inflammatory style of reviewing that he had honed in his earlier journalism brought a sense of urgency to the *Historical Register*. In his second number for August 1791, Tytler gives over twenty pages to assailing Burke's *Reflections on the French Revolution* in an extended footnote attached to the *Register*'s discussion of the French National Assembly's declaration guaranteeing that 'men have a natural right to liberty'. In this instance and throughout each number of the *Register*, Tytler makes his political points by closely analyzing the language of his opponents and exposing their hidden strategies. And his *ad hominem* attacks are unflinching, striking his quarry with an accuracy that presages the later political incisiveness of William Cobbett.

While the popularity of the *Historical Register* grew with the increasing political anxieties of the times, Tytler and Elliot encouraged their expanding circulation even more through several intriguing promotional gimmicks. The number for May 1992 was sewn together with Thomas Paine's 'Letter to the Honourable Mr. Secretary Dundas', which was offered *gratis* with the purchase of the *Register* at its usual six pence price. Printed on the blue covers was the text of a radical song, then popular in Edinburgh, 'Wha' Wants Me?', attacking Henry Dundas and William Pitt, and also a satiric squib on the slave trade in the form of an address to the sharks in the waters off the West African coast.[23] Elliot seems to have waved the publisher's right to use magazine covers to promote his other titles or for profitable advertisements in order to offer additional space for political texts that would catch the reader's attention by their outrageousness.[24] In a subsequent number, he advertised gratis an engraved portrait of Thomas Paine, suitable to serve as a frontispiece to volume two of the *Register*. Tytler's journalism, however, outstripped Elliot's promotions in its modern practice. He advertised in the *Register* for whistle blowers who would be willing to supply him with dirt on the Excise and other government departments. Tytler said that he would not accept anonymous tips; he wanted his informants to prove the integrity of their information by providing him with their names, although he assured all that he would keep his sources confidential.[25]

As one would expect, Tytler was closely watched by the local authorities who were particularly alarmed by the *Register*'s coverage of the George Square riots. And, true to his misadventuring ways, Tytler provided the government with an easy opportunity to prosecute him, when he wrote and circulated a broadsheet entitled, 'To the People and their Friends' in November 1792 for which he was arrested on 4 December under Henry Dundas's new Seditious Writings Act. Tytler was bailed by some Edinburgh booksellers involved with the *Historical Register* and was cited to appear before the High Court on 7 January 1793.[26] However, he fled over Hogmanay and was declared an outlaw. He travelled first to Ireland where he was joined by his common law wife Jean and their twin daughters before settling in Salem Massachusetts.[27]

Tytler lived in America for almost a decade, editing a newspaper and publishing works on history and medicine. His *Treatise on the Plague and Yellow Fever* is an interesting example of early medical history which contains crucial, contemporary accounts of infectious diseases in the Americas, and his *Dissertation on the Origins and Antiquity of the Scottish Nation* displays his hallmark in its assault on John Pinkerton's *History of Scotland*, calling it a text 'delivered ... in terms so pedantic, insolent and approbrious, as certainly to deserve the severest reprehension'. Tytler also attempted to find a place for Christianity in Thomas Paine's politics through his *Reply to Mr. Paine's Age of Reason*. But in America, Tytler was chiefly admired for his contributions to the *Encyclopaedia Britannica*, and his talent for political journalism and reviewing found no sufficient outlet.

So, why do we need a *post mortem* examination of a drunken Scotsman, drowned off Salem Massachusetts in the early years of the nineteenth century? Because to understand the nature of journalism and the ephemeral press in the eighteenth century, it is crucial to find out as much about the lives of the hack writers who produced this sort of work as about the physical formats of the magazines, reviews, pamphlets, and newspapers for which they wrote. This is not often an easy task. These authors are seldom identified in their texts and their backgrounds are usually shadowy, if not downright shady. Their lives are as ephemeral as the media in which they labour. Nonetheless, hack writers are just as much tradesmen as printers, typefounders, book binders or paper makers, and their 'craft' is just as fundamental to a publisher's success. While few early journalists combined whaling and ballooning with careers as chemists and encyclopaedists, most led adventurous and often bizarre lives. Their marginal and eccentric existences shape their material media undeniably, and we cannot fully understand the media for which they wrote without tracing the shapes of the hack writers' lives. Book historians need to convene more coroner's juries for this very reason. There are many James Tytlers still awaiting their book trade *post mortems*.

Notes

1. There are several brief and elliptical accounts of Tytler's life and two quite unreliable full-length studies: Robert Meek's *Biographical Sketch of the Life of James Tytler* (Edinburgh, 1805) and James Fergusson's *Balloon Tytler* (London, 1972). The entry in the New DNB is a beginning, but not without crucial faults. It is a difficult task to sort out myth from fact in Tytler's history.

2. Tytler contributed regularly to the *Edinburgh Advertiser*, the *Caledonian Mercury*, and the *Edinburgh Evening Courant*, as well as editing and writing the *Gentleman and Lady's Weekly Magazine*, the *Weekly Mirror*, the *Weekly Review*, the *Observer*, the *Glasgow Magazine and Review*, and the *Historical Register*. He also briefly edited the *Salem Register*.

3. Three of Tytler's most influential works were published in Massachusetts, after his exile from Britain. These were his poem celebrating American politics, *The Rising of the Sun in the West*, his extraordinary medical history, *Treatise on the Plague and Yellow Fever*, and his proposal for what would have been the first major work of geography to be written in America, *Proposals for publishing by subscription a New System of Geography, Ancient and Modern*. Because the latter was proposed as a serial publication which would use only eye-witness accounts of foreign geography, it is sometimes considered the forerunner of the *National Geographic Magazine*.

4. *Weekly Mirror*, Friday November 24, 1780, p. 160.

5. The only surviving issues of the Journal from this period are in the National Library of Scotland.

6. The correspondence outlining the publication history of the Journal and its demise can be found in the William Smellie Manuscript Papers in the National Museum of Scotland. The standard account taken from Robert Kerr's *Memoirs of the Life, Writings, and Correspondence of William Smellie* (1811) is seriously inaccurate.

7. The only complete run of this rare work is in the National Library of Scotland.

8. Tytler wrote most of the biographical entries for the second edition of the Encyclopaedia Britannica, and biographical essays featured strongly in most of his periodical ventures.

9. The theatre section drew upon the newspapers for coverage of London and Dublin, but the Edinburgh reviews are all original and surprisingly acute for a city that had little by way of a stage tradition.

10. Vol. 3, pp. 422-24.

11. These are some of the first instances of the style that would make notorious such later Tytler review pamphlets as *A Review of Mr Aitken's Outlines of the Theory and Cure of Fever* (1789), *A Review of Guthrie's Geographical, Historical, and Commercial Grammar* (1791), and *An Answer to the Second Part of Paine's 'Age of Reason'.*

12. In these last issues of the magazine, Tytler becomes openly critical of Edinburgh government and of the Dundas dynasty in particular, something that would haunt him later. See Vol. 4, especially pp. 369-403.

13. See 'To our Readers and Correspondents', pp. 417-19. The publication ends with this biting essay about the vicissitudes of magazine publishing.

14. See Anderson's account of Tytler in *Reliques of Robert Burns*, ed. by R. H. Cromek (London, 1808), pp. 306-11.

15. Advertisements appear in both the *Edinburgh Evening Courant* and the *Caledonian Mercury* throughout the summer of 1780.

16. Friday September 23, pp. 14-16.

17. Friday September 30, pp. 41-47. The piece on smuggling is used to set the week's historical account into an especially ironic light.

18. Beginning with the issue for 19 January 1781, the 'Historical Memoirs' become increasingly scurrilous and disdainful of the general public. Abusing the readership could hardly have been good for the periodical's already irregular circulation.

19. Vol. 1, p. 470.

20. See Tytler's correspondence with Anderson in the National Library of Scotland: Adv. MSS. 22.4.II, ff. 38-9.

21. See the file material on Tytler's balloon adventures in the Edinburgh Room, Edinburgh Public Library.

22. The attitude towards Tytler's balloon experiments sours rapidly in the Edinburgh press in September 1784.

23. The National Library of Scotland has the only known copy of this extraordinary issue.

24. Very few eighteenth-century periodicals survive in their original blue paper wrappers, but my examination of some 200 examples in the National Library of Scotland (mostly issues of the Scots Magazine), has identified a tendency toward abandoning the advertising on magazine covers and replacing it with rudimentary 'cover' stories by

1790. However, the extent of this practice on the part of the *Historical Register* is still exceptional for its daring political nature. See an account of the publisher John Murray's attitude toward magazine covers in William Zachs, *The First John Murray and the Late Eighteenth-Century London Book Trade* (Oxford, 1998), pp. 85-87.

25. *Historical Register*, July and August 1791. This would later become common practice for William Cobbett but is extraordinary for the 1790s, especially in Scotland.

26. See the manuscript for the indictment in the University of Edinburgh Library: LA Add.7, item #39.

27. There has been much speculation about the source for the assistance which Tytler received in fleeing Scotland for Ireland and then America. Throughout his career, Tytler's connection with freemasonry benefited him, and it is probable that lodges in Ireland and America – both known to be sympathetic to Tytler's politics – may have funded his passage and resettlement.

The Geographies of Promotion: a Survey of Advertising in Two Eighteenth-Century English Newspapers

IAN JACKSON

EWSPAPERS WERE KEY to the success of larger eighteenth-century provincial print businesses, and advertising was central to the viability of newspapers. Given the relatively low circulations of provincial newspapers, and the limited prospects for increase in an increasingly crowded and heavily-taxed market, increasing the revenue from advertising was the most likely way that a newspaper could be made more profitable. By 1792, the *Reading Mercury* felt able to put it more bluntly, claiming that, 'The Profits of a newspaper arise *only* from Advertisements'.[1] But where did this advertising come from? To understand the commercial basis of provincial newspapers, we must investigate the origins of eighteenth-century newspaper advertising. This in turn can inform discussion of the cultural role of the newspaper, and thus broader arguments about the commercial and social role of the provincial press. Newspaper adverts have been used as supporting evidence for two influential approaches to the problem of characterizing cultural change in the eighteenth century. Firstly, the thesis of the 'commercialisation of culture' suggests that through the eighteenth century there was a shift towards commercially organized cultural forms, such as assemblies, magazines, novels, and indeed newspapers.[2] Adverts for cultural events and products have been used to provide evidence for the expansion in this form of culture, and for the development of innovative new marketing strategies.

Newspaper advertising has also been used to underpin the hypothesis of the 'English urban renaissance'. Peter Borsay cites newspapers as both a cause and an effect of the development of a new urban culture.[3] He suggests that newspapers helped to sell cultural events and products, and were themselves an integral part of this culture. They made a polite urban culture, and through it a growing sphere of public opinion and civic consciousness, accessible to all who could afford to access them – by purchase, or in a coffee house or provincial library. Much discussion of eighteenth-century advertising has been structured around either or both of these approaches: assuming that the burgeoning newspapers of England both reflected and furthered a new consumer and urban culture. As a result, most attention has been given to advertisements for new cultural forms such as assemblies, novels, and subscription concerts, and for new consumer goods. However, reading most eighteenth-century provincial newspapers, it is striking how *few* adverts there are for such products. The commonest form of advertising is not for any new commercial product or service, but for an age-old activity: the sale of land. Furthermore, many adverts are not strictly speaking commercial at all: for example, public notices placed by local magistrates, or by candidates seeking election. The major commercial goods advertised are books and patent medicines, but these are a problematic category, because so many of the adverts are promoting the newspaper owner's own enterprises. Furthermore, the notion of the newspaper as primarily an urban phenomenon seems to be challenged by the numerous adverts placed from small villages and obscure locales.

To get a sense of the advertising market in the eighteenth century as a whole, it is important to do more than just pick out those adverts that reflect *a priori* assumptions about what is important. Rather, we need an analysis that encompasses all advertising. This in turn requires a systematic approach, surveying and aggregating adverts of different types and analysing the results. Such an approach, pioneered by J. Jefferson Looney in his work on the York and Leeds press, helps us establish the parameters of the advertising market, including the total volume of advertising, and the types of people, businesses and organizations that placed adverts.[4] This market could then also be considered spatially by plotting which areas adverts originated from. Once these commercial and geographical parameters are established, a closer examination of the strategies and language adopted by advertisers can give insight into *why* they advertised.

The *Northampton Mercury* and *Reading Mercury* are a good test-bed for such an approach. Copies of almost every issue of the *Northampton Mercury* from its foundation in 1720 until the present day survive. Survival of the *Reading Mercury* is patchier, but copies do exist from each decade from the 1720s onwards, and the file after 1767 is nearly complete. Added to the substantial continuity in the ownership of both newspapers, this enables comparisons across a long period of time to be made and greater confidence that like is being compared with like.[5]

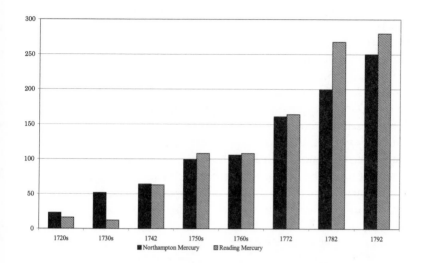

Fig. 1. Average number of advertisements per month in the *Reading Mercury* and *Northampton Mercury* from one year in each decade

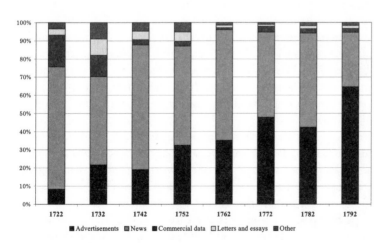

Fig. 2. Percentage of *Northampton Mercury* devoted to each type of content in each sample year

The following analysis is based on a sample of complete issues of these two newspapers. It consists of issues of the *Northampton Mercury* from every other month, in one year in every ten, from 1722 to 1792. Each issue in these months had all of its advertising logged. Thus, the sample is based on 192 issues, yielding details of over 5,600 adverts. For comparative purposes, a smaller survey on the advertising in the *Reading Mercury* for the same period was also carried out, surveying a month's worth of issues for each of ten sample years. The most obvious thing the survey tells us about provincial newspaper advertising is that there was a lot more of it at the end of the eighteenth century than at the beginning. More adverts were placed, and more space in the newspaper was devoted to advertising. This growth was enormous and consistent. In 1722 there were an average of twenty-two adverts per month, nearly one hundred in 1752, and by 1792, there were over 250 per month. Every decade saw more adverts placed than the previous one. The same trend can be found in Reading, the *Reading Mercury* increasing from around sixteen adverts per month to 280. This growth ensured that each newspaper increased its revenues and so presumably became more profitable.

There was a similar increase in the relative amount of space devoted to advertising relative to news and other forms of content, as can be seen by calculating the percentage of each individual page devoted to each type of content. A typical issue of the *Northampton Mercury* in 1722 consisted of less than ten percent advertising; but decade by decade, the proportion of advertising increased: in 1752, it was over a third, and had reached over 60 percent by the 1790s. This relative increase suggests that the simultaneous growth in the size of the newspaper may have been driven more by a desire to fit in larger amounts of advertising than by the more modest growth in the volume of news.

Where was this advertising coming from? Strikingly, more and more advertising was coming from a narrower and narrower geographical sphere. Both the *Reading Mercury* and the *Northampton Mercury* had rapidly established very wide distribution areas in the 1720s. The Northampton paper employed agents in Berkshire and Lincolnshire, while the Reading paper had a network of agents that stretched as far as Kent. Advertising patterns in the 1720s reflected this wide distribution. This is not surprising, reflecting both most advertisers' unwillingness to advertise outside their own local area, and the nature of the newspaper distribution system. The 'newsmen' – employed by the newspaper's proprietors and by agents in other towns – who delivered the newspaper also delivered goods bought from the printers, and collected advertisements, working on a commission basis – typically two pence per advert.[6] Distribution, and soliciting advertising, were thus part of the same process, and so covered the same areas. Thus, in 1732, seventy per cent of adverts in the *Northampton Mercury* came from outside Northamptonshire. Forty per cent were from the counties immediately bordering Northamptonshire, and nearly a fifth of all adverts came from still further away, in addition to the special case of the sixth of advertisements, mainly for books and medicines, which originated from London. But the *Northampton Mercury's* advertising market then became increasingly closely focused on the newspaper's own county. By 1782, forty-five percent of adverts were from Northampton-shire. A further twenty percent were from London, reflecting the growth of book and medicine advertising. Adverts from outside Northamptonshire and London had fallen back from sixty percent to under a third, and only a negligible number came from beyond the inner ring of counties around Northamptonshire. In summary, between the 1730s and the 1780s, the area from which adverts (except London adverts) might plausibly be sent in to the *Northampton Mercury* reduced from a radius of some hundred miles, to about fifty. The *Reading Mercury's* commercial range similarly narrowed.

Such concentration reflects the contraction in each provincial news-paper's 'sphere of influence', as suggested by G. A. Cranfield and confirmed in subsequent regional studies.[7] It was an ironic consequence of the further growth of the provincial press. More newspapers were established in neighbouring towns, causing increased competition for readers and advertisers from other towns. This had an impact on the self-perceived role of the newspaper. In the 1720s and 1730s the *Northampton Mercury*, for example, was a regional newspaper that happened to be based in Northampton, but was distributed over a wide area of the East Midlands and further North. By 1792, it was much more of a county newspaper focused on Northamptonshire. Not coincidentally, the space devoted to local news increased significantly. Locally-originated news stories consti-tuted only three per cent of the *Northampton Mercury's* news coverage in 1722, but this had risen to eighteen percent by 1792. It is worth noting that this concentration of markets and coverage was a concentration on Northamptonshire as a whole, not just on the town of Northampton. The proportion of adverts identifiable as coming from the urban area of Northampton levelled off after 1732, remaining between eleven and thirteen per cent. Some of the rest of the advertising came from other towns, but most originated in villages, hamlets, and rural areas. The newspaper itself may have been located in a town, but most of its advertisers – and, perhaps, its readers – were not.

This is simply another way that the pattern of advertising reflected the pattern of distribution, but it means we cannot see advertising as a purely urban phenomenon. Indeed, it could be argued that advertising was more, not less, useful for non-urban traders and vendors. For instance, inoculators worked in relatively remote locations. This made them less able to depend on word of mouth or urban advertising strategies such as passing out handbills. Consequently, there were far more adverts for inoculators in the *Northampton Mercury* – up to about twenty a year – than there were for doctors, or midwives. This was not because there were fewer doctors or midwives, but because these professions saw less need to advertise.

If advertising was not essential for all professions and trades, we should be careful not to assume that a growth in the volume of advertising simply reflects a growth in the volume of commerce. Rather, we need to investigate whether there was a growing propensity to advertise, and if so, among which groups. Investigating the decision to advertise means that we should look more closely at what exactly was advertised and then at what the strategies adopted by advertisers can tell us about their own views of the purpose of advertising. The most common single type of advertisement in both the *Northampton Mercury* and the *Reading Mercury*, throughout the eighteenth century, was for real estate. Between twenty and thirty percent of all adverts were for the sale or lease of land, farms, urban property or business premises. If other types of property advertisement, such as horses for sale, are added in, then the sale and lease of fixed and moveable property accounted for about a hundred adverts a year in the *Northampton Mercury* in 1722. By 1792, there were over a thousand a year – representing an income for the newspaper, from this sector alone, of over £100 a year. This increased propensity to advertise far outstripped any actual increase in land and other property changing hands each year through the eighteenth century. The sale of real estate and property can be differentiated from 'retail' advertising – adverts placed by retailers such as local shops, inns and fairs; and also by sellers of books and patent medicines. London vendors dominated this sector. Only about ten percent of adverts placed by retailers were what could be called 'routine' local retail advertising – that is, promoting a local shop's normal trade, or perhaps a special sale or event. A comparable number advertised a change in ownership or management of a shop or inn, usually one that did not otherwise advertise. But the lion's share of retail advertising – seventy percent in the *Northampton Mercury* – was for printed items or patent medicines, usually locally distributed, but nationally marketed.

A different type of advertising, which grew especially rapidly through-out the century was what could be classed as 'administrative' advertising: adverts which did not seek to sell anything at all, but rather to *inform* readers – about quarter sessions, turnpike meetings, political candidacies or legal settlements. New organizations, such as turnpike trusts and county hospitals, became regular advertisers, as their accounts often demonstrate. By 1792 there were almost as many administrative as retail adverts in the *Northampton Mercury*. This has important implications for how we perceive the role of advertising, as these advertisements, while accepted on a commercial basis, were not 'commercial' in subject-matter: they show that no hard and fast line can be drawn between the commercial and the non-commercial in the eighteenth-century newspaper. Advertising was provided as a money-making service, but its effects could benefit non-commercial organizations. The growth in property and administrative advertising thus kept pace with, and even outstripped, that for services. It follows that the tendency to advertise more does not simply reflect the emergence of new commercial activities. 'Old economy' activities, such as land sales and the renting of stud horses, saw an increase in advertising just as great as, if not more than, the 'new economy' of leisure and consumer goods – and so did the 'public economy' of local and national administration.

Indeed, the across-the-board growth in the volume of advertising makes it clear that neither can the overall increase in the number of advertisements simply reflect an increasing amount of commercial activity. The sheer scale of increase makes it improbable that increasing numbers of retailers, or increasing sales of goods, can account for all of it. A rise in the number of job adverts from one in the 1722 sample to 104 in the 1792 sample clearly does not reflect a hundred-fold increase in the number of jobs available. Sellers and buyers of property, services and retail goods had a range of options open to them, from alternative newspaper forums, such as the London press, to different forms of advertising such as crying and the distribution of hand-bills. Indeed, they had the option of not advertising at all, relying on contacts, passing trade, or word-of-mouth. Since newspaper advertising did increase, this must reflect an increased propensity to advertise on the part of potential advertisers – and this despite the fact that, in real terms, advertising became more expensive as the government repeatedly increased the already substantial duty on advertising. So, why *were* people more likely to advertise?

To answer this question we must try to reconstruct the decisions made by individual advertisers. In doing so, it is important to avoid simplistic assumptions about the value of advertising. For any organization, advertising was a cost, and a significant one, only worth bearing if it brought desirable results. Much of the history of advertising has been written in terms of a growing cultural acceptance of commerce, and of the emergence of increasingly sophisticated, 'modern', advertising strategies. The uneven spread of advertising in the eighteenth century is thus sometimes seen as resulting from residual cultural taboos against advertising, rather than rational commercial decisions; early eighteenth-century advertisers are sometimes characterized as unsophisticated, even naive, in their use of advertising as a marketing tool.[8]

Closer consideration of, firstly, the tactics employed by particular advertisers, and secondly, the subtle and highly self-aware vocabularies of advertising, suggests another view. It makes it more plausible that the growth in advertising reflects the aggregate effect of a series of rational and hard-headed decisions made by individual advertisers, in the confident and justified expectation that commercial or other benefits would result.

One important calculation for any advertiser to make was whether, and where, his or her competitors were advertising. There was often a noticeable clustering of particular types of advert. One schoolteacher, or inoculator, or inn would advertise; in the next few weeks, rival teachers, inoculators, or inns would follow suit. Another decision advertisers had to make was *when* to advertise. Twenty to thirty percent of adverts were repeats: that is, they duplicated adverts that had been in the previous week's paper. This proportion did not change much over the century. For the advertiser, repeat advertisements increased the chances a particular advert would be seen, and refreshed the content in the mind of the reader; for the printer, cost and time was saved if adverts could be kept standing in type, so repeat advertisers were given a discount. The relatively low proportion of repeated adverts, despite these advantages, is indicative of the strongly event-based nature of much of the advertising. It often made more sense to advertise an auction, land sale, or fair only in the week before it happened. Similarly, advertising often happened only when something disturbed a particular commercial routine. For example, a large number of localities that held autumn fairs never felt the need to advertise them until September 1752, when the change to the Gregorian calendar meant that customers needed to be told how the fair's timing would change as a result. Many types of advertising were also episodic or seasonal – for instance, horses at stud in spring, almanacs in December, and lottery tickets in the run-up to a draw.

Thus timeliness, the ability to specify a particular date when the advertising message would be delivered to readers, seems to have been an important factor in the choice of the newspaper as an advertising medium. Land adverts would always state when the land would become available, and adverts for auctions, sales, and meetings were obviously keyed to particular dates. More surprisingly, many retail advertisements were also tied to a particular event, such as a new issue of a magazine or the arrival of a shipment of goods. Here the language of advertising can offer clues to the ways that advertisers sought the attention of readers. Timeliness was almost a quality to be invented: as in the continuous present tense of 'this day is published', a linguistic convention of immediacy sat well in a paper full of news. Such timeliness was just one of a set of linguistic conventions that particular types of advertiser employed. Such conventions meant that adverts of the same type showed a high degree of uniformity, offering the reader reassurance. We can take a typical real estate advertisement from the *Northampton Mercury* as an example:

To be sold, by auction. On Tuesday the 26th of this Instant December, at Eleven o'Clock in the Forenoon, at the House of Joseph Marriott, known by the Sign of the Bull, in Kislingbury. A Freehold Messuage, or Tenement, situated in Kislingbury, in the Possession of Robert Chapman, Butcher; with a Quarter-acre land thereunto belonging, lying in Kislingbury Field. For further particulars, enquire of Mr. Markham, Attorney, in Northampton; or Mr John Chapman, in Nether-Heyford.[9]

Advertisements like this generally followed a rigid typographical and linguistic pattern. The heading is generic and will have been repeated in other adverts on the same page. There follow the basic details of the sale, and only then do we get to the question of what exactly is being sold. The language is legalistic and precise: taking more care to be correct than to make the property seem attractive. Presumably written by the Northampton attorney mentioned at the end of the advert, the approach – sober and undramatic – is tailored to the sobriety and seriousness needed for the weighty matter of the sale of valuable property.

Some adverts did consciously subvert such generic conventions. For example, a property advert in the *Northampton Mercury* of 1782 starts with a similarly generic description of an inn which is to be sold, but continues,

Such, my good Sir, is the lively and bold Situation of these Premises, that for many Years previously they have enjoyed ---- and now ---- even now, ----- while though art reading this Advertisement to thy Wife, ----- they do enjoy ---- a regular, cheerful and profitable Trade.[10]

Similarly, an advert placed in the *Northampton Mercury* in the same year formally and legalistically disavowed any debts incurred by the advertiser's eloped wife, but then, in place of the usual request for information as to her whereabouts, added tersely, 'Whoever finds her may keep her'.[11] But such deviations from convention are rare, and only point up how deeply ingrained particular forms were, that they could be so subverted.

The conventions employed for advertising services were less self-effacing. Adverts for horses at stud, for example, dwelt on the merits of each particular horse. Advertisers in this field often possessed a high degree of self-awareness. The essential problem facing any advertiser is that of being trusted: some addressed this issue head on. One horse breeder, in 1772, declared that,

The many spurious Puffs that generally attend the Advertisements of Stallions has determined Mr. Emmot to say nothing here in praise of his; it gives him pleasure in shewing them to any Nobleman, Gentleman or Breeders whatsoever.[12]

Such a claim was itself a kind of double bluff: ostentatiously avoiding hyperbole was in itself a form of boasting.

But much the most conventionally hyperbolic of adverts were those placed by the vendors of patent medicines, and of certain widely marketed types of publication such as part-works and magazines. These adverts were placed on a region-wide or nation-wide scale, and were often refined over many years; their language was thus more carefully considered than that of most advertising.[13] Some may have been inserted to fill up space, or at least on a 'standby' basis in the absence of more profitable advertising. But the evidence from the surviving office copies of the *Reading Mercury* suggests that most such adverts were indeed paid for, and many were placed by other medicine distributors and vendors, in addition to those inserted by the newspaper owner. Such adverts often sought to harness the authority of the newspaper itself to increase their credibility: for example, paid cure stories were dressed up as news items, as annotations on office copies of the *Reading Mercury* reveal. This fact may have been unknown to the readers, and the local stamp duty collector was certainly unaware, as no duty was paid on these adverts. A similar blurring of news and advertising for commercial gain appeared in the *Northampton Mercury* in June 1752. An account of the conviction of a youth for murder stated that,

He then begged the Justice to give him the little Book on the heinous sin of murder, lately published, which when he received, he shed a shower of tears, and wished he had read it before.[14]

The back cover of that issue did indeed contain an advert for the first part of a work entitled *A warning-piece against the Crime of Murder*.

The issue of credibility looms largest in patent medicine advertisements. To counter readers' suspicions, cure stories gave much detail, and signed affidavits from respectable witnesses to the effectiveness of medicines were often quoted. Delicate issues surrounded the advertising of preparations designed to treat venereal disease; such adverts had to adopt a rhetorical strategy to deal with the question of how the disease had been contracted. It was usually implied that activities long past had been to blame, attempting to defuse the charge that advertising easy and effective cures for sexually transmitted diseases could encourage sexual immorality. These different conventions and linguistic and commercial strategies show how advertisers responded to the nature of the newspaper medium itself: they exploited its timeliness, but also sought to address, explicitly or implicitly, the troubling problem of how far you could actually believe anything you read in the newspaper. One of several language registers was selected, according to the degree of trust from readers that could be expected. This implies the existence of a mature and sophisticated advertising market, with businesses placing advertisements for maximum competitive edge, and timed for greatest impact.

It thus seems that advertising came predominantly from those who thought they benefited most from it – public administrators, those selling land, and certain classes of professional service and high-value consumer goods. These groups demonstrated their belief in the effectiveness of advertising by buying adverts consistently and frequently. But were they right? Some of the most concrete evidence for the effectiveness of provincial newspaper advertising comes from a non-commercial source. John Styles has studied the role of advertising in crime detection, finding that the faster and more accurate flow of information across a region, made possible by, in particular, newspaper advertising, did have a tangible influence on detection of crime.[15] Testimonials sometimes appeared to suggest a similar effectiveness in the Reading and Northampton press. For example, in 1722 the *Northampton Mercury* printed a letter from some residents of Newmarket thanking the paper for warning them about a set of criminals, spotted in Northampton who had subsequently turned up in Newmarket.[16]

This shows the benefits of being able to place advertisements in a newspaper read primarily in the immediate region. Anyone with something to sell or something to announce could do so in the assurance that they were targeting only people near enough to matter. Handbills and town criers, the existing methods of provincial advertising, were necessarily restricted to towns, while advertising in the London press made little sense if all your potential customers were within thirty miles of you. Thus, the provincial newspaper offered a genuinely new service to advertisers, just as it offered a distinctive and novel means of cultural and political expression to its contributors and readers.

Another group of advertisers whose heavy use of the medium suggests that they felt they received tangible benefits from it were local political figures. Before elections, candidates placed adverts soliciting votes. Interest groups would also pay for the insertion of resolutions or public declarations. The expression of paid-for opinion was the most direct way that advertising could contribute to the development of forums for the expression of local opinion, and so to the establishment of some kind of local 'public sphere'. Much local political discussion and competition took place through the medium of the paid political advertisement. In 1792, the *Northampton Mercury* made its policy clear:

If the Lincolnshire graziers choose to send the substance of their late Resolution as an advertisement, properly signed, it shall be duly attended to; but we cannot otherwise interfere in the business.[17]

This has interesting consequences for how we might view the emergence of public opinion as a political force in the eighteenth century. Jurgen Habermas's account of the rise and fall of the 'public sphere' tends to idealize pre-industrial public culture, as a means of decrying the perceived commercialization of the public sphere in the twentieth century.[18] This idealization is hard to reconcile with the way that much local politics in the eighteenth century was dependent on spending hard cash on political advertising.

Other groups who gained greatly from the development of provincial advertising were magazine and part-work publishers, and patent medicine firms. Theirs was a national market, dependent on the national distribution of standardized products. People would not know that these products existed unless they advertised. Once aware that they existed, people needed to be constantly reminded of the fact, and of how they differed from the other nationally advertised products they competed against. Thus, clear branding was an essential component of all these products' advertising. Newspapers, published on a weekly basis and able to include wood-cut brand devices as part of advertisements, were well placed to offer the repetitive reinforcement of brand image that they needed. Some branded goods were advertised for very long periods of time: Rice Milliner's Horse Ointment, a staple of 1720s *Northampton Mercury* advertising, was still being promoted sixty years later.[19]

The makers of these products benefited even further by using the provincial press not just for promotion but also for distribution. The newspaper distribution network was ideally suited to the delivery of medicines, magazines, and part-works: people could place orders with their newsman, and then have the remedy or printed product delivered with the next week's paper. Almost all provincial newspaper printers became involved in providing agencies for London-based patent medicine makers, and those in Reading and Northampton went much further. John Newbery, proprietor of the *Reading Mercury*, bought the contract to be sole distributor of Dr. James's Fever Powders, probably the biggest-selling medicine of the eighteenth century, while Northampton's Diceys also made fortunes from patent medicines.[20] Through such commercial activities, but also through the increasing volume of general advertising, the *Reading Mercury* and the *Northampton Mercury* remained financially viable. By the 1790s, there were some three thousand adverts a year in the *Northampton Mercury*. This was less than the annual total for a daily London newspaper, but still represents around three hundred pounds a year in revenue, after stamp duty.[21] And this income was relatively consistent and low-risk. Office copies of the *Reading Mercury* show that it received advertising revenue amounting to three to five pounds an issue in the 1760s: a significant flow of ready money – unlike subscriptions, which were often paid months if not years in arrears.[22]

It is tempting to take the growth of the press in the eighteenth century for granted. Newspapers became so established as part of the political and public culture of Britain, and of so many provincial towns, that it is easy to buy into their own rhetoric, and see them as existing simply to provide a public-spirited and democratic service to their readers. But newspapers were run for profit, and unprofitable newspapers were closed down by their owners or by their creditors. Without advertising, the *Reading Mercury* and *Northampton Mercury* would not have been financially viable. And without provincial newspapers, an important means of cultural dissemination and expression would not exist. The role of the newspaper as both forum for, and participant in, myriad forms of political and social communication, would not have been possible without the role of the newspaper as facilitator of commercial and organizational advertising. Sermons, theological arguments, accounts of murders and executions, lists of those licensed to hunt game: these things and more were available to the eighteenth-century provinces, thanks to provincial newspapers. But these newspapers were sustained by a great volume and variety of advertising that reflected not only developments in commercial and urban culture, but also a much broader range of provincial economic, social and political activity.

Notes

1. *Reading Mercury*, 10 July 1797. Emphasis in original.

2. For the general hypothesis, see *The Birth of a Consumer Society: the Commercialization of Eighteenth-Century England* ed. by Neil McKendrick, John Brewer, and John Plumb (London, 1983) and *The Consumption of Culture, 1600-1800: Image, Object, Text* ed. by John Brewer and Ann Bermingham (London, 1995). For newspaper advertising in particular, see John Jefferson Looney, 'Cultural Life in the Provinces: Leeds and York, 1720-1820', in *The First Modern Society: Essays in English History in Honour of Lawrence Stone* ed. by Beier, Cannadine and Rosenheim (Cambridge, 1989), pp. 483-510; and Peter M. Briggs, '"News from the Little World": A Critical Glance at Eighteenth-Century British Advertising', *Studies in Eighteenth-Century Culture* 23 (1994), pp. 29-45.

3. Peter Borsay, *The English Urban Renaissance: Culture and Society in the Provincial Town, 1660-1770* (Oxford, 1989), pp. 129-31, 213-14; see also 'The London Connection: Cultural Diffusion and the Eighteenth-Century Provincial Town', *London Journal*, 19 (1994), pp. 21-35. For another conceptualization of urban culture in seventeenth and eighteenth-century England, which stresses civic and ideological attitudes over commercial diffusion, see Jonathan Barry, 'Provincial Town Culture, 1640-1760: Urbane or Civic?' in *Interpretation and Cultural History in Eighteenth-Century Britain* ed. by Pittock and Wear (Basingstoke, 1991), pp. 198-234.

4. John Jefferson Looney, 'Advertising and society in England, 1720-1820: a statistical analysis of Yorkshire newspaper advertisements' (unpublished doctoral dissertation, Princeton University, 1983).

5. The *Northampton Mercury* was owned, jointly or outright, by the Dicey family from its founding in 1721 by Robert Raikes and William Dicey, past the end of the century. The *Reading Mercury* was under the control of William Carnan by 1737, and remained either owned or printed by his former employee (and husband of his widow) John Newbery, and Carnan's descendants, into the nineteenth century. See Diana Dixon, 'Northamptonshire Newspapers, 1720-1900', in *Images and Texts* ed. by Isaac and McKay (Winchester, 1997), pp. 1-10; and K. G. Burton, *The Early Newspaper Press in Berkshire* (Reading, 1954).

6. The origins of many advertisements from agents and newsmen, and the levels of commission paid, can be seen in the manuscript annotations on the office copies of the *Reading Mercury*, which recorded the income received for each advert and its source. Some of these annotations are described in Burton, *Early Newspaper Press*, but further office copies have come to light since Burton wrote. The office copies have been microfilmed and form part of the joint sequence of microfilms produced and held by the British Library Newspaper Library and Reading Public Library.

7. Geoffrey Alan Cranfield, *The Development of the Provincial Newspaper, 1700-1760* (Oxford, 1962), pp. 203-206; C. Y. Ferdinand, 'Selling It to the Provinces: News and Commerce Round Eighteenth-Century Salisbury', in *Consumption and the World of Goods* ed. by Brewer and Porter (London, 1993); cf. Hannah Barker, 'Catering for Provincial Tastes? Newspapers, Readership and Profit in Late Eighteenth-Century England', *Historical Research*, 69 (1996), pp. 42-61.

8. For example Blanche Elliot, *A History of English Advertising* (London, 1962); E. S. Turner, *The Shocking History of Advertising!* (London, 1952). Looney's discussion of advertisers' motives in 'Advertising and society in England', Ch. 6, while more nuanced, also betrays the presumption that advertising will be beneficial to most businesses in most circumstances.

9. *Northampton Mercury*, 18 December 1752.

10. *Northampton Mercury*, 7 October 1782.

11. *Northampton Mercury*, 18 February 1782.

12. *Northampton Mercury*, 27 April 1772.

13. For the importance of branded 'patent' medicines to the provincial book trade see Peter Isaac, 'Pills and Print', in *Medicine, Mortality and the Book Trade* ed. by Myers and Harris (Folkestone, 1998), pp. 25-47. For a study of medicine advertising in a provincial town, see P. S. Brown, 'The Vendors of Medicines Advertised in Eighteenth-Century Bath Newspapers', *Medical History*, 19 (1975), pp. 352-69, and 'Medicines Advertised in Eighteenth-Century Bath Newspapers', *Medical History*, 20 (1976), pp. 152-68. Brown finds that Bath newspapers had more medicine adverts out of the social season, when there were less adverts for other goods and services ('Vendors of Medicine', p. 356).

14. *Northampton Mercury*, 1 June 1752.

15. J. Styles, 'Print and Policing: Crime Advertising in Eighteenth-Century Provincial England', in *Policing and Prosecution* ed. by Hays and Snider (Oxford, 1989), pp. 55-111.

16. *Northampton Mercury*, 20 August 1722.

17. *Northampton Mercury*, 4 February 1792.

18. Jurgen Habermas, *The Structural Transformation of the Public Sphere: an Enquiry into a Category of Bourgeois Society* (Cambridge, 1989).

19. e.g. *Northampton Mercury*, 18 October 1762.

20. See Juanita Burnby, 'Printers' Ink and Patent Medicines: the Story of the Diceys', *Pharmaceutical Journal*, 229 (1982), pp. 162-3, 169; and for James' Fever Powder, B. Hill, 'An Eighteenth-Century Cure-All', *History of Medicine*, 2 (1969), pp. 24-26.

21. For London advertising revenue see Ivon Asquith, 'Advertising and the Press in the Late Eighteenth and Early Nineteenth Centuries: James Perry and the Morning Chronicle, 1790-1821', *Historical Journal*, 18 (1975), pp. 703-24.

22. For a tabulation of six months' worth of advertising revenue, see Burton, *The Early Newspaper Press in Berkshire*, p. 256.

Medical Advertising in the Wrexham Press, 1855-1906

LISA PETERS

The patent medicine men became appreciatively bolder in the late nineteenth century. As there were no laws on the books to regulate truth in advertising here was no stopping them once they had gained access to the mass audience created and cultivated by the Victorian periodical press. The larger the audience, the more restive the quacks became. Lacking any precise notion of who it was they were addressing they promised anything and everything to anyone and everyone, vying with one another to see who could produce the most comprehensive cure-all.[1]

READERS OF THE VICTORIAN PRESS cannot fail to come across large numbers of medical advertisements. Brown estimated that advertising brought in one half of the revenue of Victorian newspapers and consequently, this dependence upon advertisers meant that many newspapers were willing to accept any kind of advertising, including the ubiquitous medical 'puffs'.[2] Medicines claiming to cure all manner of illnesses had long existed but in the Victorian period two names took medical advertising into a new era as their names and products become known throughout the world as a result of the vast sums each spent on advertising. 'Professor' Thomas Holloway began his business in 1838 and by 1842 was spending £5,000 a year on advertising, a sum which rose to £20,000 in 1850[3] £30,000 in 1855[4] and £50,000 in 1883.[5] His pills and ointments made him a millionaire and he was able to create and endow Holloway College (now Royal Holloway College, University of London). His great rival Thomas Beecham commenced his business in St. Helens in the 1850s and also spent vast sums of money on advertising, £120,000 in 1891 alone.[6]

This rise in the number of medical advertisements, fuelled by the large sums devoted to advertising by the medical companies, was reflected in the Wrexham press. Wrexham's first weekly newspaper, the *Wrexham Advertiser* (founded in 1854) saw a steady rise in the number of medical advertisements from an average of three per issue in 1855 to a peak average of thirty-seven per issue in 1880. Numbers began steadily to fall from the 1880s, reaching an average of twelve per issue by 1910. A similar pattern was displayed by the *Wrexham Guardian*, whose average number of medical advertisements per issue rose from seven in 1870 to reach thirty-six ten years later, before falling to fourteen by 1910. Medical advertisements tended make up five to eight per cent of total advertising in the Wrexham press, although at their peak in the 1880s such advertisements made up nearly a fifth of newspaper advertising. Clearly medical notices were an important part of press advertising.

Despite this, medical advertisements, surrounded by their reputation of 'quackery', were often accepted reluctantly. Joseph Corbett went so far as to refuse to accept any 'quack' advertising for the *Porcupine* despite the knowledge that this would cost him £500 a year in advertising revenue.[7] The *Wrexham Telegraph* (established in 1855) may have been addressing medical advertisers when it stated that 'all Advertisements of an exceptional nature will be scrupulously excluded' but if so, it quickly had to adjust its moral stance to its financial needs as by 1865 the newspaper contained an average of nine medical advertisements per issue.[8] A particularly high number of medical puffs often earned a newspaper a poor reputation and suggested that a lack of money had forced a reduction in advertising standards. The exceptionally high number of medical advertisements in the *Wrexham Free Press* shortly before it was sold in early 1873 could indicate that financial difficulties were the cause for the sale.

Patent medicine makers were well-known for their hyperbolic and highly unrealistic claims for their products. As Richards commented

the first thing that usually strikes one about patent medicine advertising is its indefatigable optimism. No matter what is wrong, it can be set right. Since the advertiser does not know exactly what ails his readers, he makes an effort to canvass every illness imaginable. The long lists of ills cured by pills were epic inventions celebrating the powers of the Promethean pillmaker.[9]

Although some patent medicine producers such as William Rowland of 'Rowland's Stomachic Digestive Pills' did state that their medicines could not cure all medical problems,[10] the claims of Kaye's Worsdell's Pills were typical:

Kaye's Worsdell's Pills – The experience of more than twenty years has proved that they are the most effective remedy ever offered to the public for the cure of diseases arising from the impurity of the blood or impeded circulation of the fluids, as Loss of appetite, Lowness of Spirits, Drowsiness, Heartburn, Flatulenoy, Acidity of the Stomach, Pain in the Side – Stomach – and Back, Bilious Attacks, Nervous – Periodical and Sick Headaches, Costiveness Indigestion, Rheumatism, Spansnia, Diarheorrea, Eruptions of the Skin, General Debility, Gout, Gravel, Influenza, Piles, Scrofula, Sore Legs, Ulcers, Worms, &c. They operate most beneficially on the viscera, purify the blood and stimulate it into healthy action, remove the obstruction of the stomach, bowels, liver, and other organs of the body, restoring the irregular action to health, and correct such derangements as are the first origins of disease. As a medicine for general family use, KAYE'S WORSDELL'S PILLS are unequalled. Many families have resolved never to be without them, and testimonials to their excellence are continually received.

These pills were available for 1s. 1½d., 2s. 9d. and 4s. 6d., quantities unknown.[11] Such exaggerated claims continued well into the twentieth century despite the Court of Appeal decision in *Carhill v. The Carbolic Smoke Ball Company* [1892]. The Carbolic Smoke Ball Company stated that it could pay £100 to anyone who contracted influenza whilst using their smoke ball. Mrs Carhill sued the company after contracting influenza after using the smoke ball and won her £100. Of the medical advertisements that appeared in the Wrexham press, claims that there were cures for cancer[12] and deafness[13] are clearly ridiculous.

Advertisements for 'alternative' remedies appeared irregularly in the Wrexham press but such products claimed to be able to cure as many medical complaints as their synthetic counterparts. 'Kehotah Kidney and Liver Pills' claimed to have been discovered by Kehotak, 'the mighty Indian chief and medicine man of the Upper Mississippi Valley', One large tin of Kehotak's remedy was

guaranteed to cure any irregularity if the human system, check all discharges and derangements of the Urinary organs, pains in the Back and Loins, Gravel and General Debility, and Loss of Memory of either sex … the Cure of   Diabetes   or Bright's Disease, and is a most Powerful Brain and Nerve Tonic.

The advertisement came with a small picture of Kehotak, recognizable by virtue of a feather sticking out of the top of his head. Customers were warned to be wary of imitations, the original product costing four shillings and sixpence.[14] The British Medical Association condemned these patent medicines in the publications *Secret Remedies* (1909) and *More Secret Remedies* (1912) as a waste of money and sometimes as a danger to the public. In 1914 the Select Committee on Patent Medicines organized an analysis of Fenning's Fever Cure which revealed that the 'cure' was merely a dilute solution of nitric acid and peppermint, costing an estimated halfpenny to create, yet was sold for 1*s*. 1½*d*. for eight fluid ounces.[15] The appearance of medical advertisements such as that for 'Rowland's Stomachic Digestive Pills', which assured readers that they did not contain 'a particle of Mercury or any of its preparations' may have caused them to wonder what ingredients other medicines contained.[16]

Supporting these claims of wonder cures was the personal testimonial, where companies produced either a list of those who used their medicine (or people they claimed used it) or a personal endorsement of the product by a named individual. It seems that patent medicine companies vied with each other over who could product the longest lists of aristocrats and royals using their pills. In 1843 the *Edinburgh Review* discovered that 'Mr. Cockles Antibilious Pills' were recommended by ten dukes, five marquesses, seventeen earls, eight viscounts, sixteen lords, one archbishop, fifteen bishops, the adjutant-general and the advocate–general.[17] A particularly impressive celebrity testimonial appeared in the *Wrexham Guardian* in 1900 for 'Phosferine: The Royal Tonic and Digestive' which was patronized by the Emperor of Russia, the King of Greece, the Queen of Romania, the Dowager Empress of Russia, two Russian Grand Duchesses, a Russian Grand Duke, and the Crown Princess of Romania.[18] It was not only the rich and famous that recommended patent medicines, as testimonials on the wonders of patent medicines from those lower in the social scale appeared in the Wrexham press. In 1906 the *Wrexham Advertiser* carried the tale of Jesse Rosling of Preston who claimed to have been miraculously cured from paralysis by 'Dr. Cassell's Fleshing Forming and Strengthening Tablets', which not only cured his paralysis, but also prevented 'premature greyness and delayed the appearance of old age'.[19] Perhaps medical advertisers believed that potential purchasers were more impressed by endorsements from the man in street, rather than the lofty personages of dukes and queens. If so, this concept was further perfected by 'Doan's Backache Kidney Pills' who published endorsements in the Wrexham press from various local residents who were presumably willing to supply further details on request and act as local example of the effectiveness of the pills. The endorsements were given added local character by news-like headings such as 'News Helpful to Wrexham'[20] or 'May Help Wrexham People'.[21]

Advertisers often sought to link their products with current affairs and events. Bovril, produced one of the most well-known examples of this advertising method with their famous Boer War advertisement, and the patent medicine producers also sought to associate their products with the war. The makers of one medicine declared that 'The Transvaal will destroy life – COLEMAN'S 'WINCARNUS' preserves it' without telling readers how it would do so.[22] An article published in March 1900, titled 'English Actors in South Africa – Disagreeable Experience of Two Artists', was not in fact a story on the Boer War, but a medical advertisement. The advertisement told the story of an actor, Mr Casson, who became ill in South Africa and the doctors were unable to cure him. In desperation Mrs Casson came across some boxes of 'Dr. Williams' Pink Pills for Pale People' in their luggage and Mr Casson was soon cured.[23] Advertisements for 'Dr. Williams Pink Pills for Pale People', owned by the Canadian Senator George Taylor Fulford, appeared frequently in the *Wrexham Advertiser* in the early twentieth century. The advertisements were written in the style of a newspaper article reporting a near miraculous recovery from illness. It was not until readers reached the end of the story when 'Dr. Williams' Pink Pills for Pale People' cured the sufferer that they would have realized that it was an advertisement. The stories could reflect local interests as well as current events. Several such advertisements referred to events in Wales, for example, 'Welsh Colliers and the Sliding Scale' began by commenting on the end of the sliding scale before discussing a visit by a reporter from the *Merthyr Express* to Mr Walker of Treharris, which revealed that his daughter, Mary Jane, had been cured of twitching down her right side by 'Dr. Williams' Pink Pills for Pale People'.[24] This focus of regional interest appeared in another advertisement in the same year, dramatically titled 'A Message from Welsh Americans to their Suffering Kinsmen at Home'. A title like this would usually lead the reader to expect an article promoting emigration to the new world, not one urging the 'suffering kinsmen' to use 'Veno's Lighting Cough Cure' – as sold in Boot's Cash Chemists in Wrexham.[25]

Medical books, usually available by mail-order, were regularly advertised in the Wrexham press in the 1860s and 1870s. Titles such as *A work on marriage: its duties and impediments*[26] were typical and the quali-fications of the author were similar to those of Dr Smith, the author of the *Warning Voice* who was a 'Celebrated Physician for the cure of Nervous Exhaustion, Indigestion, Rheumatism, Dimness of Sight, Functional

Disorders, Weakness, Low Spirits, Debility, Spermatorrhea, Impediments to Marriage, and all error'.[27] Books and medicines claiming to cure these 'diseases from error' were the target of the 1889 Indecent Advertisements Act. The act was aimed at those who the Earl of Meath described as sellers of cures for 'a certain class of disease of a nameless character' namely syphilis and similar diseases.[28] In studying the debates on the bill, Turner found it significant that the main objections to the appearance of such advertisements in the press was not that the products themselves were of little use, but the immoral and indecent nature of the advertisements.[29]

The passage of this act did not prevent the continued advertising of immoral and indecent notices, in particular those for abortifacients. Beecham's pills' 'Advice to Females' recommended that women suffering 'any unusual delay' should take five Beecham's pills a day, the most common cause of any delay being pregnancy.[30] In 1898 the Newspaper Society's solicitor stated in a circular that

in my view, if it could be proved that a woman obtained the medicine with a view to procure abortion in consequence of reading the advertisement of it in a particular paper, the publisher of that paper would run the serious risk of finding himself indicted for inciting the commission of a felony, or for being accessory to the commission of one, and I believe the judge would find his way to a conviction. Further, I am not sure that these advertisements are not obscene publications, for which a prosecution could be successfully maintained.[31]

However the Wrexham press ignored this warning as it continued to advertise products such as an illustrated book by P. Blanchard on birth control and abortifacients.[32]

As with other types of notices, the visual appearance of medical advertisement altered over time. Medical advertisements initially consisted of lines of small type, across one column, without illustrations, and, in the Wrexham press, often placed at the bottom of a column and therefore making them less visible to the reader. A typical example was one that appeared in the *Wrexham Advertiser* in 1855 for 'Dr de Roos Compound Renal Pills' which was placed in the bottom right corner of the front page and whose small type would have made it difficult for any reader to be attracted to the 'most safe and effectious remedy'. Only the most persistent of readers would have read the testimonials and the list of local chemists selling the pills to reach the final sentences of the advertisement which requested 'respectable persons in county places' to become sellers of the pills in return for a generous commission.[33] In contrast, by the turn of the century, illustrated advertisements with different sized type and fonts and which crossed columns were regularly seen. 'Francis' Cough Medicine' contained a picture of an old woman clutching her shawl and coughing with the phrase 'Never Let a Cough Grow Old' placed across columns to draw attention to the product.[34] Some advertisements were less adventurous in their illustrations. The slogan 'Have You a Bad Leg?' with a simple picture of a bent leg with a black spot above the ankle was not a particularly attractive method of persuading people to part with two shillings and sixpence for a bottle of 'Grasshopper Ointment and Pills'.[35] Other advertisements, such as 'Dr. Williams's Pink Pills for Pale People', as already stated, deliberately disguised their advertisements to make them appear to be newspaper articles.

An examination of the medicine advertising in the Wrexham press is a story of exaggeration, immorality, and the changing nature of newspaper advertising. Patent medicine advertisements were notorious for their exaggeration and the confidence that their pills and ointments could cure any and every illness. Dr. J. Lewis of Leeds was not the only medical advertiser to claim such confidence in his skills as to guarantee a cure if he undertook the commission.[36] Perhaps the advertisers subscribed to the view that 'the great mass of people ... will more easily fall victim to a big lie than to a small one'.[37] Not even the intervention of the law could prevent the patent medicine products from continuing to publish their outlandish claims. Patent medicine makers made fortunes from their pills and ointments and were probably richer than many of the aristocrats and royals who endorsed their products. Despite the aura of immorality that hung over it, the Victorian and Edwardian advertising world would have been far less interesting without the puffs of the quacks.

Notes

1. Thomas Richards, *The Commodity Culture of Victorian England: advertising and spectacle, 1851-1914* (London, 1991), p. 17.
2. Lucy Brown, *Victorian News and Newspapers* (Oxford, 1985), p. 17.
3. E. S. Turner, *The Shocking History of Advertising*, rev. edn. (Harmondsworth, 1965), p. 65.
4. T. R. Nevett, *Advertising in Britain: a History* (London, 1982), p. 29.
5. Nevett, *Advertising in Britain*, p. 71.
6. Nevett, *Advertising in Britain*, p. 71.
7. Turner, *The Shocking History of Advertising*, p. 50.
8. *Wrexham Telegraph*, 1 January 1855, p. 1.
9. Richards, *The Commodity Culture of Victorian England*, p. 187.

10. *Wrexham Free Press*, 2 July 1870, p. 1.
11. *Wrexham Advertiser*, 7 July 1855, p. 1.
12. *Wrexham Guardian*, 7 December 1900, p. 3.
13. *Wrexham Advertiser*, 1 December 1900, p. 7.
14. *Wrexham Guardian*, 1 March 1890, p. 7.
15. W. Hamish Fraser, *The Coming of the Mass Market, 1850-1914* (London, 1981).
16. *Wrexham Free Press*, 2 July 1870, p. 1.
17. Abraham Haywood, 'The Advertising System', *Edinburgh Review*, 77 (1843), 6. Quoted in Richards, p. 84.
18. *Wrexham Guardian*, 7 December 1900, p. 2.
19. *Wrexham Advertiser*, 15 September 1906, p. 2.
20. *Wrexham Advertiser*, 10 March 1905, p. 4.
21. *Wrexham Advertiser*, 24 March 1905, p. 4.
22. *Wrexham Guardian*, 2 March 1900, p. 6.
23. *Wrexham Advertiser*, 10 March 1900, p. 5.
24. *Wrexham Advertiser*, 21 June 1902, p. 7.
25. *Wrexham Advertiser*, 25 January 1902, p. 3.
26. *Wrexham Telegraph*, 4 March 1865, p. 7.
27. *Wrexham Advertiser*, 3 March 1870, supplement.
28. Turner, *The Shocking History of Advertising*, p. 95.
29. Turner, *The Shocking History of Advertising*, p. 93.
30. Fraser, *The Coming of the Mass Market*, p. 140.
31. Newspaper Society Circular, December 1898. Quoted in Nevett, *Advertising in Britain*, p. 114.
32. *Wrexham Guardian*, 4 March 1900, p. 6.
33. *Wrexham Guardian*, 7 July 1855, p. 1.
34. *Wrexham Advertiser*, 1 December 1906, p. 4.
35. *Wrexham Advertiser*, 15 September 1906, p. 2.
36. *Wrexham Free Press*, 2 July 1870, p. 1.
37. Adolf Hitler, *Mein Kampf* (1925). Quoted from *The Columbia World of Quotations* at http://www.bartleby.com/66

'Self-interested and Evil-minded Persons': the Book-Trade Activities of Thomas Wilson, Robert Spence and Joseph Mawman of York and the Mozleys of Gainsborough

DAVID HOUNSLOW

THE ORIGINAL INTENTION of this paper was to concentrate on the false imprints used by Thomas Wilson and his colleagues in York and the Mozley family in Gainsborough from *c.*1780 to *c.*1810; the underlying assumption being that the books involved were piracies. But this turns out not to be entirely the case, for the majority of the books published under wholly, or partially false imprints, would be better described as reprints. It is even doubtful whether many of the imprints tentatively attributed to Wilson, Spence and Mawman were printed by them and that other agencies were not also at work. It is evident too that the use of false imprints was a phase in the history of the two businesses and when circumstances changed these were abandoned as rapidly as when they were first used.

Close study shows that Wilson, Spence and Mawman and the Mozleys were two substantial businesses, but they have been largely ignored by the historians of the English provincial booktrade. Robert Davies makes only one meaningful reference to Thomas Wilson and his colleagues remarking that

Thomas Wilson was the founder of the printing and wholesale bookselling establishment in High Ousegate, which under the firm of Wilson, Spence, and Mawman, and afterwards of Thomas Wilson and Sons, was well known in the publishing world for the greater part of a century.[1]

In more recent times, John Feather for example makes no mention of either Mozley or Wilson, even though he devotes some space to bookselling in York. The exception to all this are the Sessions who provide some useful information on Wilson and his colleagues, but nowhere in any literature is there recognition of Wilson's importance on a national stage. The Mozleys have fared rather better, thanks mainly to Jim English's research and his paper, 'Chapbooks & Primers, Piety, Poetry and Classics'.[2] But it still begs the question why have these two booksellers been generally disregarded when they thrived for so long and produced so many books? The answer is that neither business fits the accepted template of what an English provincial bookseller should be like in the final decades of the eighteenth century. It is true they mirror much of provincial booktrade activity in the period, but in one significant characteristic they are unlike other provincial booksellers in that they circumvented the London booktrade whenever possible, choosing not to accept the crumbs from the London table, but deciding rather to go their own way and they did it very successfully.

The two businesses served those parts of the country market which were not being fully covered by the London trade. They realized their potential customers were likely to be price conscious and conservative and acted accordingly. So many of the books both reprinted were elderly, well-known and completely safe. Additionally, in an age of long and sometimes uncertain credit, and slow methods of production and distribution, they must have known that the more they controlled the more successful they were likely to be. From 1788 onwards the two enterprises seem to have developed an informal working agreement over the books they were reprinting, co-operating with London when it suited and involving themselves in the sale of books published by their colleagues in the northern half of the country. The first tangible outcome is the use both made of false imprints in the books they reprinted.

By the end of the eighteenth century such imprints were common-place. Typing the word 'false' in the *notes all* field of the Eighteenth Century STC brings up a brief citation list of some 4000+ titles, with the reasons for subterfuge on the part of the printer being all too obvious, with seditious libel, outright piracy and a smattering of pornography leading the way. Some, such as James Caulfield's *Blackguardiana* (*c.*1793), are simply fun, the imprint in this case being, '*Printed for, and sold by John Shepherd,... Sir John Falstaff; Sir Henry Morgan; Charles Maclean, Mary Cut-Purse; Mary Flanders; Mary Carleton and Betty Ireland.*', a veritable rogues gallery.[3] But all this aside, we are still left with a significant number of titles with probable connections to the two businesses which cannot be readily explained away. A number of these, as in an edition of Rousseau's *Eloisa*, dated 1795, take the form of a conger, with as many as sixteen familiar bookselling names listed in the imprints. But all the people listed were either dead by 1795, or given initials differing from those of the genuine bookseller.[4] Indeed there no reason to suppose either that the publication date is genuine. Neither is there any evidence linking such books with either Wilson or the Mozleys.

One name which appears in the 'conger' and most frequently in false imprints is that of Andrew Millar (c.1707-1768). Millar was one of the most prominent London booksellers of the day, involving himself in a great deal of what went on in the London trade. He was also the instigator of litigation over a reprint of James Thomson's *Seasons*, for which he claimed copyright, against Robert Taylor in 1766. *The Seasons* was the subject of further litigation in 1768, this time in *Becket v. Donaldson* which resulted in the landmark ruling by the House of Lords in 1774, effectively ending the London booksellers' claims for perpetual copyright. Millar was also a major subscriber to a scheme in 1759 to prevent country booksellers stocking cheap Scottish and Irish reprints of books for which Millar and others claimed perpetual copyright, and some of these subscribers (Johnston, Newbery, Davis and Bathurst) appear as part of the false conger.

Both the York and Gainsborough booksellers began printing and publishing works on their own account about the same time in the late 1770s, but it is John Mozley who first began using partially false imprints, employing what may have been local family names of Toplis and Bunney. These, however, were quickly dropped in favour of Osborn, sometimes used with a terminal letter e, and Griffin. Both are surnames of London booksellers, Thomas Osborn(e) (*fl.*1738-1767) being better known for the enmity shown towards him by the London bookselling establishment. He was attacked in a footnote by Pope in *The Dunciad* as:

A bookseller in Grays-Inn ... This man published advertisements for a year together, pretending to sell Mr. Pope's subscription books of Homer's Iliad at half the price: Of which books he had none, but cut to the size of them (which was quarto) the common books in folio, without copperplates, on a worse paper, and never above half the value.[5]

Even worse happened when he was flattened by Samuel Johnson: 'Sir, he was impertinent to me, and I beat him'. It was rumoured too that Osborne was persuaded to stop his piratical activities with the promise of an annuity for life and this is likely to be true, for he also subscribed to the 1759 scheme to fight off the incursions of the Scottish and Irish booksellers.

The first imprints using the names of Osborne and Griffin appear in books printed by John Mozley in 1782 and continued under his successors until around 1800, when H. and G. Mozley reverted to the more common 'printed (or published) for the booksellers (or proprietors)'. Between 1803 and 1809 John Mozley's son Henry revived the use of false imprints using, as Jim English discovered, the names of family members by marriage: Brambles (his wife's maiden name); Meggitt (his mother's maiden name) and Waters (his mother-in-law's).[6] At no point were the Mozleys ever coy about including their own names on the title-pages and, in at least one instance, made it clear they were the prime movers behind a reprint of Dodsley's *Aesop*. After 1809 the Mozleys seem to have abandoned the use of false imprints altogether and from then on their books carried only conventional imprints. Although Thomas Wilson had dealings with Alexander Donaldson's brother John (who was also into the business of cheap reprints) as early as 1775, he and his York colleagues did not start issuing reprints under false imprints until 1788 when they began using the surnames of three London booksellers, Millar, Law and Cater. These three had been targeted in 1775 in an edition of Eliza Haywood's *The Female Spectator*, but there is no evidence that Wilson was involved and it is only when he started his association with Robert Spence in 1788 that their false imprints began to appear regularly, intensifying after they were joined by Joseph Mawman in 1790. From 1800 onwards they ceased using spurious imprints altogether.

From 1790 until 1799, books were reprinted with either, '*London: printed for A. Millar, W. Law, and R. Cater; and for Wilson, Spence, and Mawman, York.*' or, '*London: printed for A. Millar, W. Law, and R. Cater* on the title-page, and while in the books with the first imprint there is ample evidence that these were being printed in York, there is little evidence in the latter, apart from the use of the word *Anno* in one imprint, and the use of a device engraved by Bewick for the company in another, that Wilson, Spence and Mawman were involved in any way. Those books which carry only the names of the so-called London booksellers are often titles which could still attract the unwelcome attention of the publishers of the mainstream London editions, Johnson's *Dictionary* (1792) and Sheridan's *Dramatic Works* (*c.*1797 and 1798) for example. Those carrying both sets of names tend to be of a more mundane nature, Fenning's *Grammar*, Walkingame's *Tutor's Assistant*; or books by authors long since dead, Defoe, Bunyan and Watts, whose *Hymns and Spiritual Songs*, and his *Psalms of David*, were regularly reprinted by others, the Mozleys included.

Although a separate clandestine business may have been at work, with Wilson, Spence and Mawman printing just some of the books, the most likely explanation for the differences in the imprints is the distinction drawn by many in the 1760s and beyond between the "original author" and the "tasteless compiler", the extent of which can be judged by Lord Hailes's scathing remarks about Thomas Stackhouse, author of *New History of the Bible*:

Herein Stackhouse, the author of this day, was an adept: he abridged the discourses pronounced at Mr. Boyle's lecture. He and his bookseller would have condemned Donaldson and his associates for encroaching on the common-law right of Bentley or Gastrell: and yet he scrupled not to make, nor his bookseller to publish, an abridgement of the arguements of Bentley and Gastrell in defence of religion! ...

The London booksellers *enlarge* the common-law right by conferring the name of *original author* on every *tasteless compiler*. Hereof there is an apposite example in Stackhouse, the author of this day.[7]

Much of the argument contained in the pamphlets which flew back and forth at the time naturally centred around questions of perpetual and limited copyright, but this other strand in the argument, about the growing importance of the author as the creator of an original work, was significant, as was the extent to which other unoriginal and older works were covered by copyright. So as late as the 1790s, the reprinting of some books was perhaps still seen as being of doubtful legality, but that others were in the public domain, as Alexander Donaldson maintained in *Some thoughts on the state of Literary Property* in 1764, 'that it was lawful for him to reprint any book of an older date.'[8] This perceived distinction between "original author" and "tasteless compiler", would help to explain why provincial reprints of children's books seemingly went unchallenged. Many early children's books, usually anonymously or pseudonymously compiled, consisted of stories lifted straight from miscellaneous sources: chapbooks, the Bible, Sarah Fielding's *The Governess*, *The Young Ladies Magazine* and so on; with the whole often being linked together by the device of a group of adults and children in conversation. If these books were changed in any way it was usually in the title, with any pages of advertisements omitted, and this happened with several reprinted by the Mozleys and by Wilson.

This also suggests that books such as William Enfield's anthology *The Speaker: or, miscellaneous pieces* could be reprinted with impunity and by extension, because who could claim copyright on the rules of grammar, or any branch of mathematics, textbooks by the likes of Fenning, Walkingame, or Thomas Dilworth. That this was a likely outcome of the Donaldson case, was predicted by Oliver Goldsmith immediately after the ruling:

The principal operation of the late decision in the House of Lords will be to set the country printers and booksellers at work in printing school books, such as spelling-books, and some other small, but necessary publications; and it is but just to give country tradesmen their share in every branch of commerce.[9]

We can only speculate on what Goldsmith would have said had he known how relentlessly his own textbooks were reprinted in the years following his death in 1774 and how his intention to move away from a catechistical form of instruction was subverted by the booksellers who republished his works.

It is most unlikely the trade would be fooled by the false imprints, for Wilson, Spence and Mawman were not the only booksellers taking Andrew Millar's name in vain. George Walker of Durham, who worked in York as a master printer from 1780-1797, has his name on the titlepage of one edition of Defoe's *History of the Devil* [*c.*1800] along with that of *A. Law, W. Miller*[sic.]*and R. Cater*. Other books with this variation on the spurious London imprint include reprints of Smollett's translation of *Don Quixote* (1793), Milton's *Paradise Lost* (1793 and 1795) and Goldsmith's *Vicar of Wakefield* (1792). Some imprints, with no apparent connection with Wilson and company, feature *A. Millar* alone, in editions of Garrick's *Dramatic Works* (1798) and *The Works of the late Doctor Benjamin Franklin* (1799), or together with fresh bookselling names as, *A. Millar, W. Cadell, and W. Cater* (1797) and *A. Millar, W. Cater, and G. Robson* (1797). To add to the confusion one book, *The Pleasing Companion* (1798), bearing the imprint of *A. Millar, W. Law, and R. Cater* is so unlike the rest, in that it is a reworking of John Newbery's *Circle of Sciences* and carries advertisements for twenty-four of Newbery's books, to suggest that Millar's name had quite widespread usage. It is almost as if *Millar* had become a brand name, synonymous with reprints, much the way *Spring Books* were in the 1960s and *Wordsworth Editions* are today. By including Millar's name in his own false imprint, was Wilson sending a signal to the rest of the trade that he was a potential source of supply for all of these books?

Although the battle to save perpetual copyright was effectively lost in 1774, the London booksellers did not concede defeat but fought back, and when John Bell published his *Poets of Great Britain*, they commissioned Johnson to write his *Lives of the Poets* (1779-81), claiming that in Bell's edition, 'the inaccuracy of the press was very conspicuous', and that 'many of [the poets] which are within the time of the Act of Queen Anne, which Martin [the printer] and Bell cannot give, as they have no property in them.' In the 1780s attempts were still being made to stem the tide of Irish reprints entering Scotland, some of which carried false London imprints and included several eventually reprinted by Wilson and Mozley. Almost certainly some of these books were destined for the shelves of English provincial booksellers.[10] Later even than that booksellers such as William Bent were still claiming rights to textbooks written at the beginning of the century:

The extensive sale of this excellent book [Dyche's *Guide to the English Tongue*] having induced many self-interested and evil-minded persons to publish and vend spurious and imperfect editions of the same, ... the public are requested to take notice, that the genuine edition ... is, by assignment from R. Ware, printed only for W. Bent, ...[11]

As late as 1827 we still see traces of this antagonism in the title page of a 'Genuine Edition' of Enfield's *The Speaker*, published in London by an authentic sixteen name conger. So even by the 1790s, when the two businesses were most actively using false imprints, the battle although lost, was not entirely over in the minds of some London booksellers.

It seems neither business felt they were behaving dishonestly in any way, but were competing against the London based trade who were operating a monopoly and deliberately manipulating other booksellers. Thomas Mozley writes that his father and Wilson, 'acted in concert, maintaining a position shared by no other country booksellers in England, and somewhat antagonistic to the London trade, then ensconced in very close lines of circumvallation'. Henry Mozley also considered himself 'a true Tory' and 'very strong against all monopolies and abuses, not holding them to be covered by the Tory creed.'[12] That they acted in concert is borne out in their booklists, where it sometimes looks as if they are leaving each other a clear run at particular titles, or are taking it in turns to reprint some books, and in the overall direction of their publishing programmes.

The principals in the two businesses were also pillars of their local communities. Thomas Wilson was an alderman and freeman of York, Robert Spence upon retirement became a Methodist preacher, Henry Mozley was a churchwarden and all were respected businessmen. Only Joseph Mawman seems to have attracted a degree of opprobrium and only then after he had moved to London in 1799. Spence, when he ran into financial difficulties found it easy to find support from a fellow Methodist, Mr. John Hall, 'who had noticed his industry, and had confidence in his integrity ... lent him double the sum he asked for.' And throughout his life in York Spence supported local charities. Similarly, Thomas Wilson earned the respect of Lindley Murray, the Quaker philanthropist:

It must in justice be observed, that the typography of Mr. Murray's works, reflect credit, not only on the author, but on the printers, Messrs. Wilson and co. of York; who were also the publishers, and, in part, proprietors of these works. Their extensive printing establishment, only about a mile from Mr. Murray's residence; the ability, promptitude, and obligingness, with which they promoted his views; were particularly satisfactory to him, and affording him great facility and accommodation, with the ordering and managing his various publications.[13]

Wilson's and Mozley's possible involvement in the reprinting of books from the established canon, was at best only ever intermittent and by the early 1800s these disappear altogether as does the use of false imprints. Increasingly manuals of religious devotion, books of a functional nature, textbooks and children's books come to dominate the York and Gainsorough lists, but again, with a few exceptions, many are reprints of earlier works. In religion, editions of Bunyan, Watts, Benjamin Keach, Joseph Alleine; the practical, Edward Hoppus' *Practical measuring*, John Evelyn's *Sylva* and Fenning's *Ready Reckoner*; and textbooks by the likes of Dilworth, Fenning and George Fisher.

Of the religious works published or reprinted by both houses, Nonconformity, and Methodism in particular, play a significant part in the lists. Many of the authors are instantly recognizable as part of the mainstream of the Protestant tradition, but others are not. In 1792, Wilson, Spence and Mawman published a single edition of Thomas à Kempis's, *Imitation of Christ* and this only makes complete sense if we know that Robert Spence was a Methodist and that Wesley thought the book, 'ought to be in every house'.[14] The Mozleys too reprinted it at least once in 1833, in the version edited and abridged by Wesley. Early on in his solo bookselling career, Robert Spence published an edition of Joseph

Alleine's *Alarme to Unconverted Sinners* and in 1785 his own abridgement of the same book, another which Wesley himself had abridged and published.

Spence also printed and sold a hymn book, known locally as the *York Hymn-book*, including in it a number composed by Wesley and this brought about a dispute between the two men, causing Wesley to remark in print, 'that the leave he had given to reprint his hymns, was to ministers of congregations; "But could anyone imagine, I meant a bookseller? Or that a *Methodist bookseller* would undertake it?" Wesley repeated his criticisms in a sermon delivered in York, upsetting Spence a great deal. But both men were eventually reconciled and after his retirement Spence preached on a Methodist circuit taking in the villages and towns around York.[15] Virtually every Protestant denomination is represented in the books published, or distributed, by Mozley and Wilson. Henry Mozley produced at least one book by a local Unitarian minister, as did Wilson for Charles Wellbeloved (1769-1858), the Unitarian minister of St. Saviourgate, York. Baptists are represented in the lists by John Johnson, a minister in Liverpool and John MacGowan Elsewhere, we find Congregationalists, Calvinists, Wesleyans, Evangelical Anglicans, the already mentioned Methodists, and even the Countess of Huntingdon's Connexion. Central to their own religious publishing and distribution for others, were devotional and instructional manuals, books of diurnal meditations and occasional accounts of godly lives. So we find both Wilson and Mozley reprinting Bogatsky's *Golden Treasury, for the Children of God ... with practical observations in prose and verse for every day of the year*, and the Mozleys re-publishing *Reflections for every day of the Year on the Works of God* by Christoph Sturm in 1816. Both at various times reprinted Thomas Adam's *Practical lectures on the Church-catechism* and both sold John Baxter's *The Young Christian's Encyclopaedia* which was printed and published in Halifax in 1818. They also regularly reprinted *The New Week's Preparation for a worthy receiving of the Lord's Supper*, a book first published in London in the 1730s.

If the spiritual world was well represented, then so was the secular. For the body there were the cookery books of Elizabeth Moxon (Mozley), Hannah Glasse (Wilson) and Elizabeth Raffald (Wilson and *Millar, Law and Cater*), and if the cooking wasn't that good, on the bookshelves there were John Hill's *Useful Family-Herbal* (1789) and Culpeper's *English Physician Enlarged* (printed London 1788 and sold by both Wilson and Mozley); for the prurient an extended version of the *Life of Bamfylde Moore*

Carew ... King of the Beggars (Mozley) and for the songster, *The Bullfinch* (published in Stamford and sold by Mozley) and the *Cheerful Companion* (published 1803 by Mozley). For self improvement and advancement, Wilson reprinted Charles Allen's *Polite Lady; or, a course in female education* in 1788; both published their own editions of Thomas Cooke's *Universal Letter-Writer; or, new art of polite correspondence* and Wilson, Spence and Mawman reprinted *The Complete letter-writer, containing familiar letters on the most common occasions of life* (1796). Both booksellers were involved in the sale of stereotyped editions of Stephen Jones's *Sheridan improved ...a general pronouncing dictionary... For the use of schools, foreigners, &c.* in 1810 and again 1820. Neither was the workplace neglected. In common with a number of other booksellers, Wilson reprinted Edward Hoppus' *Practical Measuring made easy to the meanest capacity* at least seven times, published two books and keys on landsurveying and mensuration and reprinted two others on farriery. Mozley reprinted Fenning's *Ready Reckoner* at least once and Thompson's at least three times and Thomas Crosby revised *The Ready Reckoner; or, the trader's sure guide* for Wilson in 1801 and again in the 1820s. For the young apprentice both reprinted Thomas Dilworth's *Young Book-Keeper's assistant ... for merchant's counting-houses, and young gentlemen on their first entrance on their mercantile apprenticeships.*

Between them, the two booksellers published and/or reprinted some 150 books for children which were not school related. The Mozleys reprinted Isaac Watts' *Divine Songs ... for the use of children* at least six times and Wilson at least three. Both from time to time reprinted *Goody Two-shoes*, with Wilson producing one edition which is a little mystery in itself. In their edition published in 1803, Wilson and Spence used wood-engravings attributed to Bewick. These had been used in an edition *c.*1790, 'printed for the booksellers' which carried advertisements, 'printed by and for Hall and Elliott, Newcastle.' How had Wilson come by them?[16] Both booksellers regularly plundered Newbery's list, sometimes changing the titles, but often producing their own word for word editions with mirror-image woodcuts and, in the case of Mozley, removing his 'colleagues', Osborne and Griffin to St Paul's Churchyard when he reprinted Newbery's *Valentine's Gift* in 1785. Although the advertisements were not included, the dedication from 'their old friend in St. Paul's Churchyard' was, as was the extended puff for Newbery's children's books with Osborne's name replacing Newbery's. Other books receiving similar treatment were *Tom*

Thumb's Folio, Giles Gingerbread, Be Merry and Wise and *The Fairing*, sometimes with the titles changed and sometimes not. Neither bookseller restricted themselves to the Newberys, the London bookseller John Marshall was treated in the same way, with Wilson reprinting Dorothy Kilner's *The Holiday Present* in 1797, Mary Ann Kilner's *Memoirs of a Peg-top* and *The Happy Family* (with a change in title), around the same time. Many of the others were wellworn favourites. Both did editions of Croxall's *Fables*, abridgements of *Robinson Crusoe; The English Hermit, Philip Quarl;* Thomas Day's *Sandford and Merton* in abridgements of under 100 pages; Berquin's *The Children's Friend* and Perrault's *Fairy Tales.*

From the size and scope of both booklists, we can see that these were indeed two considerable businesses and this is confirmed by evidence taken from a variety of sources. As has already been noted, Lindley Murray's biographer referred to Wilson and Co. as 'an extensive printing business' and from the same source we see that the print runs for Murray's works were very substantial indeed. His best remembered book, *English Grammar, adapted to the different classes of learners* (1st edn 1795) had gone through forty-eight editions by 1833, with new editions and *reprints* printed in runs of 10,000 copies, as was *The English Reader* (22nd edn 1833). The *Abridgement of English Grammar* (31st edn 1811) was printed in runs of 12,000; *English Exercises...* (41st edn 1832) runs of 10,000; *Introduction to the English Reader* (30th edn 1833) 10,000; *Spelling Book for Children* and *First Book for Children* 10,000 each.[17] Added to all of this, is the regular re-editing and reprinting of the textbooks by Francis Walkingame, both the original and a *Key to... Tutor's Assistant* and Thomas Dilworth, and reprint after reprint of *Pilgrim's Progress, Robinson Crusoe* and Croxall's *Fables of Aesop.* Not only that, in the first third of the nineteenth century the company was bringing along its own authors such as Elizabeth Frank (advice books, children's stories and elementary grammars), John Hornsey (yet more textbooks) and Anthony Nesbit (mensuration, practical gauging and land surveying). Throughout the history of the firm, they were also printing and publishing books by and for local authors: Tate Wilkinson (1739-1803), a local theatre manager, his memoirs in 1790 and, in four volumes in 1795, a history of Yorkshire theatres; Thomas Thompson of York, *Tithes Indefensible* in 1792, 1795, and 1796; the physician Alexander Hunter (1729-1809) *Culina Famulatrix...or, receipts in modern cookery with a medical commentary* (1804, 1805, twice in 1806, and once more in 1807), a reprint of his *Georgical Essays* in 6 volumes (1803-4) and of course the usual tracts and sermons which were often a main source of income for small provincial booksellers. Similarly, Mozley was printing and publishing religious works and textbooks and, as with the York firm, some appear with almost metronomic regularity, with Walkingame's *Tutor's Assistant* once more to the fore. As Wilson, Spence and Mawman used a local teacher to edit and revise their edition, so too did Mozley with William Birkin and he, like Thomas Crosby, headmaster of the York charity schools, produced a key to the main work. By 1851 the Mozleys were selling what they claimed was the '73rd edition, Revised, corrected and enlarged'. They also followed a similar course with Oliver Goldsmith's histories of England, Rome and Greece using Edward Coxe to revise the books and contribute, 'numerous examining questions after each section'. Ironically, by the 1830s some of these books carry the legend, 'Entered at Stationers' Hall'.

Generally the books produced in York and Gainsborough were far from insubstantial, most frequently octavos running to 250 pages or more, even in the early days. By the 1820s Wilson was capable of producing a four hundred page edition of Nesbit's *Complete Treatise on Practical Land-surveying* containing 260 woodcuts, twelve copperplates and a sixteen page engraved field book. The Mozleys had the capacity to reprint Henry's *Commentary on the Bible* in four volumes and by 1814 they were able to produce a seven page catalogue advertising eighty one 'new editions' of religious, juvenile and more general adult books. By 1825 their schoolbooks were being distributed for them in London by Cowie and Co. On a smaller scale they were regularly printing lists of books on the back cover of their own publications for children, including Thomas Day's *Sandford and Merton* in a much fuller version than the more usual abridgement in 60 pages or so which contented most small provincial booksellers.

An idea of the size of the workforce of the York business is to be found in the numbers of apprentices bound to the company and those who saw out their time. Starting in 1788 we find one bound to Wilson alone and one with both Wilson and Spence. Of these two one was freed in 1801. During the time of the partnership between Wilson, Spence and Mawman they took on twelve apprentices, of which six completed their term between 1795 and 1807. After the dissolution of the partnership with Mawman, Wilson and Spence took on a further seven, of which three saw out their term. After Spence's retirement, Wilson and his son Joseph Bilton Wilson signed up a further eleven, of which seven were freed between 1816 and

1820. This continued after Wilson's other son, Thomas Wood Wilson, joined the firm when between 1813 and 1830 the business took on a further eighteen boys with at least five completing their apprenticeships. In practical terms, this meant the business had an average of five or six bound apprentices at any given time, rising to a peak of twelve in 1815 and declining steadily to just two by 1830. However, many of the young men appear not to have finished their apprenticeships, or the fact was not recorded, so in some years the number of apprentices may have been higher than the records indicate.[18]

If we then consider the fact that Wilson *et al* were not only printers and publishers, but also retail and wholesale booksellers and from 1790 until 1799 proprietors of the *York Herald and County Advertiser*, then the infrastructure of the business must have been sizeable. We can only speculate on the number of presses, but at every stage in the regular printing of Lindley Murray's books alone, the space and manpower needed must have been considerable. Storage for paper, the drying and storage of printed sheets, type, perhaps binding materials and certainly packing materials would have required large premises. In 1787 James Fraser, a leading London bookbinder, in his pamphlets advocating the introduction of piecework in the binding trade, used a ratio of three men and two women to one errand boy or apprentice in a workshop.[19] This ratio of 5:1, would probably be too large for a provincial business, but if we allow one apprentice for every two journeymen in the workshop, then we may be looking at a workforce of twenty plus journeymen in any given year. As we cannot be sure how long some of the apprentices stayed with the firm, the overall number of journeymen and their helpers was probably much higher. Added to that would be some unskilled labour and who knows how many Pooters for the clerical work.

Neither was the reach of these businesses merely local or just regional, but what evidence exists suggests that both covered the greater part of England including the capital. Thomas Mozley records a visit of his father to Lackingtons in 1807, to South Shields in 1808 and an extended business trip north of the border to Edinburgh in 1801 where Henry found the booksellers 'very friendly' and, 'very different from London'. The business also had two or perhaps three travellers who, 'remained in his [Henry's] service so long as to become household words'. Like Wilson, Mozley had a retail shop as well as his printing, binding, publishing and wholesaling businesses and for a short time he too was involved in the production of a newspaper. In 1815, when the business moved to Derby, the Mozleys took with them some one hundred people, employees and their families. If we allow for the fact that some workers and their families may not have wanted to move with the business, Mozley was probably employing around thirty or so workers, if not more. The move, we are told, was intended to expand the business, and this in itself suggests confidence on the part of Henry Mozley that he had the resources at his disposal and was a man of substance.[20]

In his early years with Wilson, Robert Spence did most of the travelling for the business and in Burdekin's biography we find him in places as far afield as Bath and Whitby. A seemingly indefatigable traveller, Spence in his early years as a bookseller was part proprietor of an edition of Philip Henry's *Commentary on the Bible* for which 'he undertook to travel and solicit [orders] in a district one hundred miles around York.', that is effectively England from the Wash to the Scottish borders.[21] From 1805 until the dissolution of the partnership between Wilson and Spence, Richard Burdekin took up the position of traveller, and in 1812 one journey took him through England and as far as Penzance. The Sessions tell us that this particular journey took around 93 days, not only taking orders, but also collecting payment of more than £2000 in the process. His expenses for the trip were about £100, that is roughly the annual wages of two or three journeymen bookbinders. During his time on the road from *c.*1805 until 1813, he covered a total of around 70,000 to 80,000 miles, or an average of some 8-10,000 miles annually. Even allowing for an element of gloss, these figures again confirm that Wilson, Spence and Mawman, and subsequently Thomas Wilson and Sons, was a well organized and profitable business with a reach way beyond the confines of the north of England. A business of this magnitude enabled Joseph Mawman to acquire Charles Dilly's bookselling business in London, Thomas Wilson to buy a country house and Robert Spence a comfortable lifetime annuity.

If we accept the received opinion on the state of the English provincial book trade at the latter end of the eighteenth century and the very beginning of the nineteenth, then companies such as Wilson, Spence and Mawman and the Mozleys should not have existed. The picture drawn is of businesses struggling to expand, dependent on the London trade and limited opportunities presented at a local level. Everything radiates out from the metropolis. What success stories there are in the provinces, Eyres (1734-1809) in Warrington, for example, is presented as unique and unrepresentative. Tesseyman (*fl.* 1763-1811) in York is held up as an exemplar because he becomes a 'gentleman', but Wilson, who also did just that, is ignored.[22] If we look at Ellen Feepound's book stock in 1776 we find it stuffed with devotional works and 'about 140 books for scholars in English and Latin &c.', or read the catalogue for chapmen John Bew included in his edition of Benjamin Keach's *The Progress of Sin...* (1781), we find numbers of books, by title and subject, reprinted by the Mozleys and Wilson. The books Lackington's Anabaptist master had on his shelves would have been familiar to both, a ready reckoner and Watt's [sic.] *Psalms and Hymns*, a herbal and a book of physic. The pile of books John Clare acquired in his youth are frequently represented in Wilson's and Mozley's lists.[23] The conclusion can only be that these men knew the provincial trade and the market as well as, if not better than, some of their more illustrious colleagues in London.

In one respect, at least, the two businesses did resemble other provincial booksellers. When they were not producing books with partially false imprints, they printed, published and distributed books by local authors and books of primarily local interest, sermons, guides, memoirs and the like. But in the periods of their greatest activity on a wider stage, they produced virtually nothing at all of a limited or local interest, unless the author was known nationally. Significantly, they did not list London wholesalers in the imprints at those times either. If known London wholesalers appear in imprints it usually when Wilson and Mozley are listed as just two booksellers among many, and are not the prime movers in the project. They did however regularly support books published by their colleagues in the north in such places as Bradford, Leeds, Manchester, Lincoln and Stamford.

Everything changed in the first decade of the nineteenth century when they stopped the use of spurious imprints and began to forge closer ties with some London booksellers. Wilson and Spence's names appear regularly alongside that of Joseph Mawman after he had removed to London. The dissolution of the partnership had been entirely amicable and benefited both parties, even if the books published were not so diverse. The ties between the York business and Darton and Harvey, through their association over Lindley Murray's books, seemed to strengthen, with the London publisher becoming increasingly involved in production, and Longman took over publication, by assignment, of Crosby's edition of Walkingame in 1846 and a number of others.

Both booksellers appeared for a time on the titlepages of educational books published by Richard Phillips, but again they were just two among many.[24] The Mozleys, after the move to Derby, began using George Cowie and his various partners as agents in the 1820s, and as late as the 1840s they were still reprinting some titles from the early days of the business, including *Robinson Crusoe*, Goldsmith's *History of England* and a *Johnson's English Dictionary in miniature* which they had previously published jointly with Wilson and Lackington in 1822. Eventually they opened their own office in London, but still printed their books in Derby. The firm survived until the 1860s

For over fifty years, the two companies flourished and sold their books in great quantities. Today it is possible to buy some of their bestselling works for as little as five pounds, usually battered, often well thumbed and with multiple inscriptions which attest to the longevity of the books. Today we are used to the supposed rarity of eighteenth century books, but with Wilson, Spence, and Mawman and the Mozleys many of their books lie on library shelves throughout the world in quite large numbers. They were undoubtedly two of the most successful companies in the history of the English provincial booktrade.

Notes

As a preliminary to writing this paper, a checklist was prepared of the output of both booksellers. This came to a total number of new titles, reprints and new editions of 400+ for the Mozleys and 700+ for Wilson and his colleagues and this is still a far from complete listing. Most of the information was taken from ESTC (1998 ed.) and the 19th Century STC (Newcastle upon Tyne, 2002) on CD-ROM and online library catalogues. Wherever possible entries were checked against books held in the Bodleian Library, Oxford, including the Opie Collection on microfiche, and the microfilms of eighteenth century literature published by Research Publications Inc, Woodbridge Conn., USA.

1.   Robert Davies, *A Memoir of the York Press* (1868. Reprinted York, 1988), p. 265.
2.   J. Feather, *The Provincial Book Trade in Eighteenth Century England* (Cambridge, 1985). J. Feather, *Publishing, Piracy and Politics: an historical study of copyright in Britain* (London,1994) . William K. and E. Margaret Sessions, *Printing in York from the 1490s to the Present Day* (York, 1976). Jim English, *Chapbooks & Primers, Piety, Poetry and Classics* in *The Mighty Engine. The Printing Press and its Impact* ed. by Peter Isaac & Barry McKay (Winchester, 2000). Although Feather remains essential reading, his view

of the English provincial book trade in the latter part of the eighteenth century as backward and limited needs modifying.

3. *ESTC* (1998 ed.). Record No. t095154.

4. *ESTC* t136481. The imprint reads: London: printed for C. Bathurst [d. 1786], C. Nourse [d. 1789], T. Carnan [d.1788], F. Newbery [John Newbery's son retired 1779/80; his nephew d,1780], R. Cater [fictitious], R. Brotherton [fictitious], W. Johnstone [fictitious, but a W. Johnston gave evidence before the House Lords, 1774], P. Vaillant [Senior retired; junior still active in 1795], N. Conant [retired 1792], T. Davies [printer bankrupted 1775, engraver d.1785], L. Davies [fictitious?], A. Millar [d.1768], R. Tonson [d.1689], G. Keith [d.1782], W. Owen [Snr. d.1793; Jnr. not after 1792] and L. Hawis [fictitious], 1795. All were checked against standard reference works and BBTI online.

5. *The Poems of Alexander Pope* ed. by John Butt (London, 1963) p. 741 n. 167. *Petitions and Papers relating to the Bill of the Booksellers now before ... the Commons* (London, 1774), p. 5.

6. English, *Mighty Engine*, p. 160.

7. *The Decision of the Court of Sessions, upon the question of Literary Property* (Edinburgh, 1774), pp. 6-7. Mark Rose, 'The Author as Proprietor: Donaldson v. Becket and the Genealogy of Modern Authorship', *Representations* 23 (1988), pp. 51-85.

8. [Alexander Donaldson *attrb.*] *Some Thoughts on the state of Literary Property* (London, 1764), p. 6

9. *Petitions and Papers ...*, p. 19.

10. Warren McDougall, 'Smugglers, Reprinters, and Hot Pursuers: The Irish-Scottish Book Trade, and Copyright Prosecutions in the Late Eighteenth Century' in *The Stationers' Company and the Book Trade 1550-1990* ed. by Robin Myers & Michael Harris (Winchester, 1997), pp. 151-83.

11. *ESTC,* t225597.

12. Thomas Mozley, *Reminiscences...* 2 vols (London, 1885), vol. I, pp. 117, 153.

13. *Memoirs of the Life and Writings of Lindley Murray,* ed. by Elizabeth Frank (York, 1826), p. 233.

14. Isabel Rivers, 'Dissenting and Methodist books of practical divinity', in *Books and their Readers in Eighteenth Century England,* ed. by Isabel Rivers (Leicester, 1982), p. 153.

15. Richard Burdekin, *Memoirs of the Life and Character of Mr. Robert Spence, late Bookseller. Second Edition* (York, 1849), p. 33.

16. *Catalogue of a Highly Important Collection of Children's Books* [*Oppenheimer*] (London, 1975) III, lot 1205.

17. Frank, *Memoirs ... Murray*, pp. 261-2.

18. Sessions' *Printing in York*, pp. 85-93.

19. Ellic Howe, *The London Bookbinders 1780-1806* (London, 1950), p. 156.

20. English, *Mighty Engine*, p. 158.

21. Burdekin, *Robert Spence*, pp. 38, 59.

22. Feather, *Provincial Book Trade*, pp. 115, 92.

23. Feather, *Provincial Book Trade*, pp.125-8. Benjamin Keach, *The Progress of Sin, or, Travels of Ungodliness ... Seventh Edition* (London, 1781). Feather, *Provincial Book*

Trade, pp. 39-40. *John Clare's Autobiographical Writing*, ed. by Eric Robinson (Oxford, 1983), pp. 48, 169-70.

24.   Marjorie Moon, *Benjamin Tabart's Juvenile Library* (Winchester, 1990), pp. 80-3.

Lounging Places and Frivolous Literature: Subscription and Circulating Libraries in the West Country to 1825

K. A. MANLEY

EXACTLY HOW TO DEFINE the West Country is not an easy task. This paper will concentrate on libraries in Devon and Cornwall but will visit Dorset and Somerset on the way. The year 1825 marks a useful terminus, because mechanics' institutes changed the nature of library provision after that date. Three different but interlinked forms of book provision will be examined: commercial circulating libraries, usually run by a bookseller; private (or proprietary) subscription libraries where the readers bought shares in a collection of books maintained as a permanent library; and book clubs, where the books were usually sold off each year.[1] What connects these three types of book provision is that they provided a lending service of books for a fee in an age when the free public library service of today was completely undreamt of. They provided books which the user was able to choose for himself or herself, whether for education or entertainment. They were an important development along the road of freedom of choice and mutual improvement. The purchase of books was their prime aim, and so this paper deliberately excludes literary clubs where the discussion of books was the main aim, and literary and scientific institutions, because their emphasis was on lectures and learning rather than solely the provision of books.

Commercial circulating libraries came in all shapes and sizes but can be divided into at least three categories, although there are plenty of variations. The largest libraries were located mainly in London, such as John Bell's which claimed 100,000 volumes; William Lane's famous Minerva Library claimed half-a-million; Hookham's had perhaps 40,000 volumes. Of course those figures include duplicates. Their business lay in the rapid supply of the latest literature to virtually anywhere in the country. However, the majority of circulating libraries, the second type, were small High Street businesses, with between a few hundred and a couple of thousand volumes.

Many of these may not have been bookshops but haberdashers or fancy-goods sellers. They provided mostly novels and sold other fashionable items to attract the fairer sex. The largest of the provincial circulating libraries were to be found in holiday resorts such as the upmarket seaside towns of Brighton and Margate and the fashionable spa towns of Bath and Tunbridge Wells. These represent a third type because they were more than just library providers; they were also centres of fashion. They were the leaders of the pack and were looked upon with considerable envy by their smaller country cousins. Here is an extract from 'A letter from the Keeper of a Circulating Library in an obscure town, to the Keeper of a Circulating Library at a fashionable Watering Place', published in 1800:

> While you, my friend, in -----s blisful bow'rs,
> With joyful profit glad the smiling hours;
> While fashionable crowds attend your will,
> Your shew-glass empty, and your pockets fill;
> O let compassion touch your tender mind
> For one to shores less fortunate confin'd;
> Think of the place to which I'm chain'd by fate,
> And image (if you can!) my cruel state!
> For, here no beaux the library frequent,
> Who purchase useless toys at cent. per cent.
> In this dull town no belles at raffles shine;
> O town unworthy of a shop like mine!
> In vain the modish volumes I arrange,
> And wait, all day, to give and to exchange;
> [...]
> The stupor of the place confounds my care,
> And skill like mine but labours to despair.
> While thus my melancholy lot I mourn,
> Hourly to thee my envious thoughts are borne;
> While our poor nymphs, in vulgar dulness sunk,
> Scarce know the far-fam'd title of 'The Monk'.
> Your well-bred fair take each new tale to-bed,
> And not a novel crowds your shelves unread.[2]

As regards the West Country, this gloomy view of library provision matches the comments of a resident of Barnstaple writing in the 1860s about the town's libraries in the 1820s:

We had actually nothing, except the parochial library [...], and the miserable circulating libraries of a few stationers and booksellers, consisting almost exclusively of novels. The few who required more healthy, and less stimulating mental food than novels, united to form Book Clubs, but as these were in the days in which Mudie was not, the supply was miserably deficient. An attempt was made at the formation of a public [viz. subscription] library, in 1822, of which I can find no further record, than a remark in one of the periodicals of the time: 'It is not at all creditable to the inhabitants of an extensive and opulent town, that the late public library, the only establishment ever formed in it connected with letters, should so speedily have fallen to the ground'.[3]

Libraries flourished in the major rather than the minor towns. The West Country in general was not wanting in booksellers, but they were spread thinly in many parts. The pioneer of the fashionable circulating library was James Leake (1686-1764), the bookseller of Bath (which can fairly be included in the West Country), who was lending books by 1728.[4] He was the first person in England known to have organized a circulating library as a proper business; before him, booksellers lent books from their normal sale stock. Already by 1734, according to a French visitor to Bath, the booksellers were making vast profits not because they were selling so many books, but because it had become the custom for visitors to subscribe a crown or more for the privilege of borrowing books and thereby for being seen in a fashionable meeting place.[5] Leake was the epitome of sociability and sociableness, a friend of the nobility and noted for his fawning. Leake charged 5/- for the season, but 'persons of quality' paid a guinea, which led to a poem:

> Old batter'd Debauchees, says Gay,
> For what they cannot *Do* must Pay;
> So these, by L[e]ake, it is Decreed,
> Shall pay for what they cannot *Read.*[6]

Leake's circulating library was the first to become a centre of culture and fashion. His brother-in-law was to be Samuel Richardson, who had been apprenticed to the Leake family printing business, and whose novel, *Pamela* (1741), did so much to encourage the popularity of both the novel and the circulating library as a repository of light entertainment. Leake's business, continued initially by his sons, was to last until 1834. He was followed by many others.

William Frederick began in about 1740, and his lending business was to continue until 1897; many libraries only lasted a few years. In 1755 Thomas Loggan advertised:

At the Little Fan-Maker, in the Church-Yard, Bath, is a well-chosen Collection of Books, and will be all the new ones of Reputation as they are published, for the Company to read, for Three Shillings the Season [...][7]

He also offered quarterly rates and kept 'a good, warm parlour' for reading newspapers. He subsequently opened a Ladies' Tea Room at the Hotwells (later Clifton) near Bristol, complete with a collection of books to read. By 1800 there were at least ten libraries in Bath, one or two claiming to have 10,000 volumes or more. Size did not necessarily mean that demand could be satisfied. When in 1785 the sister of the playwright Sheridan wanted to read the memoirs of Mrs Bellamy, the actress, she wrote:

At Bath the Booksellers said they were sixty deep on their list before we had a chance and here [she was writing from Tunbridge Wells] I find I am at least ten too late in my application so that it will be like reading an old newspaper by the time I get it.[8]

Elsewhere in the West Country, Weymouth was to become fashionable in the 1780s. Three booksellers were vying for customers to their libraries by 1790, including John Love, a former art student whose bookshop was advertised as a house of public entertainment; he called it the 'Pantheon of Taste'. He housed a billiard room and a Public Exhibition Room, open from 6 a.m. to 10 p.m., and boasted that he received 130 newspapers two hours earlier than the Post Office. He kept lists of new arrivals and winning lottery numbers; he maintained a musical circulating library, lent tele-scopes, and insured houses and ships in the harbour.[9] When George III visited Weymouth in 1789, Love was derided by the *Morning Chronicle* for his haste in displaying patriotic flags; but he did attract Royal attention. The *Morning Chronicle*, incidentally, was not taken in his reading room. In 1791 his rival, Peter Delamotte, attracted the favours of the Royal Family and advertised that his 'gratitude for those condescensions greatly surpasses his power of expression'.[10] Their rivalry was intense, but Love died in 1793 at the age of 41, the fattest man in England, it was said, weighing 26 stone.[11] His coffin had to be slid out of a window on ropes.[12]

In Devon a couple of Exeter booksellers were circulating books before the 1780s, but the exact dates of their lending activities, as opposed to their purely bookselling businesses, are unknown. During the 1780s Gilbert Dyer and Shirley Woolmer set up rival libraries; Woolmer claimed 20,000 volumes by 1789. Dyer's library was highly regarded, and Richard Polwhele, the Cornish historian, wrote that 'for a judicious selection of books, [Dyer's] is one of the first in England'.[13] In Barnstaple the wonderfully named Fidelio Murch lent books, but although he was a bookseller by 1760 it is unknown when he began lending (though certainly before 1784). Plymouth had a handful of libraries in the 1790s, concentrated in Plymouth Dock which in 1824 became Devonport. Elsewhere on the coast, seaside resorts did not begin to develop until the 1790s. In March 1795 Rev. John Swete (who, to gain an inheritance, had changed his name from Tripe, presumably an easy decision) visited Sidmouth and found it:

the gayest place of resort on the Devon coast, and every elegancy, every luxury, every amusement is here to be met with – iced creams, Milliners shops, cards, billiards, plays, circulating libraries, attract notice in every part – and as I saw a smart Gentleman take a novel from his Pocket in the public shed – I presume such to be the fashion of the place![14]

This is almost the earliest reference to a circulating library on the Devon coast. By 1799 it had been joined by two in Exmouth and one in Kingsbridge. Circulating libraries in holiday resorts took time to establish themselves, since they were rarely just a library in a bookseller's shop, but a social centre, providing a meeting place for news and gossip. They became lounging-places, with a sea view. It took years to build up a stock worthy of an aspiring resort where the intention of the tradesmen was to attract the right clientèle. Jane Austen wrote of Dawlish that in 1802 the 'Library was particularly pitiful & wretched [...], & not likely to have anybody's publication'.[15]

As for Ilfracombe, the earliest reference to a library dates from 1810 when a Mrs Jackson, writing to one of her sons, a diplomat, found very little of anything in the town. The post was 24 hours later than in Bath, her kitchen was too small for her plump cook to turn round in, the local supply ship from Barnstaple (containing the cook) sailed past without stopping, and the only people worth knowing was a family who had been at Bath:

What is worse [she continued], although we shall have abundance of time on our hands, we shall not be able to get books to amuse us. There is certainly a *thing* called a library, but it contains far more quack medicines and articles of an all-sort description than books. Among the few they have, I could find nothing newer than two or three foolish novels of the last years of the last century.[16]

By this period (1810) Sidmouth was well on its way upwards. The 'Shed', mentioned by Rev. Swete, had been rebuilt and one end, complete with verandah, was now known as the Sidmouth Marine Library, established by James Wallis in 1809; his relations ran a library in London. A second library was run by a Miss Giles. A third, started by a Miss Rose in 1812 at the other end of the Beach, was taken over by John Marsh and became the Royal Library. Both Marsh and Wallis published opposing guides to Sidmouth, each glorifying their own handsome libraries.

Returning to Dorset, Lyme Regis developed slowly, like Sidmouth. By 1803 it boasted several libraries described as 'neither copious nor select'.[17] By 1820 only two libraries were recorded, one run by a haberdasher. Inland, the market towns had more established libraries. Robert Goadby, who had run a library in Bristol in the 1740s, opened a library in Sherborne in 1765 with 2,000 volumes, which he offered to send anywhere within the circuit of the *Western Flying Post*, which he printed.[18] He charged an annual subscription but also offered short loans. When Samuel Gould, a bookseller for 50 years in Dorchester, began lending books in around 1780, he lent books at 2d. each per night 'and on *no* other Terms'. His epitaph described him as the 'Superintendent of the Amusements of Dorchester':

> He sold Books.
> He scatter'd Jokes and promoted Mirth.
> He cemented Friendships.
> He hurt no Body.
> He wished to do good to All.[19]

Cornwall, having few towns, had fewer circulating libraries, though one run by John Hewitt in Penzance was said to have started in 1750; that cannot be proven, but he was a printer by that date. There was a circulating library in Falmouth from 1812 and also one in Truro by the 1790s, run by William Harry, who advertised:

> Books for Circulation too.
> Some are Old and others New.
> Those who have an hour to spare
> May read by Volume, Week, or Year.
> Pamphlets, New Books, Publications,
> Wrote by Authors of all Nations,
> Twice a Month, from London, I
> Can my Customers supply.[20]

Library history is made interesting by the characters who ran libraries, and one such appears in Somerset. According to the old *Dictionary of National Biography*, a worthy and respected bookseller and antiquary called James Savage was a librarian at the London Institution and then the Somerset and Taunton Institution. Savage was born in Yorkshire in 1767 and worked as a bookseller and printer with his brother, William, in Howden. William migrated to London to become a noted fine printer; he worked for the Royal Institution and wrote a treatise on ink. James followed and worked for several publishers before joining the London Institution in 1806. When the present author was asked to revise James Savage's entry for the new *Oxford Dictionary of National Biography*, a rather less rosy version of his career emerged. James Savage was not a librarian at the London Institution, but the porter, and a few years later did a runner. He had been pocketing subscriptions, but the Institution took no action on the grounds that he had defrauded individual subscribers, not the institute. He reappears as the editor of a newspaper in the Midlands (though its title has not been discovered) and as the author of a pamphlet on how to edit a provincial newspaper.[21] On the strength of that, he was invited to Taunton in 1811 to manage a new Conservative weekly newspaper. It lasted five years when it ceased for unknown reasons, though he later referred to 'peculiar circumstances in which he was unfortunately involved'.[22] He had already established a bookshop, circulating library, and reading room, all run by his wife, in Taunton, which he now concentrated on; his wife died shortly afterwards. In 1822 Savage relinquished business to become librarian of the newly-established Somerset and Taunton Institution (later the Taunton and Somerset Institution) in the Market. He wrote several local histories but had not abandoned his old ways. He was still diverting subscriptions to his own pocket, was dismissed in 1829, and whisked to a debtors' prison. On his release he was, thanks to friends, appointed editor of the *Dorset County Chronicle*, another Conservative newspaper, and died in 1845, a thoroughly respected Tory and Churchman. His career surely epitomizes so many aspects of the book trade at that period, though not the better ones.

So much for trade. In rural areas, book clubs were popular throughout England, but evidence for their existence is remarkably difficult to find. There were plenty of book clubs in the West Country, and they multiplied after 1800. One met at Swale's Coffee House in Exeter by 1765; several existed in Honiton in the 1790s. The Poole Book Society was established in 1791 but was turned into a permanent subscription library in 1799. Many met in public houses. A club in Bishops Lydeard, Somerset, by 1808 was known as the Gore Inn Reading Society, but from 1824 became the Lethbridge Arms Book Club; it lasted until 1860. Unusually we know of at least five book clubs in Plymouth by 1796, because they all appear as subscribers to the same book, John Bidlake's *The Sea*, a poem, and they were called the First Reading Society, the Second Reading Society, the Third Reading Society, and so on. A Sixth Reading Society appears later. Such formal names suggest a degree of co-operation and regimentation. Numbering book clubs is not found elsewhere, and the presence of the docks and military personnel may explain why there were so many clubs here.

Cornwall had two unusual book clubs in the eighteenth century: they catered exclusively for ladies. Such ladies' clubs were not unknown (there was one in Taunton by 1790), but they were rare. The Ladies' Book Club of Penzance was founded in 1770, and rule no. 1 read: no gentleman should be admitted as a subscriber.[23] The ladies paid 6/- a year and elected one of their number each year to take in the subscriptions, order the books or pamphlets that were chosen, and make themselves accountable for the money at the end of the year. Books were distributed by ballot, and none could be kept more than four days. Members residing outside the town could borrow books for a week, but only after the resident ladies had finished. Each year the books were to be sold to the highest bidders and, if no bidders, the remainder would be divided by lot. There were 23 original members, and the books they ordered during the first year or so included the works of the poet, Shenstone, the *Vicar of Wakefield*, Marmontel, the *Bath Guide*, a life of Cicero, *Ladies' Travels*, and such titles as the *Curate of Coventry*, the *Devil on Crutches*, *Stagnation of Matrimony*, sermon on temperance, *Man and Family*, and several magazines and reviews including the *Monthly Review* and the *Lady's Magazine*. The ladies generally ordered around fifty titles a year, and their club lasted until 1912. Incidentally, the gentlemen of Penzance had their own book club by about 1800.

The Roseland Book Club was established in 1791 and held an annual dinner at noon in the Queen's Head in the small town of Tregony, when, according to Richard Polwhele, 'the town is more than usually illumined by the splendour of carriages without, and "the feast of reason, and the flow of soul", within'.[24] It became known as the Powder Literary Society, not because its proceedings went with a bang but because its members were all ladies, with the exception of their steward, Rev. Jeremiah Trist, who was vicar of Veryan for almost 50 years. The membership was limited to 13, with an annual fee of a guinea.[25] Reading books of history, travels, biography, politics, and *belles lettres* was the society's aim, and the members were divided into two divisions, eastern and western, to help circulation. The books were sold each year, and the steward would circulate a list on which each lady would enter a price for each book they were particularly interested in, which would then be sold to the highest bidder. The club still existed in the 1850s.

Book clubs did not satisfy the need for permanent libraries, and in 1792 the Cornwall County Library was founded in Truro.[26] This was a private subscription library, as existed in many other parts of the country, with members buying shares for a guinea and paying an annual fee of a guinea; but the property was vested in the knights of the shire, because there was an aspiration of making this collection a permanent public library for Cornwall. It was also the intention to collect fossils and the like to illustrate Cornish natural history. Interestingly, the management was vested in members who paid two guineas a year, which was to lead to some friction with the one-guinea members. Three copies of all new worthwhile books were to be purchased, but only one was to be bound and preserved. There was also an intention to collect manuscripts of Cornish interest and even fund research trips to the Bodleian Library or the British Museum. The Library enjoyed an annual income of at least £100 and naturally concentrated on non-fiction, though by 1809 fiction is beginning to creep in – *Gertrude of Wyoming* is one such title from that year. In 1816 a stationer was elected as librarian and was allowed to open his shop in the library's parlour; it then had rooms in the offices of the Metal Company. In 1819 it was reported that some books in the Library were 'so trifling and insignificant' that they should never have been bought, but the rules did not permit selling off stock. Missing books were always a problem. In 1826 the Librarian put an advertisement in the local newspaper:

I am most particularly desired by the Committee to request that each Subscriber will examine his Library, lest ALBIN ON INSECTS should have crept in: it is a quarto volume bound in calf gilt, and from being unlike the binding of the Library books in general, is likely to have caused the mistake.[27]

Notwithstanding depredations, the Library was to last until about 1921.

The Penzance Library was founded in 1818 and still exists, now known as the Morrab Library from its pleasant situation in Morrab

Gardens. The Library grew slowly, though had over 2,500 books within ten years. Although the Library was open until 9 p.m., books could only be borrowed during three periods of one hour a week; by 1824 it was closed at dark because of complaints about disorder and missing books. But it still managed to have 97 members by 1825.[28] Like the subscription library in Truro, the Penzance Library had its two-guinea and one-guinea members, and clearly this fostered charges of élitism. One member certainly resented a perceived disdain for tradesmen. In 1842 he published an eight-page poem of which only an extract can be given here:

> Know, in a town just the Nor'-west of France,
> By the Mount's Bay in Cornwall, call'd Penzance,
> Britons wise, rich, and christian (?) two or three,
> Have got a most extensive library,
> Our patriots pure have long been adding to.
> How many books? I do not know: do you?
> *Christians* are ever found averse to pride:
> Whoever said they are not so, hath lied.
> So minds' purveyors never minded *caste*,
> Two guineas **your** first year, *they one* the last.
> And there's a news-room, for one guinea more,
> Admits by ballot; (papers insecure;
> And funds too low to buy a spark of fire,
> Where shivering sit few men who love the lyre;)
> So all who wish recorded mind to see,
> For the first peep must launch out guineas three:
> Thus those within are the select – d'ye see!
> Not that the rich would thus exclude *the poor*,
> For every *virtuous* man is *rich*, be sure!
> No matter how, if not by barefac'd lies,
> Keep back the truth he may, with deep device,
> And combination to keep up the price.
> [...]
> Thus blighted is provincial genius now,
> That will not deem mind's manhood very low;
> Three guineas were too great a tax, he said,
> For one who sweated for his daily bread.
> The gods assembled, and with much parade
> They talk'd awhile o those they call'd 'trade!'
> Whom they respected very, very much:
> As to poor scribes, they wept that there were such;

Plymouth Public Library, 1831. Steel engraving. © Devon Libraries

And would 'News', 'Library' consolidate:
'Till one objected, with teeth out of date,
That he'd *three* guineas paid when he came in,
And to admit for less were Sodom's sin.
[...]
Consolidate the Library and News:
Let visit both, the self-same pair of shoes.
Let the whole charge be but a guinea ONE:
Black-balling him who thus the work has done![29]

In fact the Library and Newsroom never did merge.

Subscription libraries hardly flourished in Devon, where the circulating libraries reigned supreme, but they existed. The Exeter Library Society, founded in 1776, lasted for a mere dozen years. Even though it attracted 100 subscribers in its first year, it only had 25 when it ceased.[30] The Devon and Exeter Institution, founded in 1813, and which still exists, fulfilled the functions of a proprietary subscription library, but was different, having a museum and lecture room as well. Plymouth Public Library was founded in 1810 and soon boasted a new building, opened in 1813. Its original shares cost 30 guineas, but it had accumulated 42,000 volumes and 280 members by 1910. The building was destroyed in the Blitz, but the library still exists, though as more of a newsroom. Also in 1810, the South Devon Library was founded in Totnes and still existed in the late 1880s.

A particularly interesting library is the Tavistock Library, established in 1799. The books were probably originally kept at the home of a member, next in a rented room, then in the care of a bookseller. A new building was erected in 1821, a very charming mini-Greek temple, complete with small columns. But the local landowner, the Duke of Bedford, took exception to it, and it was demolished only 11 years later. The Library then moved to the old Abbey Gatehouse, which is where the Duke had wanted the Library to go before the new building was erected. The Library still ekes out a somewhat precarious existence; in 2001 the local council tried to take over the gatehouse building and move the library elsewhere.

In the early years of the Tavistock Library, the charge was a guinea for a share, plus a guinea a year. The latter was eventually raised to £1.6s a year, though 'unmarried ladies' only had to pay a guinea. All members had to pay 2s. for a printed catalogue. Periodicals could not be borrowed until they had 'lain on the table' for a month, and new books for 14 days. Interestingly, there were reciprocal membership arrangements with the other proprietary subscription libraries in Devon and Cornwall. Today the Library is only a reading room with a few reference books of local interest; its surviving stock and archives are in Exeter. As for subscription libraries in Dorset and Somerset, the Poole Book Society and the Institution in Taunton have been mentioned, but no others are known to have existed during this period.

Although subscription libraries and book clubs were on the whole intended for the better-off (and members usually had to be voted in) their example was followed in the early nineteenth century by libraries catering for other branches of society. Regional examples include the Exeter Eclectic Library, established in 1807 mainly for young people, which was later known as the Exeter Public Select Library and merged with the Public (Municipal) Library in 1871; and the Exeter Tradesmen and Mechanics' Institute, founded in 1825 as a subscription library. Commercial circulating libraries, too, catered for all tastes and pockets. Although the majority of Devon and Dorset seaside libraries aspired to attract a fashionable clientèle, in reality most circulating libraries had differential rates which put them within the pockets of the majority of local people, not just visitors.

This abbreviated tour of the library history highlights of the West Country has hopefully revealed that the region was not badly provided with libraries and book clubs by the end of the eighteenth century. A large number lasted for many years, often for several decades. They clearly were meeting a need and were a valued part of the local cultural landscape.

Notes

1. The only comprehensive survey of such libraries in Britain will be found in Paul Kaufman, *Libraries and their Users* (London, 1969).
2. *Annual Register for 1798*, p. 40 (London, 1800), [part 2], p. 450.
3. John R. Chanter, *Sketches of the Literary History of Barnstaple* (Barnstaple, 1866), p. 79.
4. For Leake and other aspects of circulating library history, see: K. A. Manley, 'Booksellers, peruke-makers, and rabbit-merchants: the growth of circulating libraries in the eighteenth century', in Robin Myers, Michael Harris and Giles Mandelbrote [eds], *Libraries and the Book Trade* (New Castle, Delaware, Oak Knoll, 2000), pp. 29-50.
5. A. Prévost, *Le Pour et le Contre*, vol. 3, no. 38 (Paris, 1734), pp. 176-7.
6. John Winstanley and others, *Poems* (Dublin, 1742), p. 258.
7. *Bath Journal*, 18 October 1755.
8. William LeFanu [ed.], *Betsy Sheridan's Journal* (Oxford, 1986), p. 56.
9. *The Times*, 4 July 1789; *Dorchester & Sherborne Journal*, 15 June 1792.
10. *Weymouth Guide*, 3rd edn (Weymouth, c.1792), p. 56.
11. V. J. Adams, *John Love (of Weymouth)* (Dorchester, 1965).
12. *Gentleman's Magazine*, 63 (Nov. 1793), p. 1055.
13. Richard Polwhele, *The Language, Literature, and Literary Characters of Cornwall* (London, 1806), p. 97.
14. Todd Gray [ed.], *Travels in Georgian Devon*, vol. 2 (Tiverton, 1998), p. 139.
15. R. W. Chapman [ed.], *Jane Austen's Letters* (London, 1952), p. 393.
16. Lady Jackson [ed.], *The Bath Archives: a Further Selection from the Diaries and Letters of Sir George Jackson* (London, 1873), vol. 1, p. 134.
17. [John Feltham], *Guide to all the Watering and Sea-bathing Places* (London, 1803), p. 234.
18. *Western Flying Post*, 7 January 1765.
19. *Notes and Queries*, 10th ser. 5 (23 June 1906), p. 492.
20. Copy in the John Johnson Collection (Bodleian Library).
21. James Savage, *An Account of the London Daily Newspapers* (London, 1811).
22. *Taunton Courier*, 13 November 1817.
23. The rules and accounts are in the Morrab Library, Penzance.
24. Polwhele, *Language, Literature, and Literary Characters*, p. 98.
25. The rules, etc., of the club are in Cornwall Record Office.

26. The rules of the Library are in Polwhele, *Language, Literature, and Literary Characters*, pp. 98-105, and its minute books in Cornwall Record Office.

27. *Royal Cornwall Gazette*, 19 August 1826.

28. Cyril Noall, *The Penzance Library, 1818-1968* (Penzance, 1968).

29. 'Cosmopolite' [A. T. J. Martin], *The Penzance Library: a Satire* (Penzance, 1842).

30. M. M. Rowe, 'The Exeter Library Society', *Devon & Cornwall Notes and Queries*, 31 (1970), pp. 222-4.

The Production and Publication of Topographical Prints in Devon, c.1790-1870

IAN MAXTED

DEVON LIBRARY AND INFORMATION SERVICES received in 2002 from the New Opportunities Fund *NOF-Digitise* initiative a grant to locate and digitise the 3,500 topographical prints listed by the print collector John Somers Cocks in the catalogue published by the Library Service as long ago as 1977.[1] The images were also to be accompanied, where possible, by contemporary text. The resulting project, entitled 'Etched on Devon's Memory' (www.devon.gov.uk/etched) enables an overview of the changing way in which published images of the Devon landscape reached the market in the days before the arrival of photography. Works with Devon illustrations began to appear in the 1720s but these formed part of antiquarian tours of Britain as a whole. Such were for example William Stukeley's *Itinerarium curiosum*, published in London in 1724, which included a prospect of Exeter and another entitled *Moridunum*, a view of Seaton.[2] Some seventeen places in Devon were included in Samuel and Nathaniel Buck's *Antiquities, or venerable remains of above four hundred castles, monasteries palaces etc. in England and Wales*, which appeared in five volumes between 1725 and 1752.[3] Local maps and views also began to appear in the monthly magazines such as the *Gentleman's magazine*, the *European magazine* and the *Lady's magazine* in the later eighteenth century. However all these were published in London and formed part of works with a national scope.

In the 1790s regional tours begin to appear. Their appearance at this time may be explained in part by the effect of the Revolutionary and Napoleonic Wars which effectively closed the continent to those who would formerly have made Europe the destination of the grand tour, but this only served to emphasize the growing attention already being directed to regions of England such as the Lakes, the Wye Valley and the south west through the picturesque movement. A prime exponent of this manner of viewing landscape was William Gilpin who had toured Devon and Cornwall in 1775, although his *Observations on the western parts of England*

relating chiefly to picturesque beauty was only published in London in 1798.[4]
Gilpin favoured the atmospheric aquatint, often in an oval format, to
illustrate his descriptions, as did William George Maton whose *Observations relative chiefly to the natural history, picturesque scenery and
antiquities of the western counties of England, made in the years 1794 and
1796* had already appeared in two volumes in 1797 with six Devon views.[5]

There was also a growing interest in local historical writing. In 1790
Martin Dunsford's *Historical memoirs of the town and parish of Tiverton*
attracted 413 subscribers to 444 copies, seventy-five percent of them in the
West of England. This was printed for the author by Thomas Brice in
Exeter and contained three engravings.[6] So secure was the market for such
works of local history and topography that Richard Polwhele's *History of
Devonshire*, a much larger compilation than any of the earlier historical
surveys of the county, was printed by Trewman of Exeter for Cadell, Dilly
and Murray in London in three folio volumes between 1793 and 1806
with twenty-four specially commissioned plates, mostly by T. Bonnor.[7]
Here we see local printers and publishers joining the London trade in
works with topographical prints.

But tentative local steps had already been made in the 1780s. In 1782
a set of oval line-engravings by B. T. Pouncey and J. Pye showing
Plymouth waterfront scenes was issued by W. Hay in 1782 and at a slightly
later date a number of engravings by Francis Jukes (1745-1812) were issued
in Exeter. Jukes was a London based engraver, living mainly in the Fitzroy
Square area, but he had a wide range of contacts, including business connections with Switzerland, which were severed by the French Revolution.[8]
His views of Exeter Cathedral, published in 1791 were after W. Davey
while his views of the East Gate of Exeter, published in 1785 were after
J. Hayman, presumably a relative of the Exeter born Francis Hayman
(1708-76).[9] In 1806 J. Hayman provided the drawings to illustrate
Alexander Jenkins's work, *The history and description of the city of Exeter and
its environs*, published in Exeter by P. Hedgeland.[10] An important local
undertaking in these early years was the series of works by the landscape
artist and portrait painter Thomas Hewitt Williams, resident first in
Plymouth and later in Exeter, who published accounts of three series of
excursions, illustrated by about 20 etchings: *Picturesque excursions in
Devonshire* (1801), *A tour to the north of Devon* (1802) and *Picturesque
excursions in south Devon* (1804).[11] Williams did not use a horse on these
excursions, the better to become one with the landscape, but would carry

his equipment on foot 20 miles or more a day, even in poor weather. In 1827 Williams used the recently developed technique of lithography to illustrate the second edition of *Devonshire scenery*, employing Thomas Bayly, the first lithographic printer in Exeter. The work, published by W. C. Pollard, bears the statement: 'In consequence of the new lithographic establishment of Mr. Bayley, in Exeter, six drawings have been added'.[12]

However in the first decades of the nineteenth century London artists and publishers retained an important role in the production of series of fine engravings of local scenes. Leading names in this were Plymouth-born Samuel Prout (1753-1852), whose soft-ground etchings of ruinous and picturesque buildings are widely collected, and Frederic Christian Lewis (1779-1856) whose series of etchings of the rivers of Devon were published by subscription between 1821 and 1842.

It was not until the second decade of the nineteenth century that the first publisher appeared in Devon who was to make a feature of the publication of engravings and illustrated books and he set up business not in Exeter but in the infant coastal resort of Sidmouth where he established the Marine Library on the beach in 1809. The first publication of John Wallis, the proprietor of this establishment, dates from 1810 and was a guidebook entitled *The beauties of Sidmouth displayed, being a descriptive sketch of its situation, salubrity and picturesque scenery. Also a account of the environs within fifteen miles round, interspersed with authentic anecdotes* by the Rev. Edmund Butcher.[13] It contains a folded aquatint after J. Nixon of the 'View of the Beach and Peak Hill, Sidmouth' and was a modest foretaste of the publications to come. It did however take pains to describe the publisher's establishment as

a lounging-place in a conspicuous and pleasant situation, where articles of fancy, as well as information and utility, may be met with; where the news of the day may be collected and discussed, and an opportunity given to the saunterers at a watering-place to chat and gossip together. ... It is well supplied every day with the London and provincial papers. Several of the most popular periodical publications are to be found upon its tables. A variety of elegant toys and trinkets, and some articles of greater utility, occupy its shelves. Books of education, dissected maps, and a circulating library, to which new works are regularly added, complete an establishment which, with due encouragement, will be every season increasing in value and variety. The front part of the shop is appropriated to the readers of the newspapers and magazines; but, for the convenience of such as wish to do this with less interruption in the summer season, a convenient back room is also prepared.

Such thoughtfulness did indeed cause the Marine Library to flourish and the second edition of Butcher's guide, published in about 1820, contains eight aquatints and the third, published a year or two later, boasts no fewer than thirty-one, mostly by the Londoner Daniel Havell after the Sidmouth artist Henry Haseler. In the guidebook it was stated that Wallis had 'expended in excess of £900 in engraving, coloring, &c'. The most magnificent single print which Wallis produced was a panorama of the sea front at Sidmouth with Wallis's library proudly centre-stage. This was aquatinted by Daniel Havell after H. Cornish and was about 2.7 metres long.[14] A clue to Wallis's origins can be found in the illustration of his circulating library in the panorama published in 1815. Its signboard reads 'Wallis's, the original circulating library & reading room, and at no. 42 Skinner's Street, London'. In fact the London business was at that time being run by John Wallis senior and his son Edward. John junior was born in about 1780 and apprenticed to his father in 1794, becoming a freeman of the London Stationers' Company on 4 February 1806. He ran his own business at 186 Strand for a short period before moving to Sidmouth. Wallis senior had been in business in London since 1775, moving to 42 Skinner Street in 1812 where his son Edward joined him as partner in 1813. Edward and John were joint publishers of the 1815 panorama. They built up an extensive trade as map and printsellers, publishing maps by John Cary among others.[15] Beside many individual prints, including several views from his library, Wallis was responsible for several other books profusely illustrated with coloured aquatints. He commissioned the earliest lithographic illustrations to appear in a Devon series. *Sketches from Nature* were produced by Ackermann & Co. in London in 1819-20.[16]

In other resorts along the south and north coasts of Devon printers and booksellers catered with enthusiasm for the growing tourist market. Often a circulating library formed an important part of the service offered. Mr Gore ran such a library on the beach at Dawlish before the railway cut along the sea-front and in 1818 it even featured on an aquatint by Daniel Havell in Henry Haseler's *Scenery on the Southern Coast of Devonshire* published by Wallis in Sidmouth.[17] In 1831 the business was taken over by Miss Croydon, probably related to Edward Croydon of Teignmouth. Croydon's Teignmouth business had been set up by 1806 but the firm's heyday starts from June 1815, at which date the Gothick style premises in Regent Place was opened. (This survives as W. H. Smith.) Edward Croydon operated as a bookseller, printer, stationer and print and music warehouse. He operated

Gore's Library on the Beach, Dawlish, Devon, c.1819.
Aquatint by D. Havell after H. Haseler. © Devon Libraries

a circulating library and provided billiard rooms for visitors. He clearly sought to act as an important social centre for the newly formed resort. In 1819 he was selling ball tickets, his circulating library kept the London and Exeter newspapers and, prior to the establishment of the *Teignmouth arrival list* in 1849, he kept a listing of visitors at his circulating library for public consultation. He also published guidebooks. The 1821 *Guide to the watering places on the coast between the Exe and the Dart* boasted sixteen aquatints by Daniel Havell, including, needless to say, one of 'Croydon's Public Library'.[18] *The Teignmouth, Dawlish and Torquay guide* of about 1828 contains eight lithographs by L. E. Reed.[19] Croydon's son, also named Edward, established a similar business in Victoria Parade, Torquay in the later 1830s.[20]

On the northern coast one of the leading bookselling businesses was that of John Banfield in the High Street, Ilfracombe. Established by 1820, at which date he registered his press, he soon opened a circulating library and in 1830 published a guide to Ilfracombe, a second edition appearing in

1834. Benefiting from the nearness of such famous beauty spots as Lynton and Lynmouth, he became the leading publisher of illustrated guidebooks in north Devon in the period between 1830 and 1860. His *Scenery in the North of Devon,* issued in about 1835, included at least 32 lithographs by W. and P. Gauci, G. Hawkins and others which were made up into series of booklets in various combinations.[21] He was still catering for the tourists in the late 1850s, when he started to publish *Banfield's Arrival List* during the season.[22] In Devonport the firm of Byers and Saunders published a number of series of illustrations between about 1828 and 1835 and other coastal towns, such as Dartmouth and Exmouth had similar establishments to Sidmouth, Teignmouth and Ilfracombe, demonstrating that the book trade throughout Devon was not slow in making the most of tourism, which was becoming the region's major industry.

These publishers used the skills of local engravers and lithographers, some of whom set up in business independently of the other local booksellers, printers and publishers. As well as working for Wallis, Henry Haseler also published a series of twelve views of Sidmouth on his own account in 1825.[23] But there are two local artist-publishers who dominated the scene. The first was George Rowe (1796-1864) whose earliest work *Forty-eight Views of Cottages and Scenery at Sidmouth, Devon* was published in 1826 by Wallis in Sidmouth.[24] Born in Exeter, he worked first from 38 Paris Street from about 1826 and later from Saville Cottage, Mount Radford. He was the most prolific of Devon artist engravers and lithographers, being responsible for over 300 Devon scenes many of which he published himself. He moved to Cheltenham in about 1833, where he was in partnership as Rowe & Norman, lithographic, copperplate and general letterpress printers. He was also active there as a drawing master, finding time to continue his production of Devon views. In 1852, following financial setbacks, he departed for the gold diggings in Bendigo, Australia to recoup his fortunes. He returned to England in 1858, dying in Exeter in 1864.[25]

In the 1840s William Spreat dominated the Exeter scene. Born in Exeter in 1816, the son of William Spreat, bookseller, he is recorded at Premier Place, Mount Radford in 1842, with business premises at 263 High Street from 1841 where his father had his bookselling premises, his widow Jane succeeding on William senior's death in 1847. Like Rowe he was a publisher as well as an artist, and is responsible for some 200 Devon scenes. One of the earliest of his publications was the *Picturesque Sketches of the Churches of Devon*, which came out in eighteen parts with seventy-four lithographs, being completed in 1842.[26] Some of his works were after other artists, such as a series of scenes of the newly completed South Devon Railway after sketches by the engineer William Dawson, which appeared in 1848.[27] He produced extensive series of views of north and south Devon, some of them numbered as two separate series. These appear to have been issued in collections in a bewildering variety of combinations. Spreat also published jointly with London publishers such as Ackermann and in 1844 a series of views of the river scenery of Devon was published by Spreat & Wallis, the latter being Henry John Wallis who was born in the West Indies and does not appear to be linked to John Wallis of Sidmouth.[28]

Nevertheless London continued to have make a major contribution to the production of Devon topographical prints. Perhaps the most remarkable example was the concurrent publication from 1829 of two series of illustrated works. The first was Thomas Moore's *History of Devonshire*[29] published in parts in three volumes by Jennings and Chaplin between 1829 and 1833 and the second was John Britton's *Devonshire illustrated*[30] published between 1829 and 1832. Both works were illustrated by an engraved title-page and ninety-four plates; both sets were steel line engravings of virtually identical format and there was a considerable overlap in subject coverage. At least one artist, W. H. Bartlett and one engraver, Henry Wallis even worked for both projects. However the results were a series of finely engraved plates which were very popular and reprinted on a number of occasions. The works of Turner were also being engraved at this period, including his atmospheric *Picturesque Views on the Southern Coast of England* of 1826 which included seventeen line engravings.[31]

In the second half of the nineteenth century the scene is dominated by the small-scale steel line-engraved vignette. These were produced in large numbers and catered for the cheaper end of the ever-expanding tourist market. The earliest major publisher in this field was J. Harwood of London who between 1841 and 1854 published well over one thousand views in his numbered series *Scenery of Great Britain*, about forty of them covering Devon.[32] He was followed by Kershaw & Son who published a similar number of vignettes between 1845 and 1860.[33] The most successful national publisher in this field was William Frederick Rock (1802-1890), a Barnstaple man who sought his fortune in London and began his series in 1848. This would eventually include some 7,000 views, 260 of them of Devon scenes.[34]

We owe the local production of steel line-engraved vignette views to Henry Besley, one of the most innovative printers in Exeter during the 1840s, who became the only significant Devon publisher in this field. Henry's father Thomas had established his printing office in South Street in the late 1790s. In about 1825 the elder Thomas took another son Henry into partnership and by 1828 had begun the series of trade directories of Exeter which continued until 1955, after which publication was continued by Kelly until 1973. In May 1834 Thomas senior relinquished his share in the business to Henry. Within a few years Henry began to exploit the growing tourist market resulting from the arrival of the railway in Exeter in 1844 and its extension to Newton Abbot in 1846 and Plymouth in 1849. He began the publication of a series of guide books to the western counties entitled 'Route Books' in 1844 and a similar series of 'Handbooks' in 1846. Each guidebook included an account of the sights to be seen from the recently constructed railway lines, showing commendable initiative in promptly meeting a new local demand. It soon became clear that these guides would sell better if they were illustrated and so Henry Besley launched into the production of steel engraved vignettes.[35]

In 1848, the same year as Rock began his series, Besley began to publish a series of larger vignettes, mainly by the local artist George Townsend (1818-1894) whose meticulous attention to detail more than compensated for any lack of artistic imagination. His pencil sketches were copied with the utmost fidelity by the unnamed steel engravers, as comparison with original sketches shows very clearly. In the years to 1871 this ran to about a hundred views of Devon and Cornwall.[36] A smaller series was introduced in 1853.[37] Both series were used in various collections. The large series was originally intended for a publication entitled *Illustrations of Devon,* to be issued in shilling parts, each containing three views and twelve pages of text. This project, advertised in *Besley's West of England Railway Companion no. 1* never seems to have materialized but the prints were issued separately or gathered into various booklets containing four, six or twelve views, or into cloth-covered albums containing thirty or sixty engravings normally entitled *Views in Devonshire* or *Views in Devonshire and Cornwall.* The smaller series of vignettes was more versatile. Not only were they collected into booklets of six or more views with such titles as *Peeps at Exeter and Neighbourhood* or *Peeps at the Headlands of South Devon,* but they also served to illustrate the *Route Book of Devon* and the various handbooks or local guides that the firm produced from the 1840s to the 1870s. The prints were also sold separately, printed on paper or card, and were used on notepaper as letterheads. The smaller series was numbered, the Cornish vignettes being allocated numbers running from 1 to 99 but overlapping with Devon, which started at 100. The first thirty-one views of Devon appeared in 1853 and a further ten in 1854, but thereafter the pace slackened. In about 1865, when the numbering had reached the 170s, George Townsend was replaced for a short period by J. W. Tucker (1808-69) and then by S. R. Ridgway. The last number known is 215, a view of Babbacombe after an unnamed artist, produced in about 1875. The numbering may have helped to develop the fashion for collecting these vignettes and manuscript albums are known giving accounts of visits to Torquay and other resorts copiously illustrated with vignettes by Besley and others. Although the alteration of steel engravings is a difficult task, involving the careful burnishing of the steel plate before new detail can be added, Besley made several attempts to update the illustrations and plates are known in two or more states, for example the large vignette entitled *Exeter (N.W.)*, first published in about 1848, was twice altered to show changes to St David's railway station.[38] Besley also experimented with tinted versions of the plates, often used in his 'Route Books'.

The engraved vignettes represented the final flowering of the medium. Wood engravings, which had the advantage that they could be printed together with the letterpress text, had made an appearance in such works as Thomas Shapter's *History of the Cholera in Exeter in 1832* which was published in 1849 and the medium was even used occasionally by local newspapers, for example for the Royal Agricultural Society exhibition at Exeter in July 1850.[39] Already photographers such as Francis Bedford were producing albums of photographic views. These were real photographs and were relatively expensive, so there was a market for the rather unsatisfactory chromolithographed screen-folds, printed in sepia on coated paper which were largely produced in Germany in the 1880s and 1890s. Photolithography made the publication of photographic albums of views a more viable possibility from the 1880s and the arrival of the picture postcard in the 1890s ensured that this method of reproduction became cheap and widespread. The use of etching, engraving, lithography and woodcut was now reserved for art prints – a different area of study from the use of these media to provide a topographical record before the advent of photography.

Notes

1. John Somers Cocks, *Devon topographical prints 1660-1870: a catalogue and guide* (Exeter, 1977). Hereafter referred to as 'Somers Cocks'.
2. Somers Cocks, source 2.
3. Somers Cocks, source 3.
4. Somers Cocks, source 21.
5. Somers Cocks, source 20.
6. Somers Cocks, source 16.
7. Somers Cocks, source 24.
8. Somers Cocks, source 12.
9. Somers Cocks, nos 794-5, 903-4.
10. Somers Cocks, source 33.
11. Somers Cocks, source 30.
12. Somers Cocks, source 94.
13. Somers Cocks, source 62.
14. Somers Cocks, no. 2473.
15. Ian Maxted, *The Devon book trades: a biographical dictionary* (Exeter, 1991), pp. 205-6.
16. Somers Cocks, source 55.
17. Somers Cocks, source 51, no. 652.
18. Somers Cocks, source 64.
19. Somers Cocks, source 95.
20. Maxted, *The Devon book trades*, p. 210-11.
21. Somers Cocks, source 128.
22. Maxted, *The Devon book trades*, p. 154.
23. Somers Cocks, source 75.
24. Somers Cocks, source 81.
25. Maxted, *The Devon book trades*, p. 113.
26. Somers Cocks, source 156.
27. Somers Cocks, source 174.
28. Somers Cocks, source 159; Maxted, *The Devon book trades*, p. 122.
29. Somers Cocks, source 103.
30. Somers Cocks, source 107.
31. Somers Cocks, source 82. For information on Turner's tours of the region, see Sam Smiles and Michael Pidgley, *The perfection of England: artist visitors to Devon c.1750-1870* (Exeter, 1995), pp. 99-106. This work is also useful for information on Samuel Prout and Frederic Christian Lewis.
32. Somers Cocks, source 223.
33. Somers Cocks, source 224.
34. Somers Cocks, source 226, p. 9.
35. Maxted, *The Devon book trades*, p. 36.
36. Somers Cocks, source 227.
37. Somers Cocks, source 228.
38. Somers Cocks, no. 948.
39. Todd Gray, *Exeter engraved. Volume 1: The secular city* (Exeter, 2000), pp. 187-206.

John Murray II and Oliver & Boyd, his Edinburgh agents, 1819-1835

PETER ISAAC

JOHN MURRAY I had had close contacts in Edinburgh with Charles Elliot, who had acted as his agent in the Scottish capital. Elliot died, still relatively young, in 1790, and so was not able to act as the Edinburgh agent of John Murray II, who married his daughter Anne in 1807. The younger Murray first worked with Archibald Constable, and later with William Blackwood, who acted as his agent for several years. John Murray II established the *Quarterly Review* at the beginning of 1809 and soon achieved success with this 'serious' periodical. Even earlier he had been in correspondence with Thomas Campbell about the possible establishment of a 'lighter-weight' monthly magazine, but this never came to pass.[1] When, therefore, Blackwood set up his *Edinburgh Monthly Magazine* in April 1817 Murray gave his support and, in August 1818, paid £1000 for a half-share,[2] and from this time took a very active interest in the magazine and its content.

Blackwood's original editors, Thomas Pringle and James Cleghorn, had been poached by Constable and were replaced by John Wilson and John Gibson Lockhart, Walter Scott's son-in-law and later editor of the *Quarterly*. At the same time the title was changed to *Blackwood's Magazine*.[3] Murray found the editors 'clever, but abusive, and exceedingly personal in their allusions',[4] and wrote many letters of protest to Blackwood about the tone of the magazine. Murray, who has been described as that 'timorous Tory',[5] and whose name as London publisher appeared in the imprint, wrote, on 28 September 1818, in very strong terms a long letter deprecating the personality of the articles.

Murray had become an important figure in literary circles as is clear from reading the full letter, in which he writes, *inter alia*, 'You must naturally be aware that all eyes are turned to me – who am so accessible from situation and the open house I keep',[6] and he was not prepared to put up with the opprobrium created. His name as London publisher appears for the last time on issue 22 for January 1819, and, on 17 December 1819,

Murray received £1000 in repayment of his share of *Blackwood's Magazine*.[7] William Blackwood ceased to be Murray's Edinburgh agent, and the Edinburgh firm of Oliver & Boyd (Thomas Oliver and George Boyd) was appointed, almost by the way, in a letter of 15 December 1819[8] – and so begins our story. In this letter Murray asks the Edinburgh firm to advertise immediately the *Quarterly Review* which he has sent,[9] and to seek subscriptions for *Anastasius*,[10] of which he has sent eighteen copies. He includes a draft of the advertisement for the *Quarterly*, showing Oliver & Boyd as the Scottish suppliers; this is to be inserted four times each in the Edinburgh *Mercury* and *Courant*, three times in Ballantyne's *Advertiser* and twice in the *Weekly Journal*. It is also to be placed four times in the Glasgow papers, and twice each in the papers of Aberdeen, Dumfries, Dundee, Inverness, Kelso and Perth. There is also a longer draft of the advertisement for *Anastasius* to be inserted six times in the 'best Edinb. Papers'. The terms of the agency were set out as follows:

The Quarterly Review is charged 100 cop' at the price of 96 only at 4/7 – & from the amount you will have a further commission upon all that have been sold at Seven & an half p' cent –

My other Books will be charged to you at the regular Sale prices – & from these you will be allowed a commission of 7½ p' Cent also.[11]

We will settle our accounts once a year on the 31st of June [*sic*] and I shall have the liberty to draw for the balance at 3, 6 & 9 months from the first of Sept following if you will write me a few lines to say you agree to these terms.

Oliver & Boyd accepted the terms in their letter of 21 December 1819, adding 'we understand that you pay for the Advertising, of which a regular account will be rendered you'; this practice seems to have been common in the trade.[12] They go on to urge the importance of their being provided with a list of the books Murray intends them to hold in stock and ask for an up-to-date catalogue. They 'will have Travellers out from this time till the middle of March – perhaps the better way will be to receive the Books direct from yourself, and as soon as possible after the list is sent'. The prompt receipt of sufficient copies of newly published books is a topic to which I shall return. Advertisements for new books 'may be advantageously sent to the Glasgow & some other provincial papers'.[13]

Oliver & Boyd entered into this agency with enthusiasm,[14] and in their letter of 5 January 1820 describe their difficulties in getting subscriptions for Spence's *Anecdotes*, until they get copies of the work as issued and know the published price.[15] They suggest that Murray should name a sum for the advertising of each work, 'leaving it to our discretion when & where to advertise'. *Anastasius* seems to have sold well and they ask for further supplies of the book and of Hall's voyage – in general they need three times the quantity that Murray had sent, going on 'we have little doubt that they would have been all sold before now, our being unable to supply orders for new works, has the appearance of giving preference which we are in future most anxious to avoid'.[16]

In his reply of 8 January 1820 Murray promises to send the booklist on Wednesday (12 January) and says that he has shipped the books ordered. He also sends a parcel of Spence's *Anecdotes*, which he asks Oliver & Boyd to push since another edition is on the market. Enough copies of *Anastasius* have still not been received in Edinburgh, and Oliver & Boyd ask for fifty copies, of which twenty-five are to be sent by the first coach;[17] they also ask for fifty copies each of Spence's *Anecdotes* and Hall's voyage, and twenty-five copies of the *Navy List*, continuing 'the trade are a great deal irritated at the repeated disappointments, which, from the trifling quantities of Anastasius &^{c} you sent, it has not been in our power to prevent'.[18] And in their letter of 5 February 1820 Oliver & Boyd ask Murray to inform them in writing the reason for the inadequate supply of *Anastasius* so that 'we may be able to satisfy the enquiries of the trade'.[19] They go on:

When new works come out in London, and only a few copies reach this distant part of the country the literary people have no other mode of gratifying their curiosity than by obtaining a perusal of one of these copies – If a competent supply of these new works were impressed in our hands about the time of their publication in London, it would in a great degree prevent this system – We presume this has escaped your observation as it cannot take place in London, where you have always a full supply. We beg that you will take this into your serious consideration for we who live upon the spot can assure you, that the injury from this cause is by no means inconsiderable.[20]

It seems clear that Murray was having difficulty in fixing the correct size of the initial shipment of new works to his Edinburgh agents, and to judge from the number of 'returns' in the ledgers this was a continuing problem, as, indeed, is demonstrated by Oliver & Boyd in their letter of 7 March 1820, when they write 'We have received from Mr Blackwood on your account, Books pr Invoice amounting to £741.16.8, many of them so much out of condition as to prevent their sale'.

Oliver & Boyd continued to feel that they were not supplied sufficiently quickly with new publications, and in their letter of 17 April 1821[21] George Boyd writes

Now my Dear Sir I hope you will pardon me for pointing out a circumstance which has lately occurred, and which your discriminating mind will at once see the propriety of avoiding in future, as your interest is essentially connected in correcting it – what I allude to I am aware has arisen from its having escaped your observation from the pressure of other more important business at the time – It is this, soon after your sale[22] to the Trade, and some time prior to supply of Lyons Travels &c.[23] having reached us, we were a good deal surprised to find that the market was preoccupied – now nothing can be easier for your warehouseman than to send us a supply before delivering the new works sold at your sale, so as to prevent the purchasers from sending down these to Scotland, and supplying the demand <u>before your own shipment arrives</u> – and it may perhaps be proper to take into view what I have ascertained to be the fact, that in order to fill the market in the first instance a quantity is forwarded by the mail by some of the purchasers <u>to our public sale rooms</u> in order as I presume to raise money – as they are frequently sold <u>at</u> and <u>under</u> subscription price ... which gives them an instant advantage over your agents –

Surely this is a diplomatic and justified dressing-down for Murray! What was happening here was that sale copies of books from London were reaching Edinburgh before Oliver & Boyd had received their supply for examination and display; as a result orders were being taken by other booksellers in Edinburgh, damaging the agency arrangement.

It seems that in his relationship with Oliver & Boyd Murray used his clerks to write the 'nasty' letters, and only four months later, R. Glynn, Murray's clerk wrote at his order:[24]

... he also desires me again to request you will have the kindness not to order more books at a time than you really want, as in many instances your demand regulates him in printing a second edition... North G Gazette[25] we sent 100, you immediately ordered 100 more, you have now 164 on hand –

He goes on to list several further examples of over-ordering, and adds 'will you have the goodness to say if there is not some mistake in this'. He urges the rapid shipping of returns 'as many will be entirely useless if not rec[d] immediately'.

In an earlier letter Murray must have expressed the view that a 'public shop is indispensable' for the sale of his books of a 'temporary nature'. The Edinburgh firm trenchantly disabuse him of the idea, and go on:

It is perfectly true that we have not a public shop and cannot give that publicity to works of this nature, as they may require – but this so far from being a disadvantage to their publicity is directly the reverse – By not having a public shop, and standing in the situation we do, with all the respectable Booksellers we do not come into immediate rivalship with them – In place of confining works of a temporary nature to be exhibited in one shop only, it gives us the advantage, that we have it in our power to place them in every respectable shop in Edinburgh, and in the country where we may chuse to send them...[26]

Oliver & Boyd are making it clear that they are wholesalers, and the tone of their letter suggests a hurt reply from a proud Edinburgh firm to a London-centred publisher, who backs off a little by offering complimentary comments in two letters later in the same year, but he still keeps on mentioning a shop. It appears that John Murray II never quite got to grips with needs of the Scottish market, for, after the return of another clerk, Edward Dundas, from a visit to Edinburgh at the end of 1831, he writes

Mr Dundas has satisfied me also – that I do not understand the most efficient means of advertising in the Scottish Newspapers – I shall in future with great satisfaction, confide this department ... entirely to your better intelligence & discression [sic] –[27]

That advertising was important to publishers is shown by the relatively large proportion that it formed of the 'production' costs of many books, in some cases coming second to the cost of paper. Iain Beavan, who has studied the archives of Oliver & Boyd, has given illuminating accounts of the advertising of Scottish publishers.[28] It must be made clear that the agency was a one-way arrangement: Murray was not the London agent of Oliver & Boyd. Jane Millgate reminds us that Robert Cadell, the Edinburgh publisher, commented that Murray could not offer 'the facilities of a wholesale house' which were necessary in an agent in London for a Provincial Publisher'.[29] In fact George & William Budd Whittaker, of 13 Ave Maria Lane, many of whose accounts are in the O & B Archives in the National Library of Scotland, were their London agents until December 1828, when Simpkin, Marshall took over.[30]

The Scottish Book Trade Index[31] shows both Thomas Oliver, who served his apprenticeship as a compositor to James Robertson, a printer of Horsewynd, Edinburgh, and George Boyd to have been printers. For some time the firm printed *Blackwood's Magazine*, but, like Murray, broke with it and ceased printing it at the end of 1820.[32] The largest element in this agency was the *Quarterly Review*, of which 1000 copies of each issue were sent to Edinburgh, at least until 1831, when George Thornton, Boyd's nephew, asked for the number to be reduced to 800.[33] From the beginning of their association the Edinburgh booksellers – George Boyd, I think from the hand – read and commented on the issue just received. For example, their letter of 21 December 1819 ends 'I am happy to find we make our Début with so respectable a number of the Quarterly'.[34]

Later letters go into much more detailed comment, showing that at least one of the Edinburgh partners had read the issue with friendly discrimination; for instance:

We are quite delighted with the last number of the Quarterly; and if it continues to embody the same learning, judgement, and talent, which this number displays, it will in our opinion after a few vibrations very soon exceed the circulation of its rival in Edinburgh – In the last number of each of these Reviews there is an article, which brings them into immediate competition – the article in the Edin we allude to is entitled "Recent Alarms" and that in the Quarterly "On the state of Public Affairs"[35] Making every allowance for the difference of Political Sentiment in the writers, we should think it impossible for any candid person to read these articles with attention, without being struck with the contrast between the profound political wisdom, the genuine English feeling, & the clear & honest statements by which the latter is distinguished, & the miserable perversion of acknowledged principles, the rankling enmity to the present government, even where its support is identified with the support of the Constitution so dear to every Briton, & the consequent sophistry in reasoning and distortion of facts, for which the former is equally remarkable...[36]

And he goes on to praise the review of Stephen's *Thesaurus* for its richness of Grecian literature. Three months later Murray replies 'I thank you for the flattering testimony you bear towards the Quarterly Review...', and goes on 'I was getting on fast with the next number – but Mr Gifford [the editor] is unfortunately very ill at present'.[37] Such comments appear in several later letters, usually unreservedly complimentary, but occasionally indicating doubt. In his letter of 30 May 1821[38] George Boyd writes

Since it was thought not degrading to the Quarterly Review to notice such a publication as the works of the Revd William Huntington SS ie, according to his interpretation, <u>Sinner Saved</u>, or as I would have interpreted it sanctimonious Scoundrel – the review of them has been managed in a very judicious and masterly way–[39]

Having access to both 'ends' of the correspondence allows the painting of a fuller picture than one set of letters alone could produce, but, as the problems Murray seems to have had with Dr (Later Sir) David Brewster (1781-1868) show, even the fuller picture may not be the whole. John Robison (1739-1805), an important Scottish scientist and contemporary of James Watt, had published *Outlines of a Course of Lectures on Mechanical Philosophy* in 1797, and Murray decided, it would seem in 1815, to issue a revised edition, which he commissioned Brewster to prepare.[40] In June 1815 Brewster was paid £500 for the copyright of his work, and appears to have got to work fairly rapidly, the Murray ledger showing a payment of £122.0s.3d for printing to Allan & Co, of Edinburgh, on 15 March 1816, and payments on 23 September 1816 of £137.8s.0d to Cowan & Co for paper and of £77.1s.0d to Lizars for engraving plates.[41] In a letter of 25 September 1818 to William Blackwood Murray writes 'I am perfectly delighted with D' Brewster'.[42] Although, therefore, things seem to have started well Murray later became very impatient with Brewster's delays, and this is reflected in many letters from Murray to Oliver & Boyd, who, in this case, were writing as printers rather than agent. (Since Brewster was working in Scotland Murray used the Edinburgh firm to press him.)

On 7 March 1820[43] Oliver & Boyd sent Murray a memorandum from Brewster, 'who appears very anxious to have D' Robisons works finished', and who asks that Bishop Gleig (George Gleig (1753-1840), Bishop of Brechin) should be approached for permission to reproduce the article that he had written on optics for the *Encyclopædia Britannica*.[44] A summary, written on the letter in what looks like Murray's almost illegible hand, shows that volumes 1 & 4 were finished (presumably meaning printed), volume 2 was half finished, and that none of volume 3 was printed; it concludes 'the whole may be finished in 2 or 3 months' – over-optimistic as it turned out! The Edinburgh firm ask if they may go ahead with the printing of volume 3.

Three days later Murray replies that the printing of volume 3 may be undertaken and that he wants Brewster to proceed on the revision as quickly as possible.[45] He clearly does not like the idea of approaching Gleig or Robison's family 'who may be less inclined to take trouble for me ... & they have received £500 from me three years ago – pray see what you can do in this affair'.[46] On receiving Murray's letter George Boyd called on Brewster and reported 'D' B has promised to attend to your instructions without delay, but we are afraid he will require a good deal of spurring to make him move'.[47] And so it goes on, Murray remarking in his letter of 18

November 1820[48] 'Dr Brewsters conduct ... is base in the extreme – & at present arrangement [?] I have been cheated of about £1000'.[49]

At last, a year later, Murray writes:

I yesterday received a Letter from Dr Brewster giving me the long considered hopeless, intimation that "Dr Robisons Works may now be finished in a fortnight, if the printer chooses to be active".[50]

He asks the printer to complete the work 'with all possible expedition', and reports that Brewster recommends that the fifty plates should be 'put up in a separate volume'. He asks for two complete copies in quires to be sent to London by coach, and wonders whether the work extends to four or five volumes. He also requests Oliver & Boyd to 'collect the accounts from the different Printers & Stationers, Engravers &c most of them paid or partly paid' so that he can make a proper estimate of the total cost. A note from Brewster, of 19 December 1821,[51] asks Oliver & Boyd to send their 'Foreman over as early as possible tomorrow Morning to receive all the remaining copies of Robison'.[52] The work was published the following year.

Why do I suggest that this is not the whole story? Brewster was a very active experimenter and a prolific writer, as well as editing the *Edinburgh Encyclopædia*, and so it might not have been unexpected that he could not find time to carry out Murray's commission. However, his entry in the *DNB* records that the editor of the *North British Review* says:

He contributed an article to each number during the time I was editor and in each instance... the manuscript made its appearance on the appointed day with punctual regularity.

An earlier editor confirms this:

Sir David Brewster was ever remarkable for the carefulness of his work, the punctuality with which it was delivered, never behind time, never needing to write to the editor for more time or more space – a model contributor in every way.

And finally, to put a further gloss on the matter, it is worth noting that he wrote five articles for Murray for the *Quarterly Review* and two books for his 'Family Library'. I leave this with you as a topic for further investigation.[53]

While we may believe that the early nineteenth century was a time of greater politeness in correspondence than is now common, the Murray Archives show that John Murray II could write excoriating letters when he felt that circumstances called for them.[54] What is noticeable, however, throughout this correspondence is the underlying note of friendliness on both sides, George Boyd, for instance, writing on 31 May 1821[55] his sadness at hearing of the death of John Murray's son, William. Murray made a point of inviting George Boyd to his home,[56] whenever the latter came to London, even to Christmas dinner in 1826;[57] Boyd was not able to come on that occasion, but sent a cake and a volume of sacred poetry to Anne Murray, for both of which she thanks him.[58] And similar invitations were made by George Boyd to the Murray family when they were in Edinburgh.[59] As his father grew older John Murray III took a larger part in the business, including travelling to Edinburgh and elsewhere. He made gifts to George Boyd; for example, on 4 January 1828[60] he sends 'Ld Byrons Autograph as well as some Plates which as they are not to be procured any where, may assist the embellishment of your copy of his works'. (It was not until later that *Finden's Illustrations of the Life and Works of Lord Byron*[61] were issued in monthly parts each with four plates at 2s.6d.)

Time and again Oliver & Boyd show themselves concerned for Murray's good; on 27 November 1822, for instance, they write apologetically:[62]

There is a most abominable note to a review of the Liberal in the last number of Constables Magazine, insinuating that you are the proprietor of that work, because we had, unfortunately a few copies of it for sale.

The Liberal, a magazine started in 1822 by Byron and Leigh Hunt must have seemed objectionable to our 'timorous Tory', and the Edinburgh firm felt that they had damaged Murray's reputation by selling it.[63] George Thornton, Boyd's nephew, writes from Dublin on 31 August 1827:

I beg leave to enclose you a copy of a Bill which has been very generally handed about in Dublin both in Booksellers' shops and to the public on the streets. I have seen a copy of Moore's Works which is wretchedly printed. From some conversations which I have had here, not a doubt remains that these works are printed in Dublin. The person who disposes of them goes about with a gig or cart, from which he supplies the books as purchased... he goes from house to house disposing of his wares... I have thus deemed it prudent to advise you in order that your property may be protected, and that steps may be taken if possible to put a stop to such detestable traffic.[64]

And Thornton sends a printed notice of an 'American Edition' of the *Works* of Thomas Moore and of a two-volume edition of the *Works* of Lord Byron, which is subscribed 'Philadelphia, June 1st, 1827'.

Several publishers became bankrupt in 1826, a bad year for bookselling, among them the Edinburgh firm of Archibald Constable & Co, with which Hurst, Robinson & Co, of London, 'was hopelessly involved'. 'The market was flooded with the dishonoured papers of all these concerns, and mercantile confidence in the great publishing houses was almost at an end.'[65] Oliver & Boyd kept an eye on the Edinburgh developments, writing on 27 April 1826

We are afraid that Constable & Cos estate will turn out to be very bad; & we understand that the stock & copyrights will be of little value, arising from the nature of their arrangements with Hurst & Co – Mr Cowan, the Trustee, is very close at present upon the subject; but we hope to be able soon to give you more particulars. – When the failure took place, we were in their debt £8.–[66]

Murray, too, was in financial difficulty at this time, at least partly due to the failure of his attempt to establish a daily paper, *The Representative*. However, Sutherland, in his analysis of the 1826 'crash' concludes

Why, one may ask, does the 1826 crash loom so mythically large and calamitous in literature-publishing history? The reason, I suspect, is to be found in the principal sources: Charles Knight, Samuel Smiles, Lockhart, and Archibald Constable… Knight was practically ruined by the crisis; Constable's father and Lockhart's father-in-law were actually ruined. Samuel Smiles sees 1826 as the only reverse experienced by the otherwise all-conquering Murray dynasty…[67]

Even after the agency ended Oliver & Boyd were willing to assist Murray. In November 1836 Edward Dundas, one of Murray's clerks, writes asking them to advertise some of the London publisher's books, listing the books concerned, and adding 'Mr Murray will leave to your judgement & discretion the amount should not be large'.[68] A general friendliness continued after the agency had ended. Indeed, when, after the death of John Murray II, his son developed the Colonial & Home Library, Oliver & Boyd were wholesalers rather than exclusive agents in Scotland; in a letter of 6 September 1843 Murray seeks the agreement of the Edinburgh firm to his giving Griffin, of Glasgow, the same terms of sale for this Library, because of 'their connexion in the Colonies & elsewhere'.[69]

Murray's Trade Ledgers,[70] giving his accounts with booksellers, show the considerable value of the books sent to Edinburgh and the frequency of the shipments.[71] In each of the first two years Murray sent books to the value of about £5000, with 'returns' of about one-tenth of that value. Over forty shipments were made in each of these years. These figures varied from year, with highs in the early 1830s, falling off in the last three years of the agency. The unsold stock remaining at the end of each year, and the quantity of returns also varied widely. The decrease in Edinburgh sales after 1833 had not been missed by Murray, but the friendship between him and George Boyd inhibited him for some time from taking action, and, indeed, although this was the ostensible reason for ending the agency, it seems that the principal reason was that the Edinburgh booksellers could not be expected to 'push' Murray's Family Library in view of their own Edinburgh Cabinet Library.

With the wisdom of hindsight we may see the problem developing in Murray's letters. On 30 March 1829 Murray sent specimens of the proposed front and engraving for the Library, asking Oliver & Boyd to 'estimate the immediate demand for it in Scotland', while on the same day Edward Dundas gives details of the prices, with the reminder that each volume was to be published in 1s parts, though this does not seem to have been the case.[72] We do not have any replies from Edinburgh, but things must have gone on, and, five years later, the younger Murray, at that time in Edinburgh, writes

The opinion has been stated by many – not only in the South, but here in Scotland – during my visit, that it would be out of the question to expect your co-operation in the latter work [the Family Library] as you were so deeply engaged in one of so nearly similar nature yourself – I do not however lightly give ear to such insinuations – on the contrary I have perfect confidence in your zeal, & am in expectation that I shall be borne out in this, by an increase of sale in Scotland corresponding with that in England...[73]

Apparently to reinforce his belief in the Family Library he transcribes a letter from the Lord Advocate[74] to his father, which starts 'I cannot tell when I have been as much gratified by any book, as by that beautiful Life of Crabbe', which did not, in fact, appear in the Family Library.[75]

Just over a year later Murray had decided to bring the agency arrangement to an end, as we see from a letter of 1 April 1835, again written by a clerk, Edward W. Dundas, from which a long extract may be quoted here.[76]

Mr Murray has desired me to write to you on a matter of importance respecting his agency in Scotland, which you have held for several years; and, till within these few years past (since your own business has increased so largely) to Mr Murrays entire satisfaction – But Mr Murray has for sometime felt that his agency has ceased to be an object to you, and knowing that your well merited success in business has been the cause of it he has considered that he ought not to complain, and has consequently been (tho somewhat reluctantly) silent in his correspondence with you – There exists besides other reasons why Mr Murray found it difficult to express his feelings on this matter to yourselves, namely, your long connexion with him and your punctual and honorable [*sic*] conduct in the commercial transactions which have taken place between yourselves and him in your capacity as Agents – But at the same time Mr Murray has considered it but due to himself that he should endeavour to find other Agents to whom his Business would be of more prominent importance than it has appeared to be of late years to yourselves – Mr Murray has therefore made choice of Mess" Blackwood... Nevertheless, convinced as M' Murray is, that it is to his Interest and advantage to make this change it is not without some pain that he severs a commercial connexion of such duration and one, on which (at least on his part) there has been no cause for regret, except on the general grounds above mentioned. The unpleasant feelings which arise on his doing so however, are qualified by Mr Murrays considering that the cause which has led him to this determination is one, on which, rather than complain of – he can congratulate you, as it is the result of your long career of well earned success... M' Murray at the same time desires me to add that he will be happy to leave his present stock in your hands for sale by yourselves on the usual terms or he will continue to forward you such of his publications as you may require for your own use...

This letter says more to me about the friendly and hospitable, but always businesslike, character of John Murray II – but not of his politics – than does Samuel Smiles's two-volume *Memoir and Correspondence of the late John Murray* (1891).

In this short paper I have concentrated on a few aspects only of the agency. Most of George Boyd's comments on the articles in the *Quarterly Review* have been omitted, as have the frequent mentions of how well, or ill, one book or another is selling. Both topics would justify further study. In particular, the latter, together with correspondence from other booksellers in the Murray Archives, would add flesh to the financial details to be found in the Ledgers. Both archives offer rich sources of information on publishing and bookselling in the first half of the nineteenth century, and can say much on how authors and publishers interacted.

Acknowledgements

This paper could not have been written without the encouragement and assistance of Virginia Murray, Archivist to John Murray (Publishers) Ltd, of Warren McDougall and of Iain Beavan. I am also very grateful to Murray Simpson, Keeper of Special Collections at the National Library of Scotland, for easing my way into that friendly and helpful institution. I am especially grateful to Pearson Education Limited for permission to quote from the Oliver & Boyd Archives.

Notes

1. Samuel Smiles, *Memoir and Correspondence of the late John Murray* (London, 1891), 1, p. 475.
2. Smiles, *Memoir*, 1, pp. 476-80.
3. Smiles, *Memoir*, 1, p. 477.
4. Smiles, *Memoir*, 1, p. 479.
5. Dr Peter Cochran to the author – see Peter Isaac, 'Byron's publisher and his printers', *Newstead Abbey Byron Society Review* (July 2000), 86-96.
6. These letters from Murray to Blackwood are now in the Murray Archives. The letter of 28 September 1818 runs to eleven quarto pages.
7. Smiles, *Memoir*, 1, pp. 494-5.
8. Murray's letter-book (March 1803 to September 1823) transcribes only the terms of the agency; the full letter is in the Oliver & Boyd Archives in the National Library of Scotland [hereafter NLS] (ref Acc 5000/189 (1819) &c). Murray's letters to Oliver & Boyd in these Archives will be identified by date.
9. Complimentary copies of the *Quarterly Review* were to be sent by Oliver & Boyd to Miss Gillilands, James Hogg and Walter Scott.
10. *Anastasius: or the Memoirs of a Greek*; this three-volume book, published anonymously, was by Thomas Hope. The third edition was reviewed by Henry Matthews in the *Quarterly Review*, no. 48, vol 24 (Januray 1821, issued April), 511-29. The reviewer concludes 'the book … is rational and absurd, profound and shallow, amusing and tiresome, to a degree beyond what we should have thought it possible to achieve in the same performance'. Murray asks for copies to be sent to Scott and Hogg. A total of 4000 copies were printed in four editions in 1819 and 1820 by William Bulmer and Thomas Davison.
11. In the Murray Subscription Books there were normally three prices. For example, in the Subscription Book for 1814-1819 (ff. 201-2), dated 6 December 1819, is the entry for *Anastasius* '3 vols cr 8° Sells 31/6 Subscrib^d 22/3 now offered 21/- on Sale acc'; 408 copies are listed against the names of (mainly London) booksellers. Very occasionally, perhaps because a new edition was planned, there is a fourth, slightly lower, price.
12. The original letters are in the Murray Archives [hereafter MA] and will be identified by date.
13. An entertaining account of publishers' travellers will be found in Bill Bell, '"Pioneers of literature": the commercial traveller in the early nineteenth century', *The Reach of Print: Making, Selling & Using Books*, ed. by Peter Isaac & Barry McKay (New Castle, DE, 1998), pp. 121-34.
14. The greater number of letters from Murray to Oliver & Boyd in the National Library of Scotland suggests that it cannot be assumed that the Murray Archives still hold all the letters from the Edinburgh firm, but it is illuminating to note that the twenty-two letters of the Scottish agents are distributed by date as follows: 1819 1, 1820 7, 1821 6 (one of which is missing), 1822 1, 1826 3, 1827 1 (from George Thornton, George

Boyd's nephew, in Dublin), 1830 1, 1831 1, and 1833 1. The corresponding numbers of letters from London to Edinburgh are 1819 1, 1820 6, 1821 3, 1822 2 (one of which is missing), 1823 5, 1824 1, 1826 9 (including two invitations to George Boyd, who was in London, to Christmas dinner), 1827 1, 1828 1, 1829 2, 1830 2, 1831 2, 1832 2, 1833 1, 1834 1, 1835 1, and 1836 1.

15. Joseph Spence, *Anecdotes of Books and Men*, ed. by E. Malone (1820).

16. Capt Basil Hall, *Voyage to the West Coast of Corea and the Loo-Choo Islands* (1818).

17. 17. MA 11 January 1820.

18. Murrays published the Navy List from 1814 to at least 1877; John Murray II described himself as 'Publisher to the Admiralty'.

19. Murray had mentioned that a new edition was in preparation.

20. MA 5 February 1820.

21. MA 17 April 1821.

22. In the late autumn it was Murray's custom to invite a number of leading London booksellers to dinner at the Albion, in Aldersgate Street, for a trade sale; large numbers of many titles were sold at the fixed 'sale' price, the 'bidding' being on number rather than price.

23. Capt George Francis Lyon, *Travels in North Africa 1818-1820* (1821); an edition of 1000 was printed by Thomas Davison, of Whitefriars, who printed almost all the early editions of Byron's works for Murray. Murray published several other works by Lyon. We now think of this kind of book as 'serious', but travel books were then considered 'temporary' as is clearly indicated in the letter of 7 May 1799 from George Nicol to Sir Joseph Banks, discussing a second edition of Mungo Park's *Travels in the Interior of Africa*; he writes 'Besides a Book not to be bought is always borrowed, & being a Book merely of entertainment, once read is never Purchased' (see Peter Isaac, *William Bulmer: the Fine Printer in Context* (London, 1993), 48).

24. NLS Acc 5000/189 (1821), 27 August 1821.

25. *North Georgia Gazette and Winter Chronicle*, ed. by Edward Sabine (1821).

26. MA 5 February 1820.

27. NLS Acc 5000/196, 7 December 1831.

28. Iain Beavan, 'Advertising judiciously: Scottish nineteenth-century publishers and the British market', *The Mighty Engine: the Printing Press and its Impact* ed. by Peter Isaac & Barry McKay (New Castle, DE., 2000), pp. 69-78.

29. J. Millgate, *Scott's Last Edition* (Edinburgh, 1987), p. 126.

30. I am grateful to Iain Beavan for this information.

31. The Scottish Book Trade Index has been put on line by the National Library of Scotland at www.nls.uk/catalogues/resources/sbti/index/html, and is also available on CD-ROM.

32. MA 1 January 1821.

33. MA 3 May 1831; Oliver & Boyd asked permission to return a surplus of 'former numbers of the Review, which have been encreasing [*sic*] on our hands for sometime back'.

34. MA 21 December 1819.

35. The article in *Quarterly Review*, 22 (January 1820), 492-560, was by Robert Grant.

36. MA 27 March 1820.

37. NLS Acc 5000/189 (1820), 3 July 1820.
38. MA 30 May 1821.
39. The lengthy and rather savage review 'The works of the Reverend William Huntington, S.S.' (*Quarterly Review*, 24, 462-510) was by Robert Southey. William Huntington, the 'coal-heaver' preacher, eventually established a chapel in Gray's Inn Lane, where he received the support of the fine printer Thomas Bensley, who printed (probably at his own expense and, therefore, cheaply) many of his sermons.
40. See *DNB*.
41. Part of this story may be worked out from the Murray Archives, ledger B folio 7, which shows only some of the dates. There are other charges for engraving, paper and printing; both Clarke and Ballantyne are also shown as printers.
42. MA, letter from John Murray II to William Blackwood of 25 September 1818.
43. MA 7 March 1820.
44. See *DNB*.
45. NLS Acc 5000/189 (1820), 10 March 1820.
46. This payment may be found in the MA, ledger B folio 7.
47. MA 27 March 1820.
48. NLS Acc 5000/189 (1820), 18 November 1820.
49. Murray seems to have been overstating the case: this sum was made up of his advance on royalties and printing costs so far incurred. In 1822 Murray received 996 copies of the work, of which 719 were eventually sold 25 as 24 for £2.8s each, and 239 were remaindered to Thomas Tegg at 22s each, giving a loss by 1830 of £257.18s.7d; it is to be noted that this loss includes £147 interest to 10 January 1823 on the £500 advance and almost £100 for advertising.
50. NLS Acc 5000/189 (1821), 2 November 1821.
51. NLS Acc 5000/189 918 (1821).
52. He is probably using the now forgotten printer's term 'copy' for the manuscript to be set by the compositor.
53. The Murray Archives have a substantial collection of Brewster's letters to Murray, which would repay further study.
54. See, for example, his letter of 11 April 1817 to the printer, John Fowler Dove (MA, Letter Book (March 1803 to September 1823), f. 394), which was quoted at length in Peter Isaac, 'Byron's publisher and his "spy": constancy and change among John Murray II's printers, 1812-1831', in *The Library*, 6 ser, 19 (1997), 1-24 (9-10).
55. MA 31 May 1821.
56. To Wimbledon in September 1823, when Murray offered Boyd a bed for the night (NLS Acc 5000/190 (1823); Boyd was in the habit of lodging at Anderton's Coffee House in Fleet Street.
57. By this time the formal invitation is written from 14 Whitehall Place (NLS Acc 5000/192 (1826)). Soon afterwards Murray had to sell this property to recoup his losses after the failure of *The Representative*, a daily paper which the young Benjamin Disraeli, who was to edit it, had persuaded him to set up (see Smiles, *Memoir*, 2, 182 sqq, 208, 214-15).
58. NLS Acc 5000/192 (1826), letter of 22 December 1826.

59. For example, John Murray III has to refuse such an invitation because he has to go into Fife (NLS Acc 5000/193 (1827), 20 July 1827), and 'Mr, Mrs and the Misses Murray, regret very much that a previous engagement prevents...' (NLS Acc 5000/194 (1830), 18 September 1830).

60. NLS Acc 5000/194.

61. The letterpress notes to the illustrations by William Brockeden were issued later, also in parts. See also John Murray II's letter of 7 December 1831 (NLS Acc 5000/196).

62. MA 27 November 1822.

63. Four numbers only of the magazine appeared (see *The Oxford Companion to English Literature*, 4th edn (1967), pp. 130 & 407).

64. MA, letter from George Thornton of 31 August 1827 together with the printed notice.

65. Smiles, *Memoir*, 2, 212.

66. MA 27 April 1826.

67. John Sutherland, 'The British book trade and the crash of 1826', *The Library*, 6 ser, 9 (1987), 148-61 (161).

68. NLS Acc 5000/192 (1826), letter of 21 November 1836.

69. NLS Acc 5000/202, 6 September 1843. See also Angus Fraser, 'John Murray's Colonial and Home Library', *Papers of the Bibliographical Society of America*, 91 (1997), 339-408.

70. MA, Trade Ledgers F, ff. 291-9, and G, ff. 257-65, 322 & 339.

71. As the correspondence makes clear, unless especially urgent, these books were sent by sea. For example, in a brief note accompanying an order for various quantities of six titles, George Thornton writes 'We shall be obliged by your forwarding the above, by Steamer, if any, or by smack' (MA 10 November 1826).

72. NLS Acc 5000/194.

73. NLS Acc 5000/197, letter of 18 February 1834.

74. Francis Jeffrey was Lord Advocate from 2 December 1830 to 17 May 1834.

75. *The Poetical Works of the Rev George Crabbe: with his Letters and Journals, and His Life, by His Son*, 8 vols (London: John Murray, 1834). Did Murray, perhaps, give only the volume(s) containing the life to the Lord Advocate?

76. MA, letter-book (1823-1839), ff. 165-6; the letter was signed by Edward W. Dundas, another of Murray's clerks, who spent much of his time on the road for Murray.

John Murray, Richard Griffin and Oliver & Boyd: some supplementary observations

IAIN BEAVAN

PROFESSOR ISAAC, in his study of the wholesale trade agreement between John Murray II and the Edinburgh firm of Oliver & Boyd, has done bibliographical scholarship a considerable service in elucidating a number of fundamental features relating to the economics and distributional arrangements of the nineteenth-century book trade. Moreover, his paper reflects the competitiveness between, yet also the interdependence of those firms (based in England and Scotland) that were sufficiently aspiring or ambitious to aim to publish within a British (and Irish) market. But levels of interdependence differed: Murray, the majority of whose sales would have been within southern England, needed a wholesaler that could and would work at promoting his publications within Scotland, thus maximizing sales, whereas Oliver & Boyd needed George Whittaker & Co. in London (replaced, later, by Simpkin, Marshall) to provide the initial distributional point for a significant proportion of any edition that the Edinburgh firm published with the British market in mind.[1]

Recent research into the Scottish book trade has provided further contextual background to Professor Isaac's descriptions and analyses of events. In particular, Robert Cooke's letter of 6 September 1843 to Oliver & Boyd, referring to the possibility of the Glasgow firm of Richard Griffin also acting as wholesale agents for Murray's series, the Colonial and Home Library, can be more fully appreciated when set against the rapidly growing tensions in the Scottish (and British) retail and wholesale book trade.[2]

To be or not to be?

Professor Isaac draws attention to a letter of April 1835 from Murray to Oliver & Boyd that suggests that the London firm was to end the agency agreement. If the agency agreement between Oliver & Boyd and John Murray II did indeed come to an end at that time, then it was neither absolute, nor final. The Edinburgh firm was still acting for Murray a year later, as is evident from their advertising accounts. In February 1837, the proprietors of the *Edinburgh Weekly Journal* sent to Oliver & Boyd their account from July to December 1836. The account is very detailed, and lists the individual titles for which advertisements were placed. Along with notices of Oliver & Boyd's *Penny* and *Threepenny Almanacs*, their *New Edinburgh Almanac* and vol. 21 of their Edinburgh Cabinet Library (*An Historical Account of the Circumnavigation of the Globe*), the firm was charged for the inclusion of advertisements in the newspaper for an edition of Byron, Sir Alexander Burnes's *Travels into Bokhara*, Henry Knight's *Architectural Tour of Normandy*, and Sir George Back's *Narrative of an Expedition in H.M.S. Terror...[to] the Arctic*, all titles published by John Murray.[3]

Further evidence of the continuance of the agency agreement can be brought forward. In early 1843, Robert Cooke wrote twice on behalf of John Murray II to the new partners of Oliver & Boyd. The first of the two letters essentially seeks confirmation of the wholesale prices applied by the Edinburgh firm. Thus his letter of 25 February: 'Have the goodness to inform us, upon what terms Mr Murray's Publications are offered to the Edinburgh trade by you'. His note of 18 March is yet more explicit: 'Have the goodness to cause the insertion of the enclosed [advertisements] in the Scotch Papers & charge the same to our account' and continued, 'We trust to your active exertions with our publications' as your firm 'now, has solely, our Scotch agency business'.[4]

Stifling competition?
Did Griffin at any time manage to break into Oliver & Boyd's monopoly? Far from decrying Oliver & Boyd's efforts in promoting the Colonial Library, Cooke's letter of 6 September 1843 (referred to above) carefully acknowledged that the Edinburgh firm in fact wanted a further supply of prospectuses for the series, and noted that 'with the Quarterly Review you will receive 500 Copies', and then stuck a tentative and respectful tone in noting that 'Mr. Murray is anxious to consult you respecting a proposition which he has received from Messrs Griffin of Glasgow, wishing to be appointed agents for the work in Glasgow'. Cooke's final paragraph came to the essence of the matter: '[Mr Murray] would therefore be glad to hear from you by return, whether you have any objection to his giving Messr' Griffin the work on easier terms than he otherwise would, but not ostensibly making them agents. It is of course his desire not to annoy you,

but for <u>this</u> <u>work</u> so many <u>extra</u> means are required to bring it fully into play'.

John Murray III was swayed by the apparent potential of Griffin to promote the work 'owing to the nature of their business' and their connections overseas, yet clearly claimed to want to avoid any irritation to Oliver & Boyd, one of the more important and influential firms in the Scottish trade. Richard Griffin & Co. may well have had these connections, and may thereby have been able to offer extra retail outlets for the series, but, significantly, they were very evidently also trying to break from their reliance on Oliver & Boyd as major wholesalers in Scotland.

The Glasgow firm loathed Oliver & Boyd with a passion. The two firms held totally divergent and incompatible views on the principles (or, arguably, lack of them) and consequences of retail underselling (or price fixing). Oliver & Boyd, unqualifiedly in favour of the retention of the full, stipulated retail price of a book, were perceived by Griffin & Co. as coercing retail (and other wholesale) booksellers into applying (with few exceptions) that full retail price. This enforcement (which was made entirely explicit) was effected by the simple expedient of refusing to supply with stock any retail booksellers who were deemed to have been underselling. And, provided the established wholesale trade presented a reasonably united front on this issue, there was little the (dependent) retailers could do.[5] Moreover, the view of Griffin & Co. on this debate was at odds with that of John Murray whose firm had been resolute throughout in holding to a fixed retail price.[6]

Given the degree of enmity (which had been growing through the 1830s) between Oliver & Boyd and Griffin & Co.[7] it is most unlikely that the Edinburgh firm would have thought benignly of Murray's allowing, at a time of increasing commercial competition, preferential terms to a company that was perceived by many as determinedly wanting to extend the principles of free trade into the bookshop, thereby undermining what were accepted by others as long-established and beneficial trade practices. But, notwithstanding any differences of opinion on the underselling controversy, John Murray wrote to Griffin on 11 September 1843 (five days after seeking Oliver & Boyd's views) offering the Glasgow firm preferential terms on the series.[8]

A few months later, Griffin & Co. attempted to build on their discreet agreement with Murray, by suggesting that the London firm's publications were not always easily available in Glasgow (particularly in quantity), and that they (Griffin) would be prepared to act as agents for a wider range of their publications. Robert Cooke chose to tell Oliver & Boyd of this approach, and wrote to them that

as there must be a very large demand for books in Glasgow, Mr Murray is very anxious to hear from you whether it would not be worth your while to make some arrangement with a house there to keep a stock of his publications as it is by no means his wish or desire to open another account in Scotland to interfere with your agency, being perfectly satisfied with the active exertions you invariably make for the success of his works.[9]

Oliver & Boyd's response was undoubtedly both unambiguous and decisive. There was no realistic possibility of Oliver & Boyd's allowing Griffin any form of competitive edge. This much is clear from Cooke's subsequent letter, in which he states that 'Mr Murray is in receipt of yours this morning & which is perfectly satisfactory & I ~~will~~ have written by this post to decline Messrs G & Co's offer'.[10] Matters were not quickly resolved as the commercial relationship between Oliver & Boyd and Griffin further deteriorated through 1844, with the publication (compiled by John Joseph Griffin) of *Is the Glasgow Booksellers' Protection Association a Lawful Association?*, followed by *The Glasgow Booksellers' Conspiracy under a New Cloak*, which contained some bitter attacks on Oliver & Boyd themselves.[11]

Acknowledgements

First, to Professor Peter Isaac, for having granted me access to his paper in pre-publication form; acknowledgements are also due to the following for permission to quote from their papers, or from material under their curatorship: Pearson Education Ltd (Oliver & Boyd papers); National Library of Scotland; Arts Department, Mitchell Library, Glasgow.

Notes

1.   In March 1810, John Murray II complained of unfair treatment in not being offered a share in the publication of Walter Scott's *Lady of the Lake* – the work was effectively published by John Ballantyne & Co. of Edinburgh who had purchased 75% of the copyright, and had invited William Millar (rather than Murray) to become owner of the remaining 25%. In the letter, Murray made the point that Scottish sales of his publications should not be underestimated, and commented that 'you appear to forget that your engagement was that I should be your sole agent here, [i.e. London] and that you were to publish nothing but what I was to have the offer of a share in', and continued, 'the sole agency for my publications in Edinburgh is worth to any man who understands his business £300 a year; but this requires zealous activity and deference on

one side, and great confidence on both, otherwise the connection cannot be advantageous or satisfactory to either party'. Quoted in Samuel Smiles, *A Publisher and his Friends: Memoir and Correspondence of the Late John Murray*. 2 vols (London: Murray, 1891), I, pp. 174-75. In 1819, Oliver & Boyd offered Whittaker a 50% share in the copyright of Robert Mudie's novel, *Glenfergus*. The other half of the copyright was purchased by Oliver & Boyd who acted as the managing partners. Whittaker's share in the copyright of *Glenfergus* was expressed directly as physical copies, as fully half the print-run was sent south to London to be subscribed by the trade there. Such a pattern of distribution was not unusual. See the relevant Oliver & Boyd papers (Acc 5000) in the National Library of Scotland, and brought together under 'Glenfergus' in http://www.british-fiction.cf.ac.uk

2. The letter is one that passed between those only recently to have become heads of their respective firms. John Murray II died in June 1843, his firm then taken over by his son, John III. (Robert Cooke was cousin of John III, and partner in the firm.) See William Zachs *et al.*, 'Murray family (per. 1768-1967), publishers', in *Oxford DNB*. On George Boyd's death on 1 February 1843, Thomas Oliver retired as partner. The firm's partners became John Boyd (brother of George) and John's two sons: Thomas Jefferson and John (jnr). The business was effectively run by Thomas Jefferson Boyd and John (jnr). See notice to such effect in the Oliver & Boyd papers, Acc 5000/202.

3. 'Advertising A/c Weekly Journal, Jany to Decr 1836', Acc 5000/53.

4. Both letters in Acc 5000/202.

5. For a fuller discussion see I. Beavan, '"What Constitutes the Crime which it is Your Pleasure to Punish so Mercilessly?"' in *The Moving Market* ..., ed. by Peter Isaac and Barry McKay (New Castle: Oak Knoll P., 2001), pp. 71-82.

6. For several references to Griffin and Murray, see James J. Barnes, *Free Trade in Books: a Study of the London Book Trade since 1800* (Oxford: Clarendon P., 1964).

7. Leading members of the Glasgow book trade had received complaints about Griffin's underselling since the late 1830s. See, for example, letter of 4 January 1837 from Alexander Hadden to Mr Forsyth, bookseller, Trongate, Glasgow. Glasgow Booksellers' Protection Association, Mitchell Library, Glasgow. Ref. 891733.

8. Angus Fraser, 'John Murray's Colonial and Home Library', *Papers of the Bibliographical Society of America*, 91 (1997), pp. 339-408 (p. 365).

9. Letter, Robert Cooke to Oliver & Boyd, 12 January 1844. Acc 5000/202.

10. Letter, Robert Cooke to Oliver & Boyd, 18 January 1844. Acc 5000/202.

11. See Beavan, 'What Constitutes the Crime...?', *passim*.

Confessions: the Midlands Execution Broadside Trade

ALICE FORD-SMITH

THOSE HANGED BY THE STATE had their stories chronicled in execution broadsides. This distinct genre of printing reported the crime, trial and death of the condemned. There has been a tendency for execution broadsides to be eclipsed by their ballad kin. Assumptions have been made and fair assessment has been weak. This paper examines the dynamics of the execution broadside industry, under the twin themes of trade and content. Specific reference is made to the printers who worked in Nottingham and Birmingham in the early nineteenth century, reflecting the collections of gallows sheets housed at the central libraries of those cities.[1]

Before examining the industry, the defining features of an execution broadside ought first to be clarified. The gallows sheet reproduced in Fig. 1 displays many typical features.[2] On 24 August 1831, William Reynolds and William Marshall were executed at Nottingham for the rape of Mary Ann Lord. The headline, 'Some particulars of the life, trial, behaviour and execution...', wraps itself around a woodcut of a gallows scene. On one side of the flimsy sheet, the biographies, crime and execution of the two men are recorded. It is this prose that distinguishes execution broadsides from ballads. Reynolds and Marshall are presented as unremarkable characters, except for their reported indifference to their fate. Central to the broadside, in physical terms, are the trial proceedings, whilst the execution scene itself is despatched in a single paragraph at the end. The verso is blank. Needless to say, for all the 'normality' of Reynolds and Marshall's broadside, there survive other sheets that do not share the same characteristics. The printer's combination of a woodcut, uniform type and strong narrative voice, for example, are not always found in other broadsides. In contrast to the centrality of the trial proceedings in this particular broadside, another Nottingham sheet states: 'The trial of this unfortunate man has been already published and we have, therefore, purposely omitted it, as a repetition of it can be of no interest to the public.[3] Further factors such as numerous editions and the ephemeral nature of the sheets make it almost impossible to label one execution broadside as typical of its genre or period. After all, there survive at least three different versions of execution broadsides for Reynolds and Marshall including two editions from the Nottingham printer Richard Sutton. One is forced, therefore, to define an execution broadside in terms of its physical characteristics: a prose account of an executed criminal, printed on one side of a sheet of paper. Taking this definition into consideration, V. A. C. Gatrell's comment: 'Read half a dozen and you have read them all.[4] seriously undervalues the variety of execution broadsides that survive today.

Fortunately for the researcher, printers of surviving gallows sheets frequently included their name and location. In the Birmingham collection Thomas Wood of New Meeting Street, Moor Street's Taylor and Robert Heppel have a strong presence. The Suttons of Bridlesmith-Gate, New-Change's Samuel Creswell and the partnership of Burbage and Stretton are well documented in the Nottingham collection. These survivals may not correspond to a similarly large share of the market, of course, but it is likely these printers were firmly established in the execution broadside trade. The stiff competition faced by printers is demonstrated by studying the year 1817. Besides Charles Ordoyno at least three other printers of broadsides were operating in Nottingham. Daniel Diggle's execution generated broadsides by Barber, Hodson and Sutton. Meanwhile, in the same year, broadsides for a Warwick hanging were issued by Taylor, Wadsworth and Wood. Rivalry between printers was fierce, as demonstrated by the gallows sheets themselves. Birmingham's Edward Taylor certainly had a spirited relationship with one neighbouring printer. At the bottom of one of his broadsides, Edward Taylor vented his feelings:

N.B. Our readers may probably recollect that Mr. Russell, Printer in Moor Street, had the impudence to assert that his were the only correct Warwick sentences published, which I assure the public, was one of the basest falsehoods that ever proceeded from the mouth of ignorance and folly.[5]

Edward Taylor worked in the same road as Joseph Russell. Whether their hostility was confined to the printed word or spilled out into Moor Street is left to the imagination. Accuracy and authenticity were concerns claimed by others aside from Taylor. A Nottingham execution broadside warns of a 'spurious account, printed and sent into the country yesterday'.[6] Examination of the one other broadside for this execution found so far makes it unlikely that this is the rogue account referred to.[7] As both report

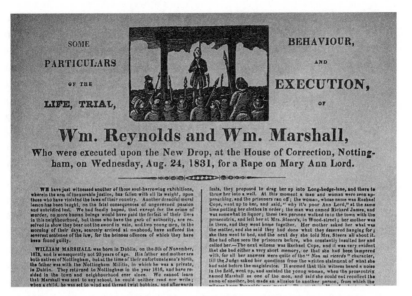

Fig. 1. Execution broadside (part) printed in Nottingham by R. Sutton, 1831.
© Nottingham City Council: Local Studies Library

the condemned man being hanged twice, after the rope slipped on the first attempt, the two accounts appear authentic. Another version may, of course, turn up. Alternatively, the warning may have been a simple ploy to increase sales and rubbish the competition.

The competitive market also encouraged trade agreements. As a result of a merger between two local newspapers, George Burbage agreed in 1775 not to print broadsides of Nottingham executions whilst Samuel Creswell remained alive.[8] The survivals suggest that this agreement was honoured. It is also quite common to find references to reprints. Nottingham's Charles Ordoyno, in particular, appears to have specialized in cooperating with other printers. A broadside of his from 1818 commemorating a hanging in Lincoln is credited as being originally the work of Drury.[9] Another Ordoyno/Drury production survives from 1823.[10] John Drury's broadside of this later execution for so called 'horrid crimes', has an almost identical narrative to Ordoyno's, even with the same italic stresses. The sheets only diverge when describing the execution. Whilst Drury's broadside expresses pity for the three men, Ordoyno concludes with: 'their limbs were trembling with agony; and as they had lived in a manner unworthy to be called men, they died as they had lived.'[11] Details missed by the Nottingham printer but included in Drury's broadside, are Arden's fortitude, Candler's stupor and Doughty's agitation. In addition to reproducing Lincoln execution broadsides, Charles Ordoyno also reprinted the gallows sheets of York printers Richardson[12] and Croshaw.[13] Ordoyno filled a niche, gaining an advantage in the market by bringing into Nottingham reports of executions from further afield. Examples of broadsides also survive of Nottingham's Barber reprinting an account of an execution in Northampton[14] and Birmingham's Russell issuing a sheet that originated in Lancaster,[15] whilst Heppel reprinted a Northampton broadside[16] and Wood reported an execution in Shrewsbury.[17] Yet to be found is a broadside acknowledging its story originated from a printing house in Nottingham or Birmingham, although there does survive one sheet from Edinburgh reporting a Derby execution.[18]

Broadsides were, of course, not the only printed form the story of an execution could take. Chapbooks, for one, were also printed. Such an operation must have been particularly cost-effective when the execution broadside and chapbook were identical in everything but format. Charles Sutton produced an execution broadside[19] and chapbook[20] of the hanging of Percival Cooke and James Tomlinson in 1812. They contain exactly the same narrative but with different arrangements of type to accommodate the two formats. It has also been observed that some of the Birmingham printers of broadsides produced books,[21] a product more commonly associated with an exclusive section of the printing trade.[22] The broadside of George Allen, for example, includes a footnote advertising the forthcoming publication of his trial proceedings, available from booksellers for a shilling.[23] According to another sheet, sixpence bought an account of the trials of some Nottingham rioters.[24] In addition to chapbooks, broadsides and books, there were newspapers to be printed. Nottingham's George Burbage, Charles Sutton, George Stretton and Samuel Creswell all produced both newspapers and gallows sheets.[25] For over fifty years, Charles Sutton and his son, Richard, managed one of England's leading radical newspapers, the *Nottingham Review*.[26] To consider a less distinguished printer for a moment, a receipt of Thomas Kirk outlines the variety of work he undertook. As 'bookseller, bookbinder and stationer', his services included:

Ledgers – Day Books – Journals – Cash Books – Memorandum Books, constantly on hand. – Ruling done, and Account Books bound on the shortest notice – Wholesale and Retail Paper Warehouse. – Genuine Patent Medicines, &c. &c.[27]

Although the receipt is silent on the matter, Thomas Kirk also printed execution broadsides.

The scale of the broadside industry is difficult to determine. To take an example from Henry Mayhew's oft-quoted sales figures, the 1849 execution of James Rush in Norwich generated an astonishing 2.5 million 'execution broad-sheets'.[28] However, it is questionable whether such a huge quantity of broadsides could be produced within the short time available.[29] After all, the most famous of nineteenth-century printers of street literature, James Catnach, only managed to keep up with demand for accounts of John Thurtell's murderous activities by working his four presses day and night for a week. At the end of such frenzied industry, an estimated 250,000 broadsides had been printed.[30] One explanation for Mayhew's sales figures, apart from simple over-enthusiasm, is his definition of an 'execution broadsheet'. The term is not clarified, and his definition may have included ballads. Even when accepting that not every hanging attracted the degree of attention bestowed on James Rush, Henry Mayhew does give a glimpse of the enormous broadside market in the nineteenth century.

Just as execution broadsides were stigmatized for being of the worst kind of literature, the people who sold the sheets were also condemned. A hawker who spoke to Henry Mayhew, distanced himself from those in the trade who sold execution broadsides: 'A man that's never been to school an hour can go and patter a dying speech.'[31] It would appear that hawkers who solely worked gallows sheets were believed to lack the skill of sellers who relied on their presentation, rather than opportunism, for sales. Moving to the question of price, on the first day of publication, 3 shillings 6 pence bought a London street seller twelve dozen broadsides. As the week progressed, and the public's interest waned, the wholesale price fell.[32] In turn, a customer was usually charged a penny, or less if the broadside was becoming difficult to sell. An obvious location to hawk execution broadsides was the gallows scene itself. Hangings attracted enormous crowds and therefore customers. The Society for Promoting Christian Knowledge claimed to have given away some 42,575 of their tracts at one execution.[33] When the immediate market petered out, hawking networks took the broadsides further afield. The pedlar would have to be brisk though; customers were not keen to buy 'old news', although it is also true that the story of an infamous criminal could be popular for months to come. The risk of peddling 'old news' may explain why the majority of surviving execution broadsides produced by London printers were left undated, whilst those printed in Nottingham and Birmingham commonly include exact dates. A dated broadside may signify a local market, whilst London productions were well traveled. Omitting details may not always have been the result of a printer's carelessness, therefore, but an indication of sound judgement. On a similar thread, it has been suggested that some broadsides were issued without an imprint so that a local printer could insert his name, and claim the production as his own.[34]

No evidence, so far, has been found to suggest that execution broadsides were purchased by any one particular group. Just as the crowd at an execution attracted men, women and children from every socio-economic class, the literature describing it could have been read by a similarly diverse number of people. This judgement, however, would have been strongly refuted by one contemporary essayist:

The purchasers of this class of literature are the lowest order of the people; the intelligent never purchase it, knowing it is seldom to be depended on for truth, and if it is true, it has already appeared, or will immediately appear, in the daily newspapers.[35]

Execution broadsides are attacked for being either outmoded or guilty of deception. Despite this account, Henry Mayhew testifies to the universal attraction of these sheets. One seller reported to him: 'A gentleman's servant come out and wanted half a dozen for his master and one for himself'.[36] The reader is left to wonder who that gentleman was and for whom the remaining five of the broadsides were destined. Of course, a person could have read broadsides without buying them. An eighteenth century newspaper advert for a coffee shop lists their stock as including newspapers, journals, monthly magazines, session papers and dying speeches.[37] The person who consulted the *Daily Advertiser*, for example, could have easily reached over to see the latest execution broadside.

The style of some of the Nottingham sheets certainly point to a relatively sophisticated audience. A typically thunderous opening to one such 'preaching' execution broadside recounts the demise of William Davies in 1806:

In this degenerate age, when vice and profaneness stalk forth with such unblushing confidence as almost to put virtue out of countenance, it is not surprising to see men frequently of education, and possessing the clearest capacities drawn into the vortex, and by a series of dissipation and wickedness brought to an untimely end.[38]

Burbage and Stretton assume a reader with enough skill to define the word 'vortex' or one, at least, who would not be discouraged by reading possibly unfamiliar words. The tone is unmistakably condemnatory; as a forger, William Davies violated the law and justice demands death. There is another category of these 'preaching' broadsides which has been ignored; those calling for reform. Reflecting the *Nottingham Review*'s policy of supporting civil liberty, the Suttons' broadsides were of a similarly radical style. Their gallows sheet of three Nottingham rioters reads:

Never, never can we be the apologists for arson and plunder, but we had fondly hoped that the Ministers of the Crown would have supposed that the justice of the case would have been amply met, by sending the guilty parties to another country, without inflicting upon them the punishment of death.[39]

In fact, in this particular case there does appear to have been great universal sympathy for the condemned. Not only does Sutton note the vigorous campaign to reprieve the men, but the broadsides printed by Kirk[40] and Heppel[41] also report the unease surrounding the executions. The style of Charles and Richard Suttons' broadsides is shaped by the family's strong combination of Reformist and Methodist beliefs. It might seem reasonable, therefore, to suppose the purchasers of these very distinct Sutton broadsides would have been sympathetic towards the principles of the printer. Before the subject of readership is cast aside, one note of caution ought to be expressed. The intricacies of the 'preaching' broadsides naturally encourage further study. However, there are other 'matter of fact' execution broadsides that may be overlooked because of their routine narrative style. The question of the audience of these sheets ought to be considered. At present, their readers are unknown.

The task of unravelling the authoring process of execution broadsides is not for the impatient. It is clear that some of the condemned had no role in the production process, past committing the crime in the first place. David Gardner's gallows sheet,[42] for example, simply reports the facts of his case. The only memorable part of the sheet is the error of type that records Gardner's execution year as 1909, instead of 1809. In other instances, the condemned would simply refuse to cooperate. Unlike his accomplice James

Brumage, William Wainer apparently would not assist in composing his broadside:

He obstinately refused to make any confession, but to God, the Saints, and the Priest... nor would he give any account of his past life, tho' much urged by the worthy gaoler and others: The printer therefore, can say no more of him than giving the following short history of his life, gathered from the conversation of those who knew him.[43]

In fact, the length and tone of the account of Wainer is not far removed from his accomplice's story, despite their differing attitudes. In his refusal to cooperate, Wainer succeeds in preserving evidence of his strength of character for the generations that followed. Other condemned prisoners cooperated with the printers of broadsides by providing specially penned correspondence. Claimed to be from the condemned to their loved ones, there is the likelihood that some of these letters were genuine. After all, the fact that the prisoner may not have been able to write did not prevent them from dictating. One of Joshua Shepherd's broadsides, for example, re-printed a letter that was purportedly: 'Addressed to his Father-in-law and Mother, the day before his Execution, as written down from his mouth, by William Mell, and attested by Mr. Cross, the jailer.'[44] Similarly, the last dying words at the gallows may have been genuine, thanks to some attentive witness. Nevertheless, newspaper reports remain the most obvious source material for execution broadsides, especially when the printers owned the local press. For those printers who worked on a smaller scale, a newspaper was relatively inexpensive and reported enough of the trial to inspire a gallows sheet. Hodson printed the same 'authentic confession' of Daniel Diggle[45] as the *Nottingham Review* in April 1817. Whether the newspaper or the broadside was printed first remains unresolved.

Printers had to work within a time frame when it was often only a matter of days between the death-sentence being passed to the day of execution. Moreover, a town could see two executions in the space of seven days.[46] Such time constraints meant the printing of broadsides was often rushed and errors were made. Nottingham's Sutton, for example, admitted on one sheet that: 'Some things through haste were omitted in a few of the first copies which are here inserted.'[47] However, small errors of typography and content should be kept in proportion. The consumers of execution broadsides were more concerned with having up-to-date news than holding a work of art. Of a more profound effect on the content of the sheets was the tendency for printers to prepare the text before the execution had taken place. Burbage and Stretton warn on a broadside of 1802: 'Beware of buying those printed the day before her execution.'[48] By the number of sheets that abruptly end, after a lengthy report of the trial proceedings, with the cursory 'launched into eternity' sentence, it was evidently a common practice. In fact, it is more common to find execution broadsides without 'last dying words' than with. It must be stressed, however, that these pre-emptive publications were not as misleading as might be expected. In terms of their content, these broadsides are similar to the ones that report the execution scene at length, albeit with a censored account of the execution. For example, one broadside of Thomas Dewey's execution records him deep in prayer at the gallows, before being sent to, in the text's words, his 'great account'.[49] However, a presumably later account, from the same printer, described a far more harrowing scene. Dewey was so insensible that the executioner had to manhandle him onto the scaffold. It was only with help from an assistant, who held Dewey upright, that the executioner could finish his work.[50] In the second broadside Dewey died wretchedly, if accurately, whilst the first allowed the man some degree of dignity, at least in printed form.

In addition to the composition of words, printers had to attend to the visual element of the broadsides. It is a widely held belief that the woodcuts used to illustrate many of the sheets often bore no relation to the subject.[51] However, it is inaccurate to assume from the images pasted on ballads, that printers applied the same philosophy to execution broadsides. From the sheets studied for this paper, when a woodcut was included the image ordinarily pertained to a hanging. Even the Mary Voce broadside, which includes a woodcut of a woman kneeling at the guillotine, identifies the broadside's subject, however inaccurate the mode of execution.[52]

It must be conceded that occasionally execution broadsides were completely fraudulent.[53] Particulars were kept to a minimum so as to appeal to the widest customer base. There survive broadsides, for example, with near identical word-for-word narratives describing the stories of two women who murdered their respective illegitimate babies. The only differing features of the sorrowful tales of Mary Jones[54] and Fanny Amlett[55] are the towns at which the women were allegedly executed. For every Fanny and Mary, however, there are many more Joshua Shepherds, Thomas Deweys and William Wainers. These so called 'cocks' should not be used to discredit all execution broadsides. Just as the accused is innocent until proven guilty, gallows sheets should be judged fairly.

Considering the question of content in more depth, although a few of the sheets may not have shied from admitting that some prisoners died proclaiming their innocence, it is rare to read any further speculation on the subject. An exceptional survival is that of Samuel Jacobs's broadside. Jacobs, executed in Warwick for raping a boy, is honoured with the following reflection:

Whether this unhappy man was really guilty of all the aggravations of his crime as they were exhibited against him in court, is difficult to determine, as he solemnly denied the charge before the Judge and continued to do the same, in a great degree all the time he remained under condemnation.[56]

It is the court most of all, not the prisoner, who is being judged in this broadside. As demonstrated by the Nottingham sheets from the Sutton family, it is more common to find accounts pondering the appropriateness of capital punishment as a whole rather than the justice of an individual case. Whether forgery warranted its capital offence appears a particular concern. A gallows sheet, printed by Birmingham's Taylor in 1817, for example, briefly reports the specifics of the forger William Stokes' criminal episode. Six lines are then devoted to explaining the evils of his crime:

The man who is foolish enough to be guilty of forgery, should consider that he is deliberately taking away his own life, in the very act, perhaps, of robbing the poor; for though a forged note may pass for a time undiscovered, yet ultimately its baseness will be detected, when in the possession of some honest mechanic or labourer, which may be his all to support the calls of a wife and a numerous family; let any man, therefore, lay his hand to his heart, and ask himself how few crimes can be more atrocious than forgery.[57]

This is not an example of a broadside simply reporting the life and death of a condemned man. The account endorses the criminal code of England. Thirteen years after William Stokes was hanged, the last person in England was executed for forgery.[58] This analysis appears straightforward, until it is made clear that the rapist Samuel Jacobs and the forger William Stokes' stories are contained in the one broadside (Fig. 2). It was argued the narrative of Samuel Jacobs is uncommon in entertaining doubts to the justice of the sentence. In contrast, William Stokes execution for forgery is supported and encouraged. By erroneously considering the two accounts as separate entities, the complexity of this broadside's text is masked. Not only

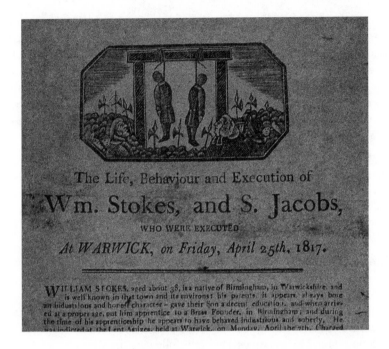

The Life, Behaviour and Execution of

Wm. Stokes, and S. Jacobs,

WHO WERE EXECUTED

At WARWICK, on Friday, April 25th, 1817.

WILLIAM STOKES, aged about 38, is a native of Birmingham, in Warwickshire, and is well known in that town and its environs: his parents, it appears, always bore an industrious and honest character – gave their Son a decent education, and when arrived at a proper age, put him apprentice to a Brass Founder, in Birmingham; and during the time of his apprenticeship he appears to have behaved industrious and soberly. He was indicted at the Lent Assizes, held at Warwick, on Monday, April the 7th. Charged

Fig. 2. Execution broadside (part) printed in Birmingham by Taylor, 1817.
© Birmingham Library Services

does this survival indicate that sheets were composed on an individual basis, but that execution broadsides may contain a multiplicity of themes and convictions.

Compared with the stylistic progress made by the printers of newspapers through the nineteenth century, the approach to execution broadsides remained largely unchanged. Birmingham printers did introduce a woodcut in which silhouettes could be added to the gallows image, but this innovation did not effect the overall character of the sheets. Leslie Shepard tells the anecdote of a broadside printer rejecting the offer of new woodblocks, saying: 'better are not so good; I can get better myself: now these are old favourites, and better cuts will not please my customers so well.'[59] The woodcuts in question were being used to illustrate carol sheets, but the response of the printer illuminates a major problem for the execution broadside industry. The sheets were trapped by the same qualities that were their selling point. By maintaining their traditional style, execution broadsides risked becoming obsolete. Tension can also felt between Henry Mayhew's buoyant mid-century sales figures and the growing unease about executions being public. Returning to Richard Sutton once again, the printer took the inspired step of using execution broadsides to help the abolitionist cause. When William Saville was executed in 1844, Sutton printed doubts of the legitimacy of the execution spectacle. In the opening paragraph of the sheet, the reader is confronted by:

Happily the criminal code of this country has recently undergone a revision, and it is now likely that we shall never more see so disgusting an exhibition as the deliberate destruction of a fellow creature in public, except for murder. It would be well even in cases of this nature also, if punishment of death were abrogated, and other punishment substituted.[60]

Sutton supported a cause that would ultimately extinguish one of his own business interests.

The year 1868 saw the end of public hangings in England. Printers continued to produce execution broadsides, but at a shadow of former quantities. In May 1876 a broadside issued to commemorate the execution of four men in London opened with the following description:

At an early hour this morning a few people collected in the front of Newgate Gaol, but not anything like the numbers on former occasions… Instead of thousands of spectators, there were only the Governor of Newgate, the Sheriffs, with their officers &c, the Executioner, the representatives of the press, and a few gentlemen who had been granted the privilege to be present.[61]

Such a muted scene was evidently not an uncommon one, as an execution broadside of around 1870 used an almost identical description for a hanging at Aylesbury.[62] Hangings held in private were not entertaining, and people stayed away. Instead, the trial proceedings were followed with added gusto. The immense fascination with crime and trials continued, but it was the newspapers that Victorians turned to.

This paper has demonstrated the need to reassess execution broadsides, in terms of their content and their trade. The people who wrote and sold the sheets have been introduced, whilst those who read them have only been glimpsed. For too long execution broadsides have been marginalized in histories of printing and society. 'Read half a dozen and you have read them all'? I think not.

Notes

1. References to broadsides will follow the following style: 'headline', place of execution, name of printer, year of execution, collection where located. Locations will be abbreviated as follows: Birmingham Central Library, BCL; Nottingham Central Library, NCL; Nottinghamshire Archive Office, NA; Kent State University, KSU; Lincolnshire Archive Office, LA; St Bride Printing Library, SB; York Castle Museum, YCM.

2. 'Some particulars of the life, trial, behaviour and execution of Wm. Reynolds and Wm. Marshall', Nottingham, R. Sutton, 1831, NCL.

3. 'The life, behaviour and execution of William Stokes, and S. Jacobs', Birmingham, Taylor, 1817, BCL.

4. V. A. C. Gatrell. *The Hanging Tree* (Oxford, 1994), p. 175.

5. 'An account of the lives and execution of William Warner, Thomas Ward, and Thomas Williams', Warwick, Taylor, 1818, BCL.

6. 'The remarkable dying words, speech, and confession of John Milner', Nottingham, n.p., 1797, NCL.

7. 'The dying speech, _____ of John Miller', Nottingham, n.p., 1797, NCL.

8. W. J. Clarke & W. A. Potter. *Early Nottingham Printers and Printing* (Nottingham, 1953), p. 18.

9. 'A right, and full account of the four unfortunate malefactors, who were executed... Richard Randall and John Tubbs, for highway robbery; and Thomas Evison and Thomas Norris', Lincoln, Ordoyno, 1818, NA.

10. 'The last dying record, and particulars of the execution of William Arden, Esq. John Doughty, and Benjamin Candler', Lincoln, C. Ordoyno, 1823, NA.

11. 'The last and true dying account of Wm. Arden, Jno. Doughty, and Benj. Candler', Lincoln, Drury, 1823, LA.

12. 'The last dying words and confession of Samuel Leatherland', York, Ordoyno, 1818, YCM.

13. 'A full account of the confession and execution of Michael Pickles and John Greenwood', York, Ordoyno, 1817, NA.

14. 'Life, behaviour, and execution of William Meadows, Wm. Gent, and Redmond Middleton', Northampton, Barber, 1822, NA.

15. 'A full, true and particular account of Susannah Holroyd', Lancaster[?], J. Russell, 1816, BCL.

16. 'Life, trial and execution of John Williams and Michael Neville', Northampton, Heppel, 1824, BCL.

17. 'The trial, sentence, judge's speech, and execution of James Davis', Shrewsbury, Wood, 1819, BCL.

18. 'A full, true, and particular account of Jeremiah Brandreth, Isaac Ludlam and William Turner', Derby, n.p., 1817, KSU.

19. 'The confession of Percival Cooke and James Tomlinson', Derby, C. Sutton, 1812, NCL.

20. 'The confession of Percival Cooke and James Tomlinson', Nottingham, 1812, NCL.

21. Trevor Jones. *Street Literature in Birmingham* (Oxford, 1970), p. 20.

22. G. A. Cranfield. *The Development of the Provincial Newspaper 1700-1760* (Westport, CT., 1978), p. 248.

23. 'An account of the life, trial and behaviour of George Allen', Stafford, Morgan, 1807, BCL.

24. 'Some particulars of the life, trial, behaviour, & execution of George Beck, George Hearson and John Armstrong', Nottingham, R. Sutton, 1832, NCL.

25. Cranfield. ref. 22, p. 91.

26. Sheila Cooke & Stephen Best. *In print I found it* (Nottingham, 1976), p. 1.

27. Receipt of Thomas Kirk, 1838, NA.

28. Henry Mayhew. *London Labour and the London Poor* (New York, 1968), vol. I, p. 284.

29. Colin Clair. *A History of Printing in Britain* (London, 1965), p. 203.

30. Charles Hindley. *The History of the Catnach Press* (Detroit, 1969), p. 70.

31. Mayhew. ref. 28, p. 235.

32. Mayhew. ref. 28, p. 220.

33. R. K. Webb. *The British Working Class Reader* (London, 1955), p. 27.

34. V. E. Neuburg. *Chapbooks* (London, 1964), p. 15.

35. Felix Folio. *The Hawkers and Street Dealers of the North of England Manufacturing Districts* (Manchester, 1858), p. 109.

36. Mayhew. ref. 28, p. 223.

37. G. A. Cranfield. *The Press and Society* (London, 1978), p. 182-3.

38. 'The life, trial, and behaviour of William Davies', Nottingham, Burbage and Stretton, 1806, BCL.

39. George Beck. ref. 24.

40. 'Trials and execution of George Beck... George Hearson...John Armstrong', Nottingham, Kirk, 1832, NCL.

41. 'The trials and execution of Geo. Beck, Geo. Hearson & John Armstrong', Nottingham, Heppel, 1832, BCL.

42. 'An account of the behaviour and execution of David Gardner', Warwick, Wood, 1809, BCL.

43. 'An account of the lives, trial, and behaviour of William Wainer and James Brumage', Nottingham, n.p., 1766, NCL.

44. 'Some particulars of the lives, trial, behaviour, and execution of Joshua Shepherd... George Milnes', Nottingham, Sutton and Son, 1826, NCL.

45. 'The authentic confession of Daniel Diggle', Nottingham, Hodson, 1817, NCL.

46. 'Particulars of the trial & execution of John Greenwood', Lincoln, Keyworth, 1831, LA.
    'Particulars of the trial & execution of Michael Lundy', Lincoln, Keyworth, 1831, LA.

47. 'An account of the experience and happy death of Mary Voce', Nottingham, C. Sutton, 1802, NCL.

48. 'The life, character, behaviour at the place of execution and dying speech of Mary Voce', Nottingham, Burbage and Stretton, 1802, NCL.

49. 'Some particulars of the trial, behaviour and execution of Thomas Dewey', Nottingham, Sutton and Son, 1825, NCL.

50. 'Some particulars of the trial, behaviour and execution of Thomas Dewey' II, Nottingham, Sutton and Son, 1825, NCL.

51. Maurice Rickards. *The Encyclopedia of Ephemera* (London, 2000), p. 138.

52. Mary Voce. ref. 47.
53. Hindley. ref. 30, pp. 44-45. Records that Mrs. Catnach and two hawkers were reprimanded by police for circulating false news.
54. 'The heart-rending execution of Mary Jones', Chester, D. Dyson, n.d., YCM.
55. 'Execution of Fanny Amlett', Gloucester, n.p., n.d., YCM.
56. William Stokes and S. Jacobs. ref. 3.
57. William Stokes and S. Jacobs. ref. 3.
58. John J. Burke. 'Crime and punishment in 1777', in *Executions and the British Experience from the 17th to the 20th century* ed. by William B Thesing, (Jefferson, 1990), p. 75.
59. Leslie Shepard. *John Pitts* (Pinner, 1969), p. 64.
60. 'Some particulars of the life, trial, behaviour, and execution of William Saville', Nottingham, R. Sutton, 1844, NCL.
61. 'Trial and execution of the Lennie Mutineers', London, W. Fortey, 1876, SB.
62. 'Trial and execution of John Jones', Aylesbury, n.p., n.d., SB.

Station to Station: the LNWR and the Emergence of the Railway Bookstall, 1840-1875

STEPHEN COLCLOUGH

HISTORIANS OF THE BOOK TRADE have long been familiar with the important role played by railway bookstalls in the distribution and sale of texts, and of 1848 as the year in which W. H. Smith made a successful bid to run the bookstalls on the London and North Western Railway (LNWR) between Euston Square and Manchester. Indeed, in many accounts the two have become synonymous and form the official history of distribution in the railway age.[1] This paper aims to explore the nature of newspaper and bookselling on the LNWR stations before the arrival of W. H. Smith using evidence from the bids submitted to the railway company when the line was put out to tender in August 1848. It also uses documents from the Smith archive in order to investigate the way in which the railway bookstall business expanded during the 1850s and 60s and describes the new print environment that was created as the company established chains of bookstalls on almost all the major English lines.[2]

Much of what we know about the bookstalls in the late 1840s and early 50s has been derived from a small number of articles published in contemporary magazines and newspapers which constructed an image of the pre-Smith's bookstall as the source of 'cheap' books or 'improper' fiction that has continued to influence the way in which we think about their development and operation. As Lynda Nead has argued, 'cheap' literature was associated with obscenity throughout the 1850s – the decade in which the Obscene Publications Act was made law – and the theme of dangerous 'trash' runs through much of this early commentary.[3] For example, the account of the London termini published by *The Times* in August 1851 was primarily concerned with the influence of the stalls upon the 'mental development' of the nation.

Is the most made of the finest opportunity yet offered to this generation for guiding awakened thought and instructing the eager and susceptible mind? The question forcibly occurred to us the other day in a first-class carriage, in which two young ladies and a boy, for the space of three mortal hours, were amusing themselves and alarming us by a devotion to a trashy French novel, most cruelly and sacrilegiously misplaced. A volume of 'Eugene Sue' was in the hands of each. The colour of the books was light green, and we remarked to have seen a huge heap of such covers as we hastily passed the book-stall at the station on our way to the carriage.[4]

The correspondent went on to report that he had spent the next few days searching out 'trash' at the various London stations and that it was to be found everywhere except at the stall run by Smith's at Euston Square. Murray republished this article a few weeks later as a *6d* pamphlet entitled *The Literature of the Rail,* which included a discussion of the 'gradual rise of the Railway book-trade' that had not appeared in the original article.[5] This new preface argued that the first vendors, 'whose profits had been as varying as their punctuality', had been replaced by newspaper men who established permanent stands on the platforms, and that they in turn had been replaced by the 'deserving' amongst the railway's employees:

A cripple maimed in the Company's service, or a married servant of a director or secretary, superseded the first batch of stragglers, and assumed a business for which he had no previous qualification.[6]

It goes on to argue that these unqualified booksellers made 'large sums of money' from the sale of cheap 'French novels' and were themselves superseded when the railway companies decided to put the bookstall privileges out to tender. It was on these new stalls that Eugene Sue's novels and other items of 'literary trash' were found in the original article, but the new preface ends on an optimistic note by drawing special attention to the role being played by W. H. Smith ('the proprietor of the North Western book-stalls') in the improvement of the 'literary tastes of the people'.

As a polemical piece *The Literature of the Rail* presented contemporaries with an attractive narrative of the triumph of 'culture' over obscenity, and of the professional bookseller over the disabled amateur, and it was this version of *The Times* report that established a way of writing about W. H. Smith as the saviour of the railway reader that was to be continued throughout the rest of the century and beyond. For example, the review of this pamphlet that appeared in the *Athenaeum* talked of Smith's 'interest' in maintaining the 'dignity of literature by resolutely refusing to admit pernicious publications amongst his stock' and argued, in a direct echo of the first passage quoted above, that until the 'Great Northern copied the good precedent [of the LNWR], and entered into a contract with Mr Smith and his son, the greenest literature in dress and digestion was all that was offered to the wants of travellers'.[7] Several passages from *The Literature of the Rail* were reproduced in the *Illustrated Exhibitor and Magazine of Art* in 1852, and the recurrence of the central narrative of the replacement of 'illiterate amateurs' with professional staff in a number of articles published in the 1860s, suggests that this idea of moral and intellectual progress was very attractive to a contemporary audience that was nervous about the way in which print culture was proliferating.[8] This association of the Smith's bookstalls with moral progress passed into the twentieth century via a number of books on the life of the second William Henry Smith and echoes can be found in most accounts of Victorian print culture including Charles Wilson's history of Smith's, *First With the News*.[9] Using evidence from the LNWR's meetings, Wilson was able to substantiate the claim first made in *The Literature of the Rail* that 'former railway employees' sold improper literature at the pre-Smith's bookstalls, but only a single bookseller, Samuel Mayhew of Euston, was 'severely reprimanded for his misconduct' during this period.[10] The minutes of the LNWR confirm that the privilege of vending books and newspapers at Euston was often awarded to former employees, but the fact that no other bookseller was disciplined for selling 'improper' texts during the early 1840s, and the willingness of employees of the railway company to act as referees for those bidding to maintain their business at the stations, suggests that such occurrences were unusual, at least outside London.[11]

A large number of the booksellers and newsvendors already working on the line, including those at Coventry, Crewe, Euston, Liverpool, Rugby, Stafford, Warrington, Wolverhampton, and Wolverton, submitted bids to the LNWR when the entire line was put out to tender in August 1848.[12] Because many feared that they were about to lose their livelihood, they included letters and references with the standard forms, and these reveal a great deal about the nature of their business, as well as the number of years that they had been on the station. The referee for Samuel Rowse of Stafford, for example, claimed that he had sold books and newspapers at the station for seven years. A member of the LNWR staff who supported the bid by the resident at Crewe, stated that James Grimes had been:

News Agent at this Station, upwards of five years [and] has always conducted himself with propriety & given general Satisfaction to the Public, and I have no hesitation in recommending him to continue his present occupation (Bid 31).

Such recommendations suggest that the railway bookstall's reputation for impropriety may have been something of an exaggeration.

Both Rowse and Grimes described themselves as 'booksellers', although neither is listed in contemporary trade directories of Stafford or Crewe, and the amounts that they offered to the LNWR in order to continue their business suggests that both had a significant amount of available capital. Indeed, of the nine firms who reapplied to the LNWR in 1848, only four described themselves as 'newsvendors', and of these only John Utley of Warrington and William Staniforth of Wolverhampton offered less than £5 for their annual rent.[13] The rest included a number of well-established book trade figures, such as Henry Lambert Horsfall of Coventry, who declared that he was:

the party that has hitherto the privilege of selling newspapers &c at the Coventry Station, and that having a news and Bookstand in connection therewith, I am probably enabled to supply it better and more profitably than another party would be (Bid 31).

Horsfall, who also ran a bookshop, news agency, and a circulating library in the town, offered £20 for the continuation of his business at the station, and his bid, with its references to both 'a news and bookstand' suggests that, even before the arrival of Smith's, some vendors offered a number of services to the railway reader. Similarly, John Edmunds Curtis of Newport Pagnel, who described himself as a 'printer, bookseller and stationer' as well as the 'holder of the bookstalls at Wolverton', was prepared to pay £880 to extend his concerns to Euston and Rugby (Bid 31). Of course, the bidding process itself was probably designed to exclude the 'illiterate' vendors of 'improper' texts described by *The Times,* but the bids submitted by those already working on the line suggest that such vendors (if they existed on the LNWR) were already beginning to be outnumbered by legitimate booksellers who ran the stalls as part of a larger business.

However, the letters to the LNWR from those holding stalls outside the major towns and cities were keen to draw the company's attention to both their meagre profits and the cramped conditions in which they worked. For example, William Tait, of Rugby, who, like Horsfall, also ran a business in the town, thanked 'the company for the privilege I have held as newsvendor at Rugby Station', but added

Fig. 1. W. H. Smith's bookstall at Knottingley Station, *c.*1885.
© W. H. Smith Archive

I shall be glad to retain it by paying a rent of £30 per annum and £10 more ... if I might have the use of a small light room. At present I am on sufferance among the luggage in the 3rd class room (Bid 33).[14]

Utley of Warrington made a similar request for 'more convenient accommodation', and a number of vendors also asked to be allowed to 'contract for the carriage' of their papers as well as the stall, in order to increase their profits.[15] Staniforth of Wolverhampton, who offered just £1 in rent, argued that 'the amount of my receipts do not warrant me in offering more' and Rowse of Stafford complained that he was frequently left with a large number of unsold newspapers because alterations to the timetable had diverted most of his trade to the nearby Tamworth station. Complaints about 'the exceedingly exaggerated views many entertain respecting the profits to be gained at railway stations' are noted by a number of bookstall holders in the Midlands.[16]

These 'exaggerated views' were undoubtedly founded upon some knowledge of the profits that could be made in London. In December 1847 both *The Times* and the *Railway Times* reported the rumour that the 'sale of newspapers and periodicals at the London-Bridge Station returns a profit of 10 guineas a week' in articles that also referred to the 'rent payable for this privilege at the Euston station' and it is significant that the majority of new bidders made an offer for the London terminus.[17] I have been unable to find any other records relating to those booksellers who owned railway bookstalls prior to 1848, but some idea of the extent of the business at Euston can be found in the legal records detailing the battle between William Gibbs and the LNWR that came to court at the Guildhall in December 1849. Gibbs, a former employee of the railway company, had acquired a stall at Euston in 1846, but refused to give up his business when the line was transferred to Smith's in November 1848. Because he attempted to recover both his stock, which was confiscated, and what he saw as lost earnings, the legal record provides the most detailed evidence that we have of both the contents of a bookstall during this period and the scale of profits to be made in London before the takeover by Smith's. John Gibbs, the plaintiff's father, declared in court that his son's net profits amounted to over £1021 for the ten months from 1 January to 1 November 1848, and he implied that most of this profit came from the sale of a range of newspapers including the *Daily News,* the *Express* and the *Times,* of which he had sold over 53,000 copies at 6d (or a profit of over 2d per copy).[18]

The stock was not limited to newspapers, however, and Gibbs senior provided details of both the physical structure of the stall itself and the books it contained in order to emphasize that his son was running a permanent business from the station:

He had a very large stall on the platform; it was fixed to the wall. There was a table with cupboards underneath ... There was one book in the cupboard valued at £2, and there were several other books.

This description confirms that the business was primarily concerned with the sale of newspapers, but the permanence of the fixtures and the expensive nature of the book stock reveal that the London trade was well developed by the late 1840s, and both the bids and the LNWR minutes confirm that Euston was able to support at least two bookstalls during this period.

Fig. 2. W. H. Smith's bookstall at Finchley Station, *c.*1895.
© W. H. Smith Archive

Taken together, this evidence suggests that while the LNWR bookstall business was already well established at the major termini in the 1840s (particularly at Euston with at least one permanent stall on the platform), the provincial stalls were still in the early stages of development, with new tenants attempting to sell newspapers and other goods from a range of impermanent or inhospitable venues such as the '3rd class room' occupied by Tait at Rugby. Consolidation of the business into the hands of a single operator, as the LNWR, Smith's and a number of other large companies recognized, would help to stop many of the problems experienced by the proprietors of individual stalls, such as the loss of business to a rival stall on the line.[19] Although Smith's bid was for 'the entire line', a letter to the LNWR from September 1848 suggests that they planned to open only fifteen stalls including those at Euston and Manchester.[20] However, the other bids reveal that up to twenty-one stalls were already in operation on the line, and it is significant that Smith's excluded Wolverhampton, the stall that had performed so poorly for William Staniforth.[21] We do not know how Smith's worked this line in the first few months of the contract, but it is likely that they operated a system in which 'boys with newspapers' were sent from the larger stalls to serve the under performing stations that 'would not justify a bookstall', as occurred on the Great Eastern in the 1860s.[22]

This evidence suggests that when Smith's reorganized the line as a single business in 1848 they displaced some booksellers, such as Staniforth, who were struggling to make money but, as the letter accompanying their bid makes clear, Smith's had hoped to take on the current bookstall staff 'to continue in their several positions, as far as may be possible', and their willingness to do so provides further evidence that the proprietors of the pre-Smith's bookstalls on the LNWR deserve to be remembered as much more than the illiterate purveyors of 'improper' books who figured in contemporary representations.[23] Indeed it could be argued that they were at the cutting edge of a new form of provincial bookselling and that it was their determination that allowed the bookstall business to expand enough for the entire line be put out to tender in 1848.

After acquiring the stalls on the LNWR and the Midland in 1848, W. H. Smith expanded their business to include a number of other lines and by the end of the 1850s they had contracts with twelve companies including the Great Northern.[24] Part of Smith's achievement during this decade was to bring a sense of disciplined uniformity to the railway bookstall business that had previously been lacking, and as the *Saturday Review* noted in 1857, their name had already become synonymous with railway reading:

In these days of universal travelling [at] almost all the larger railway stations, bookstalls – which in some instances attain the proportions of shops – are established. Nearly all ... are branches of the single firm of Messrs W. H. Smith and Son, who have for some years past supplied an enormous proportion of English railway travellers with their light reading.[25]

During the 1860s and 70s Smith's rapid expansion continued and they increased the number of stalls that they owned from 167 in 1861 to 385 in 1874.[26] This extension of the bookstall business throughout much of England and Ireland during the mid-Victorian period had a major impact on the way in which texts were purchased in the provinces and helped to create a new print environment in which a variety of texts, from books to handbills, vied for the reader's attention. I now want to examine the way in which this print environment was articulated by drawing on documents held in the archives of W. H. Smith, which reveal both the range of texts available at the stalls, and the ways in which they were marketed. Most of the early bookstall contracts allowed Smith's to sell 'newspapers, books, periodicals, pamphlets & prints', but we know remarkably little about the specific titles that they sold during this period.[27] However, some details about these texts and the way in which the bookstalls operated can be reconstructed from the instructions that Smith's issued annually to the 'clerks in charge' of their bookstalls. The earliest known copy of the *General Rule* dates from 1855 and, as Elizabeth James has argued, it reveals that each clerk had to combine the skills of 'wise selection and careful display' if he was to obey the rule preventing the 'accumulation of Dead Stock' and uphold his responsibility for the 'good condition' of the books and papers.[28] Keeping the stock clean was obviously very difficult in the railway environment and 'books, soiled from exposure at their bookstalls' were regularly advertised for sale in the 1860s 'at one-third of their original published price'.[29]

The *Rules* stipulated that books in pristine condition should be 'charged at the London published prices', but newspapers were more expensive at the railway station than anywhere else. Smith's 1848 contract allowed them to charge '6d for a 5d paper' (as *The Times*) and '4d for a 3d paper' (as *The Daily News*), and most daily papers were still being sold at these prices in 1855.[30] Newspapers were sold both at the stall and by boys who patrolled the platform, and the *Rules* record that their cries were restricted to the words 'London or morning papers' in order that 'no Daily Paper is mentioned by name at the carriages' . The titles of the dailies are not recorded, but a surviving return from the Bletchley bookstall lists ten (including The *Times* and the *Daily News)* that appear to have been available throughout the system in 1855.[31] By contrast, weekly publications such as *Punch* and *Household Words,* which could be returned to the publisher if they remained unsold, were sold at the 'regular fixed charges', but a further twenty-two texts could not 'be returned or allowed for' and needed to be 'ordered accordingly' by the clerk. In other words, the texts that dominated the stalls in the 1850s were those dailies and weeklies that could be returned if unsold. However, that the *Rules* also stipulated that the clerks could be made to pay for 'excessive returns that appear to arise from want of care' , suggests that the number of titles available at each stall was carefully regulated in order to limit the hidden costs that occurred when texts needed to be returned to the publisher.

Of course, the *Rules* can only provide a very general picture of the texts available at the stalls, but during the 1850s Smith's also began to issue 'Weekly' statement forms that had to be completed by each bookstall manager. From the 1860s these recorded the numbers of daily, local and weekly papers received, returned and sold, as well as details of trade customers, private subscribers and new members of the subscription library. Unfortunately, only a very limited number survive, but those returned by the Bradford stall record that by 1868 Smith's could supply twenty-one daily and fifty-eight weekly papers to their stands.[32] However, they also reveal that in practice, only those texts that could be guaranteed a regular sale were allowed to take up valuable space on the stall. At Bradford less than half the available dailies were regularly ordered, although small numbers of many of the weeklies appear in the returns, and it was the fourteen local papers that produced over half the stall's turnover from newspapers during the whole of 1868. For example, during the week ending 10 October 1868 the sale of local papers contributed £8 6s 7d to a total turnover of £15 13s 11d, and the local *Bradford Observer* sold more than twice as many copies as its nearest national rival, the *Telegraph,* although additional sales of the latter to trade customers need to be added if the total of actual sales is to be calculated.[33] The Bradford returns thus demonstrate the importance of newspapers and local publications to the bookstalls in the 1860s and are an important reminder of the way in which the print environment of each stall reflected the culture of the town or region in which it was situated.

The least well documented of all the texts sold on or around the bookstall in the Smith's archive is the book itself, but a number of contemporary reports contain details of the titles that they sold in the 1850s. For example, in 1857 the *Saturday Review* used information supplied by Smith's to describe the contents of the stalls and had much fun with those customers who bought copies of expensive texts such as the two-volume *Book of the Farm* (1851), of which it remarked, 'we should expect the person who made such a purchase to go into the refreshment-room at Swindon and ask for a barrel of salt pork and a puncheon of rum'.[34] The author of this piece assumed that all books bought at the stalls were to be consumed in the carriage, but the purchase of such expensive books suggests that readers used the stalls in much the same way as they used any other bookshop, and the *Review* goes on to give estimated sales figures for books of a 'more moderate size and price' such as the *Complete Works* of Thomas Moore which had sold twenty copies at *12s 6d* during the previous six months (p. 101). However, the main focus of this article is the 'shilling and eighteen-penny novels' that formed 'the great bulk of the sales on railways', and it draws particular attention to the display of famous names such as Walter Scott, whose *Waverley Novels* are listed as having sold 'as many as 200 a month' in an 'eighteen-penny edition', and popular novelists such as Edward Bulwer Lytton, whose work could sell 'from 1200 to 25' copies each month.[35] It concludes with a discussion of texts in which the 'external decorations' were better executed than the contents, such as the aptly named *Language of the Eye*, which it claimed had sold '4,000 copies at Messrs Smith's stalls alone' (p. 101).[36] This text comes in for particular criticism, and the conclusion to this article reconfirms contemporary anxieties about the role of the bookstall in the dissemination of cheap fiction or books of 'mere amusement' (p. 102).

Unfortunately, there are no detailed financial records for the early years of the bookstalls, but later accounts reveal that newspapers contributed much more to the turnover of the stalls than books.[37] Figures from the 1870s record that the rapid expansion of the bookstall business led to a vast increase in their profitability, but it was the newspaper business that grew most rapidly during this period, accounting for nearly 57% of total turnover by 1875.[38] By contrast, the share of turnover generated by books in the same period dropped by nearly 2%, despite an increase in sales from £109,042 to £159,998 per annum. However, a series of notes accompanying these accounts suggest that up to one-third of the increase in the profits made from bookselling during the period 1870-1875 had in fact been derived from the sale of magazines, periodicals and other goods and services, such as bookbinding. Thus, although the accounts prove that newspapers were the most profitable part of Smith's business, they also confirm that the other services offered at the bookstalls were important to their success. How the various goods offered by the stalls were displayed in the mid-Victorian period is difficult to reconstruct because the photographic evidence does not begin until later in the century, but a catalogue of 'Engravings, Chromotypes and Colored Photographs' issued in 1868 gives some idea of the kinds of texts that were on offer, other than books, newspapers and magazines, and I think we can assume that at least some of these prints would have been displayed on the larger stalls in much the same way as they were in the 1880s and 90s (see Figs. 1 and 2).[39]

In 1851 Smith's entered into agreements with the LNWR and the Midland that allowed them to display 'advertisements, handbills and placards' at and around the railway stations and advertising played a very important role in defining the print environment that surrounded the stalls in this period.[40] Spectacular advertising, such as that represented in the frontispiece of Sampson's *History of Advertising* (1875) was probably restricted to the termini of major cities during this period, but photographs taken in the 1860s and 70s suggests that even at relatively minor stations advertising was the most visible aspect of contemporary print culture on the platform and that, unlike the bookstall itself, it could not be avoided.[41] Despite an agreement with the LNWR in 1849 for the free carriage of library books, Smith's did not introduce a library to their stalls until 1860 and a letter from W. H. Smith II dated 20 December 1861 suggests that they did so at this time in order to attract new customers by altering the way in which the stalls were perceived by the public:

My great motive in establishing it was to increase the general advantages of the system of business connected with the Bookstalls, on the principle that the more the wants of the Public are met by the business the broader will be its basis in public estimation.[42]

The role that Smith's wanted the library to play in the improvement of their standing in the 'public estimation' is clear from the way in which it was used in advertisements soon after its introduction. This publicity strenuously avoided the phrase 'circulating library', which was still negatively associated with novel reading in this period, and instead directed 'especial attention to the Subscription Library which is intended to promote the reading of the higher class of literature'.[43]

However, in the same letter Smith also noted that the library had involved 'a larger outlay than any return' and the earliest surviving accounts reveal that in the first six months of its existence the cost of buying books and the expenses incurred in running the business came to almost twice what was made in subscriptions and sales, leaving a debt of £2054 to be carried over to the next year.[44] These accounts also show that part of the library's turnover during the period July-December 1860 came from 'sales of reduced books'. As Simon Eliot has argued, during the 1870s and later, the library department was often rescued from insolvency by the selling on of library materials as 'second hand' books, but the books sold in the first few months of the library's existence would not have had enough time in circulation to recoup the cost of their purchase.[45] It is possible that these were books that had become damaged in circulation or 'soiled' on the stalls, but the fact that the library had begun to budget separately for 'Purchases for reading' and 'Purchases for sale' by 1866 suggests that the sale of books was essential to the library from the very beginning and that not all books were intended for circulation.

The library accounts thus reveal that by the autumn of 1860 the range of texts on offer to the railway reader at the stalls included discounted library books. By the summer of 1861 Smith's were issuing lists of 'Library Books at Greatly Reduced Prices', which allowed customers to place orders 'at any of the Railway Bookstalls' and the list issued on 1 July 1861 included a number of texts first published for the Christmas market at the end of 1860, such as Oliphant's *The House on the Moor,* which was reduced from 31s 6d to 8s 6d.[46] This suggests that part of the library's function was to attract customers to the stall with the promise of recent titles at cheap prices, and this role was made explicit in the 'Rules' issued to the bookstall clerks in 1868 that required them to display library books 'prominently' so that they could be sold to 'the Public as well as to Subscribers at a discount of *not more* than 25 per cent (3d in the Shilling) off the *retail price',* and which allowed them to sell 'New Books just received' at their discretion.[47]

The establishment of the library in 1860 meant that Smith's could offer their bookstall customers a wide range of texts, in various material forms, at a range of different terms (from renting at subscription rates, to purchase second hand), but it was also a marketing tool designed to bring in new customers by offering the appearance of an older distribution system, the subscription library, which was associated with the careful selection of texts for a family audience. It is this combination of the targeting of specific audiences with the creation of a new commercial space that makes the Smith's bookstalls such an important phenomena in the history of the distribution and retailing of texts in England.

Notes

1. John Feather, *A History of British Publishing* (London, 1988), pp. 136-7.

2. Smith's withdrew from Scotland in 1857, see Leslie Gardner, *The Making of John Menzies* (Edinburgh, 1983). For Ireland after 1850, see L. M. Cullen, *Eason & Son: A History* (Dublin, 1989).

3. Lynda Nead, *Victorian Babylon: People, Streets and Images in Nineteenth-Century London* (London, 2000), 149-161.

4. *The Times*, Saturday 9 August 1851.

5. *The Literature of the Rail Re-Published by Permission from the Times of Saturday 9th August, 1851, with a Preface* (London, 1851), pp. 4-8.

6. *Literature of the Rail*, p. 5.

7. *The Athenaeum*, No. 1245 (6 September 1851), 947-48.

8. *The Illustrated Exhibitor and Magazine of Art*, Vol. 2 (1852), 394-96; *Once a Week*, 2 February 1861, 161-63.

9. Herbert Eustace Maxwell, *The Life and Times of The Right Honourable W. H. Smith, M P.*, 2 vols, (Edinburgh, 1893); Eric Chilston, *W H. Smith* (London, 1965); Charles Wilson, *First With the News: the History of W. H. Smith*, 1792-1972 (London, 1985).

10. Wilson, pp. 101-103; Public Record Office, Rail 410/141, records that on 19 August 1846 Mayhew was 'severely reprimanded for his misconduct, and his sale of books on the Euston platform confined to Railway Maps and Guides', fol. 104.

11. PRO, Rail 384/97. In 1845 George Backer was given permission 'to supply newspapers' at Euston because of his 'excellent conduct during the long period of his employment in this company's service', fol. 3001.

12. PRO, Rail 410/873. The bids from those already established on the line are: Bid 3, Henry Horsfall, Coventry; 4, John Utley, Warrington; 14, Samuel Rowse, Stafford; 18, Samuel Mayhew, Euston; 19, Bradshaw & Blacklock, Manchester; 20, John Edmunds Curtis, Wolverton; 31, James Grimes, Crewe; 33, William Tait, Rugby; 42, Henry Noble, Liverpool; 43, William Staniforth, Wolverhampton. Further references are included in the text.

13. Rowse offered £44 for Stafford and Tamworth, Grimes £35 for Crewe and Stafford. Utley offered £4 and Staniforth £1.

14. *Hodson's Booksellers, Publishers & Stationers Directory* 1855 (London, 1855- OBS Reprint) lists a William Taite as a printer in Church Street, Rugby.

15. Horsfall (Bid 3) and Edward and David Smith of Liverpool (Bid 23) made this request.

16. This remark is made by Rowse of Stafford (Bid 14) but Horsfall and Staniforth echo it.

17. *The Times*, 24 December 1847, records that the rent at Euston was £60 p.a. Of the surviving forty bids, twenty-one include Euston.

18. Extracts from the trial were included in *The Times*, Wednesday, 19 December, 1849, p. 7.

19. The newspaper agent Joseph Clayton wanted to send parcels free of charge, 'to prevent a deficiency or surplus of periodicals at one station while at another there may remain a superabundance of both (Bid 22).

20. W. H. Smith Archive (hereafter WHS), 56/4, 'The stations at which we should at once arrange to sell newspapers & books are Bedford, Birmingham, Coventry, Crewe, Euston, Liverpool, Manchester (Victoria and London Road), Northampton, Rugby,

Stafford, Tamworth, Warrington, Watford, and Wolverton'. References to materials held at the W. H. Smith archive are reproduced with their permission.

21. William Donald of Euston Square tendered for 18 stations including four (Chester, Leamington, Stockport and Wolverhampton) not referred to by Smith's (Bid 10).

22. WHS 37/1, fol. l.

23. PRO, Rail 410/873, Bid 13.

24. For a comprehensive survey of the expanding bookstall business, see Wilson, pp. 88-179.

25. *Saturday Review*, 31 January 1857, pp. 100-102 (100-101).

26. A list of 167 'Railway Bookstalls' is included in WHS, 248/2; WHS, x108 records that '385 bookstalls' were 'open in 1874'.

27. This phrase comes from PRO Rail 410/835, a contract with the LNWR dated 14 June 1860.

28. Elizabeth James, 'An Insight Into the Management of Railway Bookstalls in the Eighteen Fifties', *Publishing History* 10 (1981): 65-69 (67); WHS, PA 1(3), *General Rules to be Observed by those Engaged at the Railway Bookstands of W. H. Smith & Son* (W. H. Smith, 1855).

29. Advertisements for 'Soiled Railway Books' are included in *A Catalogue of Modern Books New & Second Hand ... Offered at Reduced Prices by W. H. Smith & Son, July* 1868 (n.p., 1868).

30. WHS, 56/4, fol. l.

31. WHS, A46 'Weekly Statement ... Monday 14 May to Saturday 19 May 1855', also lists thirty-five weeklies, f.10.

32. Only two sets of statements have survived, WHS A38, 'Weekly Statements Book, Bradford Station, 30 December 1867 – 30 December 1868', and WHS 490: 'Weekly Statement Book, Hatfield Station, 3 January – 25 November 1876'.

33. The stall sold an additional 126 copies of the *Telegraph* to the trade, bringing the total number of copies sold to 302; the *Observer* sold 594 copies. During the week ending 10 October 1868 the turnover for newspapers at the Bradford stall was made up of £5.0s.1d for dailies, £2.4s.7d for weeklies, and £8.6s.7d for local papers.

34. *Saturday Review*, 31 January 1857, pp. 100-102. Further references are given in the text; Henry Stephens, *The Book of the Farm*, 2 vols. (Edinburgh, 1851).

35. The *Review* contains a list of bestsellers: 'Sir E. Lytton ... is at the head of the list. Next comes Captain Marryat; after him – *longo intervallo* – Mr James, Captain Grant, Miss Sinclair, Mr Haliburton, Mrs Trollope, Mr Lever, Mrs Gaskell, and Miss Austen.' (p. 101).

36. Joseph Turnley, *The Language of the Eye* (London, 1856).

37. WHS, x108 includes the 'Annual Accounts' for '1867-1877'.

38. WHS, x108. The sale of newspapers accounted for 53.8% of total turnover in 1870, and had risen to 56.8% in 1875.

39. The catalogue of engravings is included with the British Library's copy of *A Catalogue of Modern Books New & Second Hand ... by W. H. Smith & Son, July* 1868 (BL, RB.23.1.a. 4863). For illustrations of the stalls in the 1890s, see Wilson, p. 240.

40. For the growth in advertising, see Wilson, pp. 112-17.

41. Henry Sampson, *A History of Advertising from the Earliest Times* (London, 1875). For images of the stalls in this period, see Jeoffry Spence, *Victorian and Edwardian Railway Travel* (London, 1977).

42. WHS, 66/7, fol. 2.

43. WHS, 248/3, 'Printed Circular, January 1862', p. l.

44. WHS, A102, includes 'Library Balance Accounts 1860-67', ff. 1-2.

45. Simon Eliot, 'Bookselling by the Backdoor: Circulating Libraries, Booksellers and Book Clubs 1876-1966', in A *Genius for Letters: Booksellers and Bookselling from the 16th to the 20th Century*, ed. by Robin Myers and Michael Harris (Winchester and Delaware, 1995), pp. 145-66. Eliot suggests that at Mudie's the 'average' novel needed to circulate for nine months to recover the cost of purchase and overheads.

46. WHS, 248/1, p. 2. Oliphant's, *The House on the Moor* (London, 1860) was advertised as a new work in the *Publishers' Circular* on 1 December 1860, p. 614.

47. WHS, A38, p. 2.

Imagined Local Communities: Three Victorian Newspaper Novelists

GRAHAM LAW

Y THEME HERE is novels serialized in local newspapers and their role in reinforcing a sense of regional identity, in the face of metropolitan pressures to adopt national and imperial perspectives. As the title suggests, focusing on newspaper fiction in this way involves an engagement with Benedict Anderson's theories on the origin and spread of nationalism. Anderson finds a primary contributory factor in the development of 'print-capitalism, which made it possible for rapidly growing numbers of people to think about themselves, and to relate themselves to others, in profoundly new ways'.[1] He draws particular attention to the novel and the newspaper as the 'two forms of imagining which ... provided the technical means for "re-presenting" the kind of imagined community that is the nation'.[2] Extrapolating from Anderson's insights, in his recent *Atlas of the European Novel*, Franco Moretti has attempted literally to map the geographical development of national consciousness in European fiction in terms of both forms and markets. In doing so, he recognizes more explicitly than Anderson that the imagined national community emerges through the wresting of fictional space 'from other geographical matrixes ... just as capable of generating narrative'.[3] Nevertheless, Moretti tends to see the forces of economic centralization and geographical polarization as working 'implacably' within the development of the modern media.[4] He also seems unconscious of the irony that much of his evidence for the spread of national consciousness in fiction derives from the book holdings of the national libraries.[5] Most importantly for my purposes, Anderson never recognizes that news and novels often occupied the same publishing space, while Moretti seems only able to conceive of narrative fiction in the shape of the bound volume. Yet if the emergence of the novel is rather seen as intimately involved with the complexities of serial publication, a rather different picture begins to emerge, in which the tension with both sub- and supra-national identifications is persistent.

Not long ago, I wrote a general account of the publication of instalment fiction in the Victorian weekly newspaper, a print medium that had been largely overlooked in the extensive previous scholarship on serialization.[6] That account focuses mainly on the mechanisms of syndication, which allowed groups of provincial papers to compete with London periodicals for the latest works by authors with established metropolitan reputations. However, the book also contains a certain amount of discussion not only of the overseas markets penetrated by the major syndication agencies, but also of the persistence of local themes treated by local authors. In this latter case, the writings were often amateur and the methods of acquisition informal. But clearly the demand for local tales in local papers was such that more regular sources of supply were sought. One method was for writers already on a paper's editorial staff to write novels of local interest to order. These often show strong antiquarian or folkloric interests, like the various stories written for the *Aberdeen Free Press* by its editor William Alexander.[7] Another avenue, explored regularly in Scotland from as early as the late 1850s but in the English provinces perhaps only from the early 1870s, was the readers' fiction competition.[8] Here, however, I wish to focus not on these avenues but on a trio of professional novelists who took a much more systematic approach to the production and distribution of local fiction. Each was individually responsible for more than forty full-length newspaper serials. The writers in question are David Pae from Scotland, James Skipp Borlase in the English Midlands, and J. Monk Foster, a former coal-miner from Wigan in Lancashire.[9] These newspaper novelists, portrayed in Plates 1-3, can be seen not so much to exploit existing methods of syndication for their own purposes as to pioneer new modes of distribution which were often taken up by the professional agencies themselves. Though the three accounts inevitably begin with a certain amount of attention to biographical and bibliographical detail, the aim in each case is to move towards the narrative content of their work and its complex contribution to the formation of regional identities.

David Pae (1828-84) and the rise of syndication

A number of London weekly newspapers had experimented briefly with the idea of carrying original serial fiction during the 1840s but the still heavy burden of the 'taxes on knowledge' had forced them either to price themselves out of the popular market, like the sixpenny *Sunday Times*, or to risk legal action in the case of unstamped papers like the *Penny Sunday*

Fig. 1. Portrait of David Pae.
People's Journal, 17 May 1884, p. 3

Fig. 2. Portrait of James Skipp Borlase.
Derby and Chesterfied Reporter, 11 November 1887,
p. 3

Fig. 3. Portrait of J. Monk Foster.
Frontispiece to his *Passion's Aftermath* (London:
Digby, Long, 1892)

Times. As a result, by the end of the decade, the penny weekly magazine, which contained no news and thus escaped the tax, was found to be the format best suited to bringing serial fiction to a broad popular audience.[10] Thus serial fiction was rarely found again in the London newspaper press until the later 1870s. Things were very different further north. William Donaldson, the only previous scholar to have studied Pae's writings in any detail, proposes as a working definition of popular literature in Victorian Scotland the phrase 'material which has been written specifically for publication in newspapers'.[11] According to Donaldson, a major reason for the earlier rise to prominence there of the newspaper novel is to be found in the increasing orientation of the Scottish bourgeoisie towards English metropolitan culture, and the concomitant slump in the indigenous book and serial markets.[12] One consequence was a marked decline in locally produced fiction, whether in volume or in periodicals. With the removal of the taxes on knowledge in the mid-century, the Scottish newspaper press moved quickly to fill this gap with new cheap miscellaneous weekly journals combining news summaries, political discussion, and literary material.[13] They were distinctively Scottish in tone and content, predominantly radical in political affiliation, and aimed mainly at the upper-working and lower-middle classes. The most popular and consistent contributor of serial tales to these papers was undoubtedly David Pae.[14]

Pae was born in Amulree, Perthshire in 1828, but raised by his mother among her family in Coldingham, Berwickshire, after his father, a miller, died in an accident when the child was only a few weeks of age. A solid education in the parish school enabled him to be apprenticed to Thomas Grant, an evangelical Edinburgh bookseller, who was to publish several of Pae's early works. Once in Edinburgh, Pae became influenced by liberal trends in contemporary evangelicalism, both anti-Calvinist and millenarian, and issued a number of widely circulated pamphlets on these subjects. Pae's novels unmistakably reveal the same religious and political preoccupations, and, particularly in their endings, partake of the quality of the religious tract. A handful seem to have appeared first in volume form, but, as Table 1 shows, the vast majority ran as serials in popular newspapers, like the *Edinburgh North Briton* which began to carry his first novel *Jessie Melville* in 1856.[15]

Pae became a full-time professional author only in 1859 when he took on the editorship of the *Dunfermline Saturday Post*, where *Annie Gray* made its first appearance. By 1864 he had already produced around fifteen

Table 1. Serials by David Pae first located in newspapers in the 1850s and 1860s

	Serial	Newspaper serializations located
1	Jessie Melville, or the Double Sacrifice	NB56, PP63, BWT69, RA71, BWJ73
2	Clara Howard, or the Captain's Bride	NB57, GP59, PP59, PF71, AR72, ST72, MWG72
3	Helen Armstrong, or the Rose of Tweedside	BJ57, AWN68
4	Lucy the Factory Girl, or the Secrets of the Tontine Close	NB58, GT58, PJ63, AR63, AWN64, ST68, BWG73, MWG82, NDT86, LWP91
5	The Heiress of Wellwood, or Swindlers and their Victims	NB59, GT59, HA62
6	Annie Gray, or Sunshine and Shadow	DSP59, PP61, RA71
7	The Heir of Douglas	NB60, GT60, HA60, AWN64, PJ65, ST65
8	The Forged Will, or the Orphan and the Foundling	NB60, GT62, AR70, KT73
9	Nelly Preston, or the Lawyer's Plot	NB61, HA62, AWN65, BWP69, PF72
10	Caroline Frazer; or, the Witch of the Eccleston Moor	NB61,GT61, AWN65, BWP65
11	Flora the Orphan, or Love and Crime	PP61, NB62, BWG76
12	Norah Cushaleen, or the Murdered Wife	NB62, PP62, HA64, KT66, PF72, BWG78, MWG83
13	Biddy Macarthy, or the Hunted Felon	NB62, PP62, HA67, BWJ72
14	Basil Hamilton, or the Ticket of Leave	NB63, PP63, BWP64
15	The Merchant's Daughter; or Love and Mammon	GT63, PRG69, BWT71
16	Very Hard Times, or the Trials and Sorrows of the Linwood Family	NB63, PP63, AR63&71, ST71, BWG74&84, NDT86
17	Mary Patterson, or the Fatal Error	PJ64, PP64, ST65
18	Captain Wyld's Gang, or Mysteries of the Black Boy Close	NB64, PP64, BWP68
19	The Rose of Glenlee	HA64
20	The Gipsy's Prophecy, or the Hermit of the Glen	PJ65, HA65, AWN65
21	Eustace the Outcast	PJ66, HA66, ST66, BWP68, MWG82, NDT87
22	Effie Seaton, or the Dark House in Murdoch's Close	PJ66, HA66, ST67, BWJ73
23	The Haunted Castle, or a Brother's Treachery	PJ66, HA67, ST67, AR68, BWJ72, MWG81
24	George Dalton, or the Convict's Revenge	PJ67, AR77
25	The Laird of Birkencleuch, or the Maiden's Choice	PJ67, HA68
26	Jeannie Sinclair, or the Lily of the Strath	PJ68, AR69, ST69, HA69, MWG69, AWN69, BWP70
27	Cast on the World, or, the Border Marriage	PJ69, AR69, HA69, AWN69, ST70, PRG70, BWP70, MWG70, LE72
28	Clanranald or, The Fugitives	PJ69, PRG70, HA70, RA73

Paper Codes:

BWG = Bolton Weekly Guardian
GP = Galloway Post
LE = Leeds Express
NDT = (Blackburn) Northern Daily Telegraph
PRG = Paisley & Renfrewshire Gazette

AR = Ashton Reporter
BWJ = Bolton Weekly Journal
GT = Glasgow Times
LWP = Liverpool Weekly Post
PF = (Dundee) People's Friend
RA = Rotherham Advertiser

AWN = Ayrshire Weekly News
BWP = Belfast Weekly Press
HA = Hamilton Advertiser
MWG = Middlesborough Weekly Gazette
PJ = (Dundee) People's Journal
SP = (Dunfermline) Saturday Press

BJ = Berwick Journal
BWT = Bradford Weekly Telegraph
KT = Kendal Times
NB = (Edinburgh) North Briton
PP = (Glasgow) Penny Post
ST = Sheffield Telegraph

Year Codes: Two digit numbers following paper code indicate year of commencement of serial run, but not necessarily year of completion

instalment novels, including his most popular work *Lucy, the Factory Girl,* which was serialized simultaneously in Edinburgh and Glasgow. He then resigned his post in Dunfermline and entered into a long-standing agreement to write new serials exclusively for John Leng, the English proprietor of the Dundee *People's Journal.* But the arrangement must have left Pae free to sell on his second serial rights to other newspapers. Pae thus seems almost immediately to have set up informal syndicates with both Leng's brother William at the *Sheffield Telegraph* and other English proprietors like John Andrews of the *Ashton Reporter* in Lancashire, where Pae's new serials appeared in roughly the same sequence following their completion in the Dundee papers.[16] By 1870 Pae had printed an advertising leaflet offering a choice from among twenty-nine serial tales, the majority of around forty chapters, and listing a dozen existing client newspapers, several of which provided testimonials.[17] From around this time Pae's old work begins to show up regularly in a wide range of other weekly journals all over Scotland and northern England, and more occasionally further afield.[18] Pae was thus single-handedly responsible for a significant proportion of the serial fiction published in newspapers north of the Trent up until the early 1870s and can thus make a reasonable claim to be one of the most widely read novelists in mid-Victorian Britain. In 1869 Pae also became the founding editor of John Leng's latest periodical venture, the popular weekly literary miscellany *The People's Friend,* which went on to carry a number of old and new works by its editor. When Pae died of a heart attack in May 1884, he had published around fifty full-length serial novels, of which the most popular must each have been purchased by over half a million newspaper subscribers.

Indeed, the practice he had developed of selling the same stories either in series or in parallel to papers with complementary circulations was to provide the model for the professional fiction syndication agencies that were to emerge in England from the early 1870s.[19] It is significant that when Tillotsons of Bolton began to carry fiction in their *Bolton Weekly Journal* from 1871, they turned to David Pae for each of their first three stories. In 1873 they were to found the 'Fiction Bureau', the first and most successful of the northern agencies. And their biggest rivals from the mid-1880s proved to be the 'Editor's Syndicate', the agency started up by John Leng's brother William at the *Sheffield Telegraph,* one of the first English papers to carry Pae's work. By the later 1870s the dominant mode of instalment publication in Britain (whether measured in terms of the number of works issued, size of audience reached, or remuneration offered to authors) had shifted unmistakably. The shift was from serialization in single metropolitan magazines - whether monthlies like *Temple Bar* or weeklies like *Chambers's Journal* - to syndication in groups of provincial weekly papers, and this dominance was to last into the 1890s. In the process, distinguished metropolitan authors were attracted into the newspaper market with some regularity. Yet even in this company Pae's stories seemed able to hold their own. As Jesse Quail, editor of the *Northern Daily Telegraph*, put it, the most popular newspaper novelists of the Tillotson era, 'William Black, James Payn, Walter Besant, and even Miss Braddon … cannot hold up a candle to David Pae'.[20]

Putting Pae alongside Braddon obviously raises the question of the relationship between the evangelical melodramas found in the Scottish newspapers and the phenomenon of 'sensationalism', which erupted in the London literary magazines in the early 1860s. While they are clearly not quite the same thing, there are significant points of similarity.[21] Pae does not encourage the frisson of sexual and social transgression that Braddon exploits so effectively; he prefers the pure, blushing heroine to her angels of darkness; but in both forms there is the same unsettling combination of documentary and melodrama, fantasy with realism. If the sensationalist typically offers Gothic events within respectable domestic settings, Pae most characteristically gives us urban fairy-tales, dreams of fulfilment against a backdrop of the grim city streets. As Donaldson has already argued forcefully, traditional accounts of fiction in Victorian Scotland, reflecting only novels issued in book form for a bourgeois audience, see it as devoted to 'a nostalgic, sentimental vision of the rural past', and entirely oblivious of the nature of urban industrial life.[22] Pae's serials prove how distorted this picture is.

Finally, we need to consider the limits to Pae's social realism by returning for a moment to the 'Scottishness' of his stories. For here Pae contrasts markedly with William Alexander, the novelist-editor of the *Aberdeen Free Press*. As Donaldson has shown in detail, Alexander took great pains to ground his narratives in the community in which he lived, and to reproduce as accurately and consistently as possible Scots dialect forms specific to Aberdeenshire.[23] Pae's work, on the other hand, was not restricted in setting to a single local community, nor written to any significant extent in the Scots vernacular. His *mise-en-scène* ranges not only all over Scotland from Edinburgh to Glasgow and from the Highlands to Tweedside, but shifts on occasion to the north of Ireland or the Lancashire cotton towns. Pae's narratorial voice is unwaveringly in standard literary English, and his villains' speech seems to owe as much to the Newgate novels found in the *London Journal* as to authentic Glasgow thieves' slang. These qualities perhaps help to explain how Pae was able immediately to reach and touch audiences across such a wide range of Scottish and northern English communities.

James Skipp Borlase (1839-?) and self-syndication

The dominance of Tillotsons from the mid-1870s should not be seen as signalling a total defeat for the concept of local newspaper fiction. This is for two reasons. In the first place, though the Bolton firm clearly made their largest profits from the distribution of original novels by popular metropolitan authors, they in fact supplied a wide range of newspapers and needed to offer an eclectic mix of material. Tillotsons' regular clients included many smaller country journals who could not afford the substantial sums required to obtain serials rights to the latest work from the pen of a Braddon or a Collins. These tended to be concentrated beyond the Trent, and preferred to purchase cheaper stories with a general or specific northern flavour. In the early days, Tillotsons thus marketed a number of serials set in the Bolton area by anonymous local writers, and in the 1880s they were offering fiction by Lancastrians who had established national reputations, including veteran Mancunian authors Harrison Ainsworth and Isabella Banks.[24] The second sign of the resilience of the local imagination in newspaper fiction, is the fact that, throughout the Golden Age of newspaper fiction in the 1870s and 1880s, it remained possible to by-pass the syndication agencies altogether. As they had been in the 1850s and 1860s, authors were free to make direct approaches to individual provincial newspaper publishers, and vice versa. In the late 1870s, for example, the *Glasgow Weekly Mail* and *Manchester Weekly Times* each avoided the big agencies but had an informal agreement to share fiction by both Scots writers like George MacDonald and Lancastrians like William Westall. A number of buccaneering writers like Captain Mayne Reid and J. E. Muddock resented dependency on the agents and consistently sold their own work to different newspaper proprietors, though much of it was in the form of exotic tales of adventure. There were, however, several lesser-known authors who were happy to produce custom-written tales with a particular local theme for a

Table 2. Three genres of newspaper serial by James Skipp Borlase

Genre	Serial	First located in	Year
Australian Tales	Tales of the Bush	Sheffield Times and Iris	1873-4
	The Adventures of a Mounted Trooper	Sheffield Weekly Independent	1874
	Who Killed John Cameron	Hull Packet & East Riding Advertiser	1882
	The Love that Killed	Derby and Chesterfield Reporter	1886
Russian Romances	Both Princess and Police Spy; or, By Command of the Czar	Sheffield Weekly Telegraph	1881
	Darker than Death: A Tale of Russia Today	Hull Packet & East Riding Advertiser	1882-3
	Nina the Nihilist: or, Death in the Palace	Sheffield Weekly Telegraph	1883
	The Black Hand: A Tale of the Secret Societies	Sheffield Weekly Telegraph	1883
	From Riches to Ruin	Yorkshire Weekly Post	1884
Local Stories	Force and Fraud; or the Luddites in Leicester	Leicester Chronicle	1884-5
	The Lily of Leicester; or, A Wife for an Hour	Leicester Chronicle	1885-6
	The Nevilles of Nottingham	Nottinghamshire Guardian	1886-7
	Exeter House; or, The Pretender in Derby	Derby & Chesterfield Reporter	1886-7
	Babington's Conspiracy; or, Dark Days in Derbyshire	Derby & Chesterfield Reporter	1887-8
	The Lancashire Mill Girl	Liverpool Weekly Post	1894

specific provincial readership. Notable among them was another literary buccaneer, James Skipp Borlase.[25]

Borlase is an interestingly dubious character, whose lively literary imagination seems frequently to have infected his own autobiographical statements.[26] He seems to have been born into a Catholic family in Cornwall in 1839, a descendant of the antiquarian William Borlase. Skipp Borlase emigrated to the Australian colonies for five years in the mid-1860s, and lived in Brighton for much of the rest of his life. Lucy Sussex convicts him during his colonial period not only of occasional plagiarism but also of deserting his wife.[27] It also seems likely that he tried to practise there as a solicitor, perhaps without taking the trouble to qualify for the profession.[28] However, his claim in 1895 to have produced 'eighty nine serials, published in periodicals and newspapers' seems likely to be more or less true, even if some were not entirely from his own pen and others were old wine in new bottles.[29] Only a small proportion of these ever appeared in volume form, several under the pseudonym of J. J. G.Bradley.[30] Before sailing for Australia Borlase seems to have been already contributing regularly to penny fiction miscellanies like the *Family Herald* and *London Journal*. In Melbourne and Hobart he seems to have been instrumental in starting up journals of a similar character, most notably the *Australian Journal*. By 1868 he was to be found in Sydney, 'supplying up-country papers with supplementary sheets full of fiction and miscellaneous literature, each paper having its own special imprint, a scheme which Messrs. Tillotson and Son, of Bolton, conceived and started in England very nearly ten years later'.[31] On his return to Britain he regularly contributed adventure stories for boys to *Peter Parley's Annual*, probably the oldest of the children's gift annuals, and to many children's weeklies.[32] But, as Table 2 suggests, even more of his writing seems to have found its way into provincial newspapers by one means or another.

In the 1870s, to both Tillotsons and Leaders of Sheffield he sold tales of the Australian bush such as *The Adventures of a Mounted Trooper*, many of which had already appeared in the *Australian Journal*.[33] In the 1880s for both William Leng and Cassells of London he wrote exotic romances, several set in Czarist Russia like *Nina the Nihilist*. When demand for his serials by the major syndicators began to wane, he was the first of several authors to place advertisements in the trade paper *The Journalist* offering lists of his wares to all-comers. But for our purposes, his most interesting products are those historical romances with local settings which he

Table 3. Lancashire serials by J. Monk Foster carried by Tillotsons, 1889-1899

Serial	First located in	Year
A Pit Brow Lassie	*Leigh Journal and Times*	1889
For Love of a Lancashire Lass	*Bolton Weekly Journal*	1890
Slaves of Fate	*Bolton Weekly Journal*	1890-1
Children of Darkness	*Cannock Chase Mercury*	1891
A Miner's Million	*Bolton Weekly Journal*	1891-2
A Crimson Fortune	*Bolton Weekly Journal*	1892
That Bonny Pit Lass	*Ripon Observer*	1893
The White Gipsy: A Tale of Mines and Miners	*Ashton Reporter*	1893
The Lass that Loved a Miner	*Liverpool Weekly Post*	1894
Judith Saxon: The Pitman's Daughter	*Bolton Weekly Journal*	1894-5
Through Flood and Flame	*Manchester Weekly Times*	1895
The Watchman of Orsden Moss	*Bolton Weekly Journal*	1897
The Cotton King	*Bolton Weekly Journal*	1898-9
The Forge of Life	*Bolton Weekly Journal*	1899-1900

produced to order for major journals in the Midlands in the mid-1880s. For both the *Leicester Chronicle* and the *Derby Reporter*, for example, he wrote at least two full-length local serial tales, in addition to a larger number of short stories of a similar character. It seems likely that he continued this practice well into the 1890s, as I have also located a serial of mill life especially written for the *Liverpool Weekly Post* as late as 1894. Borlase was clearly a resourceful writer, for there seems no evidence of any communal link between Borlase and the Midland counties or Merseyside. Clearly the taste for local and regional fiction was not entirely eradicated despite the increasing availability of more exotic fruits of the literary imagination in the later Victorian decades.

It is difficult to make any great claims for the quality of Borlase's output, and he is clearly a much inferior writer to Pae. When advertising his wares, Borlase seems commonly to have adopted the following line: 'I have never written a story that I have been unable to sell, even though I have not a spark of true genius but merely a power of mechanical construction, which has perhaps served me in better stead'.[34] The term 'mechanical' seems entirely appropriate. All of Borlase's local serials that I have looked at start off with a striking scene on a well-known bridge over the local river, and more than one involves a rescue from drowning either suicidal or homicidal. The Nevilles of Nottingham in the *Nottinghamshire Guardian* from late 1886, for example, bears more than a passing resemblance to *The Lily of Leicester* in the *Leicester Chronicle* from Christmas 1885.

A typical local effort from Borlase's pen is *Babington's Conspiracy; or, Dark Days in Derbyshire*, a serial beginning in the *Derby Reporter* in November 1887. This is set in Elizabethan Derbyshire, at the time of the detention of Mary Queen of Scots at Wingfield Manor in the hands of the Earl of Shrewsbury. The hero is the historical personage Anthony Babington, the brave and handsome local squire, who attempts to rescue the Scottish Queen but in the end suffers execution for conspiracy. In his narrative, Borlase evokes a good deal of sympathy for the persecutions suffered by both Catholics and non-Conformists, and his opening chapter is little more than a catalogue of cruelties committed during the reign of 'Good Queen Bess'. There is also an attempt to include local detail of antiquarian and folkloric interest. In the end, though the tale remains more of a rollicking romance in which one of the principal interests lies in Babington's attraction to both pale Rose Renshaw, the daughter of an

Anabaptist, and bouncing Bessie Pierrepoint, the Papist companion of Mary Queen of Scots. Almost inevitably the narrative opens with a scene in which Rose is rescued by Babington from being drowned as a witch in the Derwent by St Mary's Bridge, during which her clothing becomes torn in a manner bordering on the pornographic. Perhaps because of these enticements as well as for the local interest, both the proprietors of and subscribers to the *Derby Reporter* seemed keen to come back for more. Nevertheless, the announcement of the publication of *Babington's Conspiracy* stated: 'We need scarcely add that this is the seventh serial, and fourth specially LOCAL romance that Mr. Borlase has contributed to our columns, wherein he has made his mark as a very especial favourite in local tale writing.'[35]

John Monk Foster (1858-1930) and the decline of syndication
By the 1890s the power of the provincial syndicates was on the wane, and there was a clear shift of commercial power back to the London publishers. Inevitably, given the metropolitan political context, this process was accompanied by an upsurge in national and imperial themes in the fiction concerned. The new generation of news miscellanies published in London included both 'class' and 'mass' journals, that is, papers aimed at either the distinct professional classes or the undifferentiated masses. Among the more expensive and respectable class weeklies featuring instalment novels from the mid-1870s were pictorial papers like *The Graphic* or *The Illustrated London News*, which soon claimed circulations approaching 250,000 copies. The mass penny weeklies which began to include serial fiction slightly later included both old radical journals like *Lloyd's Weekly* and the new fragmentary entertainment miscellanies led by George Newnes's *Tit-Bits*, both of which were already achieving sales of well over half a million by 1890.

The provincial syndication agencies reacted to these challenges in different ways. Leaders were soon to close down their syndication business and sell off their newspapers. Like Cassells with their new *Saturday Journal*, Lengs in Sheffield attempted to get a piece of the action by starting up their own national *Weekly Telegraph*, along the lines of *Tit-Bits*, though with slightly greater pretension to respectability. But, for our purposes, the most interesting development was the change of policy adopted by Tillotsons in the late 1880s. Even before the founder W. F. Tillotson's death in early 1889, Mary Braddon had deserted the 'Fiction Bureau', lured away by a more generous offer from Lengs, who wanted to use her name to kickstart their new paper. The Bolton agency thereafter refused to compete with the fancy prices obtained by name authors from the metropolitan journals. This entailed a slow retreat back into their home market in the northern and western regions of the United Kingdom, and a growing emphasis on local and regional fiction by authors with a limited reputation in London. The most obvious marker of this process is that the Fiction Bureau began to contract with a number of reliable regional authors to produce a given amount of fiction per year at a pre-determined salary. One of them was J. Monk Foster, a former miner from Lancashire writing local industrial serials.[36]

Foster was born in Wigan in 1858, and started to work at the local Moss Hall Colliery from the age of nine.[37] While in his twenties he began to write short stories of colliery life, several of which were bought by London weekly journals.[38] Around the same time he had written an outspoken article attacking the pit inspection system, in which he claimed that he had worked down the pit for seventeen years but had never once seen a mining inspector.[39] After the article was published in the *Nineteenth Century*, he lost his job as a mining contractor and started to make his living as a professional writer. In 1888 his first long serial *A Miner's Million* was published in a couple of Lancashire newspapers, and the author came to the attention of W. F. Tillotson, who offered him a contract to write exclusively for the Bolton firm. At a regular wage of around two pounds a week, for sixteen years Foster contracted to provide the Fiction Bureau with an annual full-length novel and a short story or two. As Table 3 indicates, these appeared regularly in Tillotsons' series of *Lancashire Journals* between 1889 and 1904, and were also sold on during the same period to many smaller papers in the Midlands and North. After leaving Tillotsons's employ, Foster continued to sell mining and factory tales freelance to other publishers and agencies, including both the Lengs and D.C. Thompson in Dundee. He seems to have found fairly ready buyers for his wares until the eve of the Great War, when the market for newspaper fiction collapsed and he was forced to seek charity from the Royal Literary Fund. He wrote from Salford to the secretary:

You will see that laziness has not been one of my sins, for, after I had spent 21 years in the coal mines, I wrote – or have written, between 45 and 50 long serials of from 80,000 to 120,000 words. But with the year 1913 misfortune overtook me and has had me fast ever since. At the present moment I have many stories written – serials, short novels, short stories – running to a quarter of a million words or more, and yet, somehow or other, I am, and have been unable to 'place' them.[40]

Perhaps thanks to the lukewarm praise of his sponsors – 'A high literary achievement would hardly be expected from an author who has had to educate himself, as I imagine, in later life', wrote Owen Seaman of *Punch* – he was granted the magnificent dole of £10.[41]

Although Foster states that a number of his industrial serials were afterwards issued in cheap volume form, perhaps from provincial publishers, only one of his novels is found in the British Library – *Passion's Aftermath* (1892) published in London by Digby, Long, though printed in Bolton by Tillotsons. But this is a romance of bourgeois life presumably considered more appropriate for a metropolitan audience, and which seems never to have been serialized.[42] In my opinion it is inferior as well as unrepresentative. A more typical example of Foster's narratives can be found in *A Pit Brow Lassie*, his first long serial for Tillotsons, which appeared in the *Lancashire Journals* from April.

The setting is contemporary, at and around the King Pit, Ashford, a fictional but precisely detailed Lancashire location, and much of the dialogue is in broad Lancashire dialect. The narrative includes elements of mystery, concerning the missing relatives of the heroine Kate Leigh, the pit brow lassie of the title. Her father turns out to have perished among the labyrinthine but unmarked air tunnels of the mine (a further dig at flaws in the inspection system) and her uncle to have escaped to Australia to make his fortune. But the central interest lies in Kate's romantic choice between the honest miner Luke Standish and the scheming rake Arthur Willesden, who has secretly learned that Kate will inherit her uncle's wealth. Arthur seduces another mining girl, fast Molly Sheargold, but craftily fastens the blame for the fathered child on Luke and thus wins the hand of the heroine. Later Molly is murdered and Luke is arrested and sentenced to death, but at the last moment the heroine is able to prove that her evil husband is guilty of the crime. She is thus reunited with her first love and together they are able to enjoy her uncle's fortune.

Of particular interest is the way this melodrama is intertwined with the themes of popular reading and self-culture. Both Luke and Kate are shown to have improved themselves through their 'passion for reading' (ch. 1). Kate's moral superiority to Molly derives in part from her subscriptions to popular penny-fiction journals like the *London Journal* and *Bow Bells*, while Luke borrows non-fiction from the local Free Library, dreaming of, and eventually succeeding in becoming, a mining manager. Arthur, on the other hand, insinuates himself into Kate's affections by covering up his idleness with the pretence that he is 'an author who had come to Ashford especially to study the habits and life of pit-folk, with a view to putting the knowledge gleaned into a novel he was writing' (ch. 11). The scenes of both active employment at the pit and leisured domestic reading both seem enlivened by Foster's own personal experience. While we might agree with Foster's sponsors in his applications to the Royal Literary Fund that his novels are hardly masterpieces, his career as a newspaper novelist can still provide a respectable example of the resurgence of local themes in the material provided by the major syndicators during their period of decline.

Conclusion: North and South
The conclusion must be that, as reflected in the rise and decline of syndication in the Victorian market for newspaper fiction, developments in print capitalism did not determine a unilateral shift towards nationalist perspectives. Rather they provoked a tension between different models of imagined community to which allegiance could be given. In the process, we have had to recognize that the local or regional community itself is not simply and organically there, but needs to be shored-up and rebuilt through mechanisms that parallel those used in the construction of imperial identities. The late nineteenth century is a period of the reinvention of local and regional traditions as well as the invention of national ones.[43] In the end, though, it must be recognized that the techniques of syndication reveal a closer affinity with regional than local consciousness. Thus, it is apparent that, above all, the provincial newspaper novel both reflected and contributed to a sense of a broad 'Northern' cultural identity, covering the inhabitants of both Scotland and England 'beyond the Trent', in contradistinction to and often in antagonism with that of 'Southern' culture centred on the metropolis and the Home Counties.

Evidence for the continuing existence of this imagined community of North Britain includes the wide circulation enjoyed by Pae's tales, the specific arrangements for the sharing of fiction between papers in, say, Dundee and Sheffield, or Glasgow and Manchester, and the nature of the 'home territory' of agencies like Tillotsons. We should recall finally, that, in contrast to the focus on industrial fiction at the time of the Chartist disturbances in the mid-century, when novels like Gaskell's *North and South* are allowed a key cultural role, mainstream literary history of the later

Victorian decades has tended to discover provincial themes predominantly in relation to the Southern market town or the rural Southwest. Thus authors like Trollope and Eliot, or Hardy and Blackmore, tend to take centre stage, while writers like George MacDonald in Scotland, or Isabella Banks in Lancashire, are largely overlooked – not to mention, of course, my entirely unsung heroes, the newspaper novelists Pae, Borlase, and Foster.

Notes

1. Benedict Anderson, *Imagined Communities: Reflections on the Origin and Spread of Nationalism* (London,1991; revised edition), p. 36.
2. Anderson, *Imagined Communities*, pp. 24-5.
3. Franco Moretti, *Atlas of the European Novel 1800-1900* (London, 1998), p. 53.
4. Moretti, *Atlas*, pp. 170-1.
5. Moretti, *Atlas*, pp. 174-85.
6. Graham Law, *Serializing Fiction in the Victorian Press* (New York, 2000).
7. See William Donaldson, *Popular Literature in Victorian Scotland: Language, Fiction and the Press* (Aberdeen, 1986) pp. 101-44.
8. See Law, *Serializing Fiction*, pp. 45-7 & 51.
9. Unfortunately K. D. M. Snell's recent *The Bibliography of Regional Fiction in Britain and Ireland, 1800-2000* (Burlington, VT, 2002) is of little assistance concerning these writers, since it ignores work published in periodicals but not reprinted in volume form. Thus, neither Borlase nor Foster appears there at all, while Pae is represented only by a single work in the Glasgow section.
10. See Law, *Serializing Fiction*, pp. 19-23.
11. See Donaldson, *Popular Literature*, p. 154, n. 31.
12. See Donaldson, *Popular Literature*, p. 14.
13. There were even short-lived experiments with similar journals before the removal of the newspaper stamp, notably the Perth *Saturday Journal*, which appeared from summer 1841 to the end of 1844 and featured unsigned historical serials by Robert Scott Fittis, including *The Mysterious Monk* and *The Mosstrooper*. See A. H. Millar, 'Robert Scott Fittis', in Robert Scott Fittis, *The Mosstrooper: A Legend of the Scottish Border* (Perth, 1906) v-xv.
14. For earlier discussions of Pae's work, see Donaldson, *Popular Literature*, pp. 72-100; and Graham Law, 'Introduction' to his edition of David Pae, *Lucy, the Factory Girl; or, The Secrets of the Tontine Close* (Hastings, 2001) vii-xiv. The chief biographical sources of information concerning Pae are: obituaries in the Dundee papers (notably, Andrew Stewart, 'Death of the Editor of the "Friend"', *People's Friend* (14 May 1884) pp. 33-4; reprinted in Pae *Lucy*, ed. by Law, pp. 301-6); and documents in the possession of Pae's great granddaughters, Judith Cooke in Dundee and Tricia Englert in Watford. I am extremely grateful to both for generously allowing access.
15. The British Library Catalogue attributes to Pae the novella *George Sandford; or, the Draper's Assistant*, published by Thomas Grant in Edinburgh in 1853, an attribution accepted by Donaldson (*Popular Literature*, pp. 80-1). However, although there is no

doubt that the work shares some of his evangelical preoccupations and was issued by his employer, I argue that the work is unlikely to be by Pae (Law, 'Introduction', viii).

16. See: Edward Fletcher Cass, 'The Cotton Factory Times, 1885-1937: A Family Newspaper and the Lancashire Cotton Community', Unpublished Ph.D. Dissertation, Edge Hill University College, University of Lancaster, 1996, pp. 129-55; and Law, *Serializing Fiction*, pp. 44-50.

17. See 'List of Serial Stories, Written by David Pae for Publication in Newspapers' (Ardrossan: Ayrshire Evening News Office, [1870]), found among the documents held by Tricia Englert.

18. For example, *Annabel, or the Temptation* was serialized in the (Plymouth) Western Weekly Mercury in 1881, while *Lucy, the Factory Girl* has even been located in Sydney, in the *Australian Town and Country Journal*, though this was in 1891, several years after Pae's death.

19. See Stewart, 'Death of the Editor of the "Friend"', p. 33.

20. Cited in William Westall, 'Newspaper Fiction', in *Lippincott's Monthly Magazine*, 45 (January 1890) pp. 77-88; 81.

21. See Pae's spirited defence of sensation fiction in his Preface to the volume edition of *Mary Paterson; or, The Fatal Error* (London, 1866).

22. Donaldson, *Popular Literature*, p. 99.

23. Donaldson, *Popular Literature*, pp. 101-44

24. See Law, *Serializing Fiction*, pp. 64-84.

25. See Law, *Serializing Fiction*, pp. 93-100.

26. The main biographical sources concerning Borlase are: 'Some Interesting Notes about Mr. James Skipp Borlase', *Derby and Chesterfield Reporter* (11 November 1887) p. 2; and Clifford Craig, *Mr Punch in Tasmania: Colonial Politics in Cartoons, 1866-79* (Hobart, 1980) p. 131. These were pointed out by Lucy Sussex, another modern scholar who has investigated Borlase's career. See her 'Whodunit?: Literary Forensics and the Crime Writing of James Skipp Borlase and Mary Fortune' (with John Burrows), in *Bibliographical Society of Australia and New Zealand Bulletin* 21:2 (2nd Quarter, 1997) pp. 73-105 and 'Whodunit?: A Postscript', in *Bibliographical Society of Australia and New Zealand Bulletin* 22:2 (2nd Quarter, 1998) pp. 111-13.

27. Sussex and Burrow, 'Whodunit?: Literary Forensics', pp. 74-5.

28. See Craig, *Mr Punch*, p. 131; the documents Craig cites have Borlase claiming to have been admitted as attorney of the Court of the Queen's Bench and solicitor of the High Court of Chancery simultaneously in June 1862 (i.e. at the age of only 22 or 23, which seems somewhat premature.)

29. ALS to George Redway, 1 January 1898, National Library of Australia, MSS 7661.

30. See the entry on Borlase in E. Morris Miller, *Australian Literature from its Beginnings to 1935: A Descriptive and Bibliographical Survey*, 2 vols (Sydney, 1973).

31. 'Some Interesting Notes', p. 2.

32. Miller, *Australian Literature*.

33. Toni Johnson-Woods, *Index to Serials in Australian Periodicals and Newspapers, Nineteenth Century* (Canberra, 2002).

34. ALS to George Redway, 1 January 1898, National Library of Australia, MSS 7661; similar sentiments are expressed in 'Some Interesting Notes'.

35. 'Some Interesting Notes', 2.

36. See Law, *Serializing Fiction*, pp. 84-91.

37. My principal source of biographical information is File 2944, John Monk Foster, the Royal Literary Fund Archives, British Library Manuscripts.

38. A typical example was 'The Moss-Pit Mystery' which appeared in James Henderson's *Penny Pictorial News* on 20 December 1886.

39. J. Monk Foster, 'Mining Inspection a Sham', in *Nineteenth Century* 17 (May 1885) pp. 1055-63.

40. ALS to A. Llewelyn Roberts, 6 August 1914, Royal Literary Fund Archives.

41. ALS to A. Llewelyn Roberts, 14 October 1914, Royal Literary Fund Archives.

42. Provincial newspaper proprietors often acted also as publishers of fiction in book form, including three of the major syndicators, Tillotsons in Bolton, John Leng in Dundee, and W.C. Leng in Sheffield, while popular metropolitan proprietors such as Newnes also issued series like the *Tit-Bits Novels*.

43. See *The Invention of Tradition*, ed. by Eric Hobsbawm & Terence Ranger (Cambridge, 1983).

Index

References to illustrations are in *italic*

205